PAUL: MISSIONARY OF JESUS

AFTER JESUS, VOLUME 2

PAUL

Missionary of Jesus

Paul Barnett

William B. Eerdmans Publishing Company
Grand Rapids, Michigan / Cambridge, U.K.

Published 2008 by

Wm. B. Eerdmans Publishing Co.

2140 Oak Industrial Drive N.E., Grand Rapids, Michigan 49505 /
P.O. Box 163, Cambridge CB3 9PU U.K.

Printed in the United States of America

14 13 12 11 10 09 08   7 6 5 4 3 2 1

Library of Congress Cataloging-in-Publication Data

Barnett, Paul (Paul William)
    Paul: missionary of Jesus / Paul Barnett.
        p.   cm.   — (After Jesus ; v. 2)
    Includes bibliographical references and indexes.
    ISBN 978-0-8028-4891-8 (pbk.: alk. paper)
    1. Paul, the Apostle, Saint.   I. Title.

    BS2506.3.B375   2008
    225.9′2 — dc22

                  2007026627

www.eerdmans.com

In memory of Brian King, bishop (1938-2006)

CONTENTS

   Paul, a Christ-Shaped Emissary   159

11. Romans: Paul's Final Answer (ca. 57)   181

12. Paul's Achievement   198

   APPENDIX A: "Saul, Who Is Also Paul" (Acts 13:9)   205

   APPENDIX B: The Acts of the Apostles and the Letters of Paul   208

   APPENDIX C: Mind and Spirit: How Paul Made Decisions   211

   APPENDIX D: Paul's Asian Epistles (Philemon, Colossians,
               Ephesians)   215

   APPENDIX E: Paul's Names for Jesus   218

   Bibliography   220

   Indexes

      Subjects   225

      Modern Authors   228

      Scripture and Other Ancient Writings   230

PREFACE

Historians of Christian origins are fortunate that Paul was such a major force in the early stages of the movement begun by Jesus of Nazareth. Thirteen of Paul's letters have survived,[1] and these provide a series of windows into his mind as well as the circumstances of the churches that belonged to his mission. As well, his friend Luke gives us a contemporary external narrative of the most critical part of Paul's missionary thrust into the Greco-Roman world. Few figures of antiquity are as accessible to inquiry as Paul of Tarsus.

So powerful a figure is Paul that some authorities regard him as the true founder of what Christianity was to become. Those who make this assessment, however, tend to do so not to praise Paul. On the contrary, they complain that he hijacked the religion of Jesus and made it into something that was never intended or envisaged.

When I began this book, I did not expect to discover too much that was new about Paul. How wrong this proved to be. The discipline involved in tracking Paul's career *chronologically* has been quite eye-opening. It has been a revelation to reflect on the number of years Paul lived in Jerusalem before he became a persecutor, on the number of years he passed in relative obscurity, and on the astonishing brevity of his missionary career. Furthermore, curiosity about aspects of Paul's life has produced interesting hypotheses for questions like: Why did Paul persecute the disciples when

1. Some scholars question the authenticity of Ephesians, Colossians, and the Pastoral Epistles, while also acknowledging significant Pauline influence in their authorship.

his teacher Gamaliel advised against it? Why did Paul *eventually* begin his westward mission? Why did he use strategies different from those of other missionaries? And why were he and the countermissionaries locked in such determined struggle?

ABBREVIATIONS

ABD	*Anchor Bible Dictionary*
Annals	*Annals of Imperial Rome* (Tacitus)
Ant	*Jewish Antiquities* (Josephus)
b.	Babylonian Talmud
BBR	*Bulletin for Biblical Research*
BC	P. Barnett, *Birth of Christianity,* vol. 1, *After Jesus* (Grand Rapids: Eerdmans, 2005)
CBQ	*Catholic Biblical Quarterly*
CurBS	*Currents in Research: Biblical Studies*
ET	English translation
ExpT	*Expository Times*
HE	*History of the Church* (Eusebius)
HTR	*Harvard Theological Review*
ICC	International Critical Commentary
JBL	*Journal of Biblical Literature*
JSNT	*Journal for the Study of the New Testament*
JSNTSS	Journal for the Study of the New Testament Supplement Series (Sheffield)
JTS	*Journal of Theological Studies*
JW	*Jewish War* (Josephus)
LCL	Loeb Classical Library
Life	*Life* (Josephus)
m.	Mishnah
NIGTC	New International Greek Testament Commentary
NovT	*Novum Testamentum*
NSBT	New Studies in Biblical Theology

NTS	*New Testament Studies*
RB	*Revue biblique*
RTR	*Reformed Theological Review* (Melbourne)
SBLDS	Society of Biblical Literature Dissertation Series
SBLSP	*Society of Biblical Literature Seminar Papers*
SBT	Studies in Biblical Theology
SNTSMS	Society for the New Testament Studies Monograph Series
TDNT	*Theological Dictionary of the New Testament* (ed. Kittel and Friedrich)
TynBul	*Tyndale Bulletin*
WBC	Word Biblical Commentary
WUNT	Wissenschaftliche Untersuchungen zum Neuen Testament
ZNW	*Zeitschrift für die neutestamentliche Wissenschaft und die Kunde der älteren Kirche*

MAPS

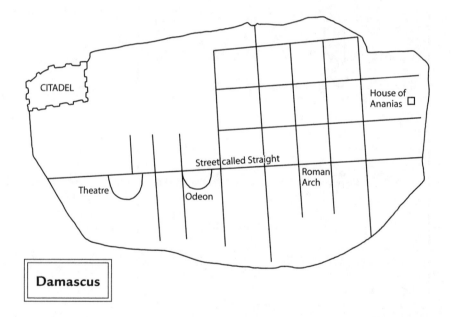

CITADEL

House of
Ananias □

Street called Straight

Roman
Arch

Theatre

Odeon

Damascus

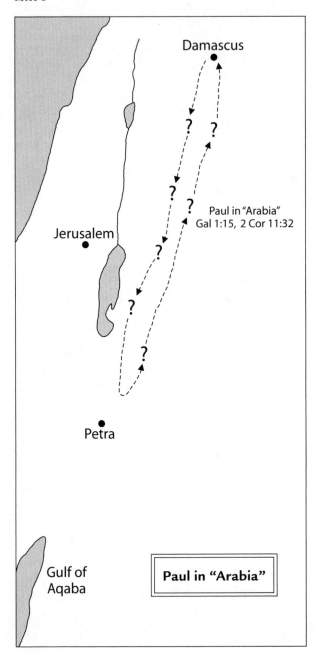

Damascus

Jerusalem

Paul in "Arabia"
Gal 1:15, 2 Cor 11:32

Petra

Gulf of
Aqaba

Paul in "Arabia"

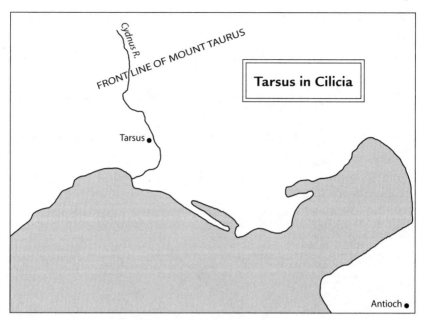

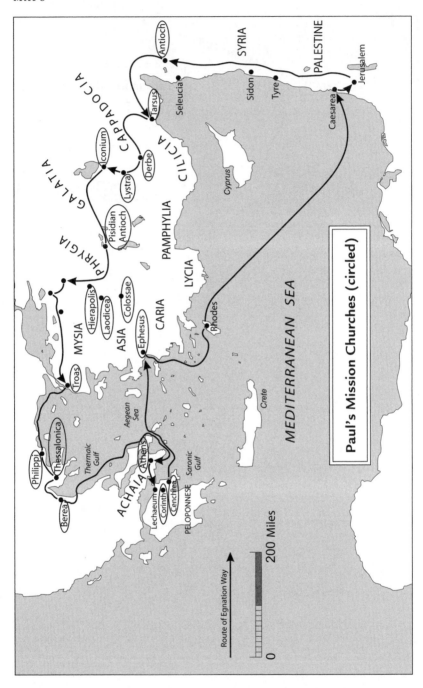

Paul's Mission Churches (circled)

Paul: Historical Enigma

What missionary is there, what preacher, what man entrusted with the cure of souls, who can be compared with him, whether in the greatness of the task he accomplished, or in the holy energy with which he carried it out?

Adolf von Harnack[1]

There is no abatement. Books on Paul — large books — keep appearing. This book, however, is not large. It addresses some theological issues along the way, but it is not a "theology of Paul,"[2] and although it adopts a diachronic approach, it is not a biography of Paul.[3]

---

1. Adolf von Harnack, *What Is Christianity?* (New York: Harper and Row, 1900), 179.

2. See, e.g., J. D. G. Dunn, *The Theology of Paul* (Grand Rapids: Eerdmans, 1998); U. Schnelle, *Apostle Paul: His Life and Theology,* trans. M. Eugene Boring (Grand Rapids: Baker Academic, 2005); M. J. Gorman, *Apostle of the Crucified Lord* (Grand Rapids: Eerdmans, 2004).

3. See generally F. F. Bruce, *Paul, Apostle of the Free Spirit* (Exeter: Paternoster, 1977). For a stimulating biography see J. Murphy-O'Connor, *Paul: A Critical Life* (Oxford: Oxford University Press, 1996), who, however, adopts a negative stance toward the reliability of the Acts of the Apostles. For Paul the preconvert, see M. Hengel, *The Pre-Christian Paul* (London: SCM, 1991); for the short time between the first Easter and the Damascus event, see M. Hengel, *Between Jesus and Paul* (London: SCM, 1983); Barnett, *BC,* 55-85; and for Paul's "unknown years," M. Hengel and A. M. Schwemer, *Paul between Damascus and Antioch* (London: SCM, 1997).

Questions about Paul

Paul is an enigmatic figure because we have more questions about him than answers.[4] There is an interesting question about Paul, however, for which an answer can be found and which this book seeks to address. It is this: Was Paul a true missionary of Jesus? Embedded in that question are others. Did Paul know about Jesus' life and teaching? Did Paul preach Jesus' message? Was Paul true to Jesus' intentions? Did Paul continue in the trajectory begun by Jesus?

Many people drive a wedge between Jesus and Paul, preferring Jesus and dispensing with Paul. They contend that Paul did not know Jesus' teachings but that he willfully struck out in his own idiosyncratic direction in pursuit of his own mission. William Wrede called him the "second founder" of Christianity in terms that were uncomplimentary (see 13). If Paul was not true to Jesus' teachings and intentions, we might justifiably dispense with him. But was he?

This main question is critical in its own right. Apart from that, however, it is a question I must address in this the second volume in my trilogy called *After Jesus*. The first volume was entitled *The Birth of Christianity: The First Twenty Years,* and the third (please God) will be *Finding the Historical Christ.* This short essay on Paul logically comes between the other two.

---

4. Many questions about Paul will likely never be answered to everyone's satisfaction. Who was his father and what had he done to achieve *Roman* citizenship? Was Paul always his name, or was he renamed in Cyprus (see appendix A)? Were his parents, siblings, and other relatives living in Jerusalem? Was he married? Was he doing "Jewish evangelism" before he began persecuting the church in Jerusalem? Had he met (or at least heard, or heard about) Jesus? Was he solely dependent upon the heavenly vision for his information about life "in Christ"? If he was influenced by disciples of Jesus, were they from Jerusalem or Antioch? What was he doing during the time (the "unknown years") between the Damascus event and when he embarked on his westward missionary journeys? Why, at last, did he decide to become a traveling missionary? Why did he leave his churches so soon after founding them? Who were the Jewish believers in Jerusalem who opposed him, and why? What was the relationship between his Jewish Christian opponents in Jerusalem and the "pillar" apostles, James, Cephas, and John? What was the "thorn in [or for] the flesh"?

The Importance of Paul for History

Despite the many unanswered questions about Paul (that make him an enigmatic figure), he is the fulfillment of a historian of antiquity's dream. This is because so many good sources are available (Paul's own letters), because a useful contemporary secondary source is also available (the Acts of the Apostles), and because the manuscript sources for both are quite early.

First, there are early copies (of copies?) of Paul's original letters that have survived and are safely housed in museums around the world. Furthermore, as well as their earliness,[5] the number and wide geographic distribution of editions of the whole NT[6] mean that textual critics are able to reconstitute versions of Paul's original texts that are for practical purposes what Paul actually wrote. Disputed readings of Paul's texts are minimal and are usually limited to isolated words.[7]

As well, the next wave of Christian writers (in the early second century) quotes extensively from Paul and provides a further check alongside his manuscripts. For example, Polycarp, bishop of Smyrna, wrote a short letter to the Philippians circa 110 and quoted from or alluded to ten of Paul's thirteen letters (Romans, 1 Corinthians, 2 Corinthians, Galatians, Ephesians, Philippians, Colossians, 2 Thessalonians, 1 Timothy, 2 Timothy).[8] The integrity of Paul's letters, based on the earliness and number of manuscripts and patristic citations, gives historians good grounds for their study of Paul.[9]

Second, Paul's letters are not intentional historical chronicles but "written sermons" to be read to congregations in the absence of the writer, addressing doctrinal and ethical matters. They do, however, contain his-

---

5. The manuscript known as 𝔭46, which is kept in the Chester Beatty collection in Dublin, is the earliest collection text of Paul's letters, dating from the late second century.

6. The editions of the NT known as Codex Vaticanus and Codex Sinaiticus date from the fourth century, but the texts on which they depend are necessarily earlier.

7. For example, reading Rom 5:1 as "*We have* peace with God" or "*Let us have* peace with God" depends on the reading of one vowel (omicron or omega) and scarcely affects the overall meaning of the passage.

8. Based on cross-referencing in the margins of Kirsopp Lake, *The Apostolic Fathers*, LCL (Cambridge: Harvard University Press, 1977), 282-301.

9. By contrast, the earliest manuscripts of the letters of Pliny the Younger (early second century) date from the late fifth century, although there is an earlier isolated citation from those letters by Tertullian (*Apology* 2) in the late second century.

torical, autobiographical, and geographical information that is gratuitous to the intent of the letters. The secondary nature of this data is of special interest to historians. At that time people tended to write history not only to narrate events but also to communicate a message; for example, much of Josephus's *Jewish War*, written in the mid-70s, is thinly veiled propaganda presented as history. Personal letters, business documents, and official correspondence from that era are innocent of the bias we find in intentionally written history.

Paul's letters belong (broadly) to one of the various categories of letter writing and are of special interest to historians. As a result, a large amount of authentic information can be gleaned, for example, the many places and people and events that Paul mentions in passing.[10] Consider, for example, the autobiographical, historical, and geographical information about Paul available to us in his letter to the Galatians.

Thirdly, there is an external narrative of Paul's life for circa 34-62 found in Acts 8–28. Furthermore, if it is granted that the author Luke was Paul's traveling companion circa 57-62 (as implied by the first-person "we"/"us" narrative in Acts 20–28), this likely means that Paul himself was the source for the earlier years (including Paul's childhood and pre-conversion years) that the author narrates.[11]

Historical information (gleaned) from Paul's letters in turn provides a reciprocal check on the accuracy of Luke's narrative about Paul, which proves to be reliable. When Paul's letters and relevant sections of Acts are considered side by side, we are able to reconstruct a chronology of Paul's life and establish when he wrote his letters.[12] These reconstructions are not complete in every detail, but, compared to other influential figures of that era, we are relatively well informed about Paul. There is no comparable parallel in antiquity to the nexus between an external narrator (Luke) and a letter writer (Paul) that yields such extensive information.[13]

10. See P. Barnett, *Jesus and the Logic of History* (Grand Rapids: Eerdmans, 1997), 15-28.

11. Barnett, *BC*, 187-205.

12. See J. B. Polhill, *Paul and His Letters* (Nashville: Broadman and Holman, 1999), for an account of the relationship between Paul's life and his letters.

13. See appendix B.

A Chronology of Paul

circa

5	Born in Tarsus of conservative Jewish parents
17	Moves to Jerusalem for study under Gamaliel
34	Leads persecution against disciples of Jesus
	Converted and "called" at Damascus
34-47	"Unknown Years" — Syria, Arabia, Judea, Syria-Cilicia
47-57	Missions in Galatia, Macedonia, Achaia, Asia
	Writes nine (extant) letters
57-64	Years of imprisonment — Caesarea and Rome
	Writes four (extant) letters

Scholars quibble about the details of this chronology, but the broad narrative about Paul is historically secure.[14]

This reconstruction indicates that Paul was in Jerusalem during the period of Jesus' public ministry (ca. 29-33). This raises the question whether Paul met Jesus, heard him, or heard about him. We do not know for certain, but the probability is high that he had at least heard about him. Be that as it may, we are on firmer ground in dating Paul's persecutions and subsequent conversion to circa 34, about one year after the first Easter. This means that Paul's persecutions and conversion occurred closer to the historical Jesus than we might think, based on the Acts narrative, which does not introduce "Saul" until chapter 8.

The Significance of Paul

Whether or not we view Paul positively, we reasonably regard him as one of history's truly remarkable figures.

First, Paul was determined to achieve what he set out to do, that is, to establish Christianity in the Greco-Roman world. During his decadelong burst of energy he walked thousands of kilometers (about thirty per day) across forbidding mountain ranges and through arid wastelands pro-

14. See R. Riesner, *Paul's Early Period: Chronology, Mission Strategy, Theology* (Grand Rapids: Eerdmans, 1998), for a comprehensive study of chronological issues, and E. Schnabel, *Early Christian Mission* (Downers Grove, Ill.: InterVarsity, 2004), for an expansive account of Paul's travels.

claiming the message of the crucified but risen Messiah. For preaching a message that was offensive to both Jews and Gentiles he was repeatedly and severely flogged, and on one occasion stoned. Virtually penniless, he labored throughout the night to earn money to preach by day. This ex-Pharisee brought the message about Jesus the Christ to the eastern provinces of the Roman Empire, and wanted to repeat this achievement in the western province, Spain. Apart from Paul's herculean efforts, it is difficult to imagine how the gospel of Christ would have taken root so comprehensively in the Greco-Roman world.

Paul's intrepid and energetic travels and tireless work, however, do not in themselves explain his achievements. Here we must understand that for Paul his relationship with Christ and his work for him were inseparable. He regarded all that he did as "the work of the Lord" (1 Cor 15:58) that the risen Christ was doing "through" his servant, Paul (Rom 15:18).

Christ, not Paul, initiated the relationship between them ("I was seized by Christ Jesus" — *katelēmphthēn hypo Christou Iēsou* — Phil 3:12), on Damascus Road.[15] He saw himself as the object of Christ's love because Christ was "made sin" for him so that he might participate in the "righteousness of God" on the last day (2 Cor 5:14, 21), which he confidently expected to do. It was Christ's initiative and love that drove him on in his missionary work (2 Cor 5:14; 6:3-10). As a prisoner in Rome thirty years after the Damascus event, Paul's zeal for Christ was undiminished: "I count everything as loss because of the surpassing worth of knowing Christ Jesus my Lord. For his sake I have suffered the loss of all things, and count them as refuse, in order that I may gain Christ and be found in him, not having a righteousness of my own, based on law, but that which is through faith in Christ" (Phil 3:8-9).

In short, to understand Paul's achievements we need to appreciate his driving passion, which was that Christ loved him and seized him, and that he could never be separated from his love (Rom 8:35, 39), sinner though he was and persecutor though he had been. For Paul that "love" *(agapē)* of God directed to him through the Son of God (Gal 2:20) became the key to his understanding of God's dealings with Adam's lost tribe (Rom 5:8; cf. 8:32) but also the basis of all human relationships (1 Cor 8:1) since "love" is that quality of God that "never ends" (13:8).

---

15. See chapter 5.

Closely connected with his relationship with Christ and equally basic in explaining those achievements was Paul's spiritual intelligence. His considerable native intelligence may be inferred by his precocity as a younger rabbi in the prestigious school of Gamaliel (cf. Gal 1:13-14) as well as by his multilingual abilities (Hebrew, Aramaic, Greek, and Latin [?]). Through that rabbinic school Paul became a master of the Old Testament, from which he makes more than one hundred identifiable quotations, more than half being from the Septuagint, the Greek translation of the Tanak[16] (Hebrew Bible). Additionally, his writings contain innumerable echoes from and allusions to biblical texts. Frequently these quotations, echoes, and allusions do not reproduce the original text exactly, suggesting that Paul was in many cases relying on a well-stocked memory; carrying voluminous OT scrolls was likely not practical for a penniless itinerant preacher who *walked* everywhere!

Through the Holy Spirit this man "in Christ," who was steeped in the OT, and who had likely been catechized at his baptism, became the first theologian in the early church, and arguably the greatest in the history of Christianity. Paul's genius is not found so much in his innovation as in his adaptation and application of traditions that had come to him from the Lord ("handed over" by earlier disciples) that he in turn reshaped for use in the churches, both by oral catechesis and by his letters. That adaptation and application usually arose in response to the theological, ethical, and relational crises within the churches of his mission. The occasional and responsive nature of Paul's thought is true even in his most "systematic" of letters, Romans.[17]

Paul and Theology

Indeed, Paul is to such a degree a "dialectic" thinker that it must be questioned whether the attempt at creating a "theology of Paul" is a viable enterprise. In my view, the most practical approach to Paul is to read his letters on a case-by-case basis and attempt to grasp their intent as originally formulated to the initial readers. There is an inherent danger that, in too

16. Acronym (TNK) formed from letters of the titles of the three major divisions — Torah ("Law"), Nebiim ("Prophets"), and Ketubim ("Writings").

17. See chapter 11.

closely "joining Paul's dots," important elements of his theological genius will be lost.[18]

It is true that we can make a list of Paul's beliefs, and this is useful to do. Our difficulty is to arrange these tenets as a hierarchy in a theological statement ("Paul's theology").

Rather than attempt to restructure Paul's theology from his letters, it may be more profitable to recover his initial kerygma and *didachē* and parenesis (ethics) from his letters (with reference also to the book of Acts). In that vein, of special importance are those passages that Paul reintroduces by way of reminder (e.g., 1 Cor 15:1-5 — "I would *remind* you . . . what . . .") and those texts where he appeals to the things they "know" that point to initial missionary instruction (e.g., 1 Cor 8:4 — "as to the eating of food offered to idols, we *know* . . ."). Analysis of his kerygma and *didachē* proves helpful in establishing Paul's initial missionary preaching and the theological and ethical foundations he laid upon which he built the superstructure of his thought (in his letters).

Paul, the Historical Jesus, and Earliest Christianity

The arrangement of the texts in the New Testament obscures the critical fact that Paul's letters were written before the Evangelists wrote their Gospels. That is to state the matter in broad terms, for it is possible that (an early version of) Mark preceded Romans (written ca. 57).[19]

Most of Paul's letters were written during his "missions decade" (ca.

---

18. Contra Dunn, *The Theology of Paul*, 13-19, who contends that it is possible to detect various "window-opening" stories like the story of Israel and Paul's own story. Dunn's own theology that follows, however, does not appear to be informed by his perception of the stories he thinks underlie and give unity to Paul's thought. As it happens, however, Dunn gives special attention to one of Paul's letters in particular, Romans, which he calls "a kind of template on which to construct our own statement of Paul's theology" (26). Here, though, there is a problem. Romans is indeed Paul's most comprehensive statement, but it is one that needed to be made against the pernicious influence of the Jewish-Christian countermission (see chapter 9). 1 Corinthians, however, written about three years earlier, is also a carefully constructed statement that is addressed to an entirely different ecclesial situation. If we attempt to formulate a single theological statement from such different arguments as we find in Romans and 1 Corinthians, it is hard to say what our starting and finishing points should be in ranking the items of his beliefs so as to recapture his "theology."

19. See Barnett, *BC*, 157.

47-57) and so provide the earliest known references to the historical Je-sus.[20] If, as I argue, Galatians is Paul's earliest letter (written ca. 47), it means that only a decade and a half separate that letter from the first Easter (33). If, as a majority believe, 1 Thessalonians is Paul's first letter (written ca. 50), the period of separation must be extended by a few years. By the standards of documentation of that era, this is a relatively brief pe-riod.

As Paul is the nearest chronological witness to Jesus, his passing ref-erences to his life and death and his echoes of his teachings are historically valuable, especially since they are generally given incidentally rather than intentionally, as noted earlier.

As well, Paul's missionary career (as reflected in his letters) has af-fected the broader documentation of early Christianity through the writ-ings of Luke. Luke wrote the book of Acts because he wanted to narrate the passage of the word of God to the Gentile nations. Since Paul is the chief bearer of that message, we conclude that he was Luke's inspiration for both the Acts of the Apostles and its predecessor, the Gospel of Luke. That is to say, Luke wrote his first volume to establish the rationale for what he nar-rates in his second volume, Paul's mission to the nations. Without Paul there would have been no urgent need for Luke to write about Jesus since there was at least one other Gospel already in circulation (Mark's).

This point, though indirect, is significant. Luke's Gospel-Acts alone establishes the nexus between Jesus and the rise of earliest Christianity. Without Luke-Acts it would not be possible historically to connect early Christianity with Christ or to explain the relationship between them.

Conclusion

Although Paul is an enigmatic figure about whom there are many unan-swered questions, there is no more important issue than his relationship with Jesus of Nazareth. Paul is the most powerful figure in earliest Chris-tianity, and I am interested to know whether his mission and message were Jesus' mission and message.

To answer this question I will (briefly) trace Paul's career, reflecting on a number of theological issues along the way. This book is not a "theol-

20. See chapter 2.

ogy of Paul," however, since it may not be possible to formulate such a theology given the uneven, dialectic nature of Paul's writings.

Historians of Christian origins are fortunate to have the writings of Paul, given their extent, earliness, gratuitous character, and early manuscript attestation. Furthermore, we have the external narration of Paul's missions in the writings of Luke. In consequence we are able to piece together much of Paul's life and thought. Not least, Paul himself is our earliest witness to the one he served, whom he called the Christ.

Paul and Jesus

It is hard to think of a more pressing theme in the whole field of New Testament study than the relationship of Paul to Jesus.

A. J. M. Wedderburn[1]

Jesus have I loved and Paul I have hated.

With apologies to Malachi

Giants Build a Wall

Since the beginning of the critical era, the titans of biblical scholarship have declared that Paul struck off in his own idiosyncratic direction, ignorant of or disobedient to the intentions of Jesus, the one he claimed to serve.[2] The keyword to the view of Baur, Harnack, Wrede, Schweitzer, and Bultmann on the Jesus-Paul relationship has been "discontinuity."

1. A. J. M. Wedderburn, foreword to *A Theology of Inclusion in Jesus and Paul: The God of Outcasts and Sinners,* by W. A. Simmons (Lewiston, N.Y.: Mellen Biblical Press, 1996), v.

2. The commencement of the Jesus-Paul debate may be dated to 1831, with publications by F. C. Baur about the place of Paul in the early church. For a historical survey of the Jesus-Paul question, see, for example, D. L. Dungan, *The Sayings of Jesus in the Churches of Paul* (Oxford: Basil Blackwell, 1971), xvii-xxix; J. W. Fraser, *Jesus and Paul* (Abingdon, Berks, England: Marcham Books, 1974), 11-32; S. G. Wilson, "From Jesus to Paul: The Contours and Consequences of a Debate," in *From Jesus to Paul,* ed. P. Richardson and J. C. Hurd,

11

True, the views of these famous scholars have not gone unchallenged. Yet, to generalize, the challengers have seldom made the same impact as the radical views they have attempted to answer. Apart from a few notable exceptions, the New Testament academy has adopted this skepticism as its critical orthodoxy.[3]

For these scholars the "resurrection" represents a wall between the historical Jesus and Paul the apostle, separating the one from the other. They see the Jesus-Paul discontinuity as part of the global discontinuity between Jesus and the early church. Jesus and the church belong to different sides of a barrier, with just a few gleams of light coming through from Jesus' side.

Nowhere is the wall of separation more evident than between Jesus and Paul, the apostle who was the dominant voice in the early church. The giants of the study of the New Testament argue that a virtual hiatus exists between Paul and Jesus in three matters. Paul's letters reveal that he knew almost nothing about Jesus' *life*, his *teachings*, and his *mission*.

This present study will concentrate on Paul's mission and its relationship to Jesus' mission. Nonetheless, we must first address the related questions about Paul's knowledge of Jesus' life and his teachings.

Loving Jesus and Hating Paul

In general these noted scholars as well as lesser-known Continental scholars had warm feelings about the historical Jesus (as they saw him) while regarding Paul as a misguided zealot who sent Christianity off in a direction that was far from the mind of its true founder.

Toward the end of the nineteenth century many Continental scholars came to emphasize Paul's isolation from Jesus. Jesus' teachings were simple and ethical and attainable, whereas Paul's were idiosyncratic and preoccupied with redemptive theology.[4]

Festschrift for F. W. Beare (Waterloo, Ont.: Wilfred Laurier University Press, 1984), 1-21; V. P. Furnish, "The Jesus-Paul Debate: From Baur to Bultmann," in *Paul and Jesus*, ed. A. J. M. Wedderburn, JSNTSS 37 (Sheffield: JSOT Press, 1989), 11-50; M. Thompson, *Clothed with Christ*, JSNTSS 59 (Sheffield: JSOT Press, 1989), 15-18; D. Wenham, *Paul: Follower of Jesus or Founder of Christianity?* (Grand Rapids: Eerdmans, 1995), 1-15; M. W. Yeung, *Faith in Jesus and in Paul* (Tübingen: Mohr Siebeck, 2001), 5-10.

3. Cf. Thompson, *Clothed with Christ*, 15-17.

4. See Fraser, *Jesus and Paul*, 12.

At that time Harnack attempted a more mediating approach. He attributed greater influence to "primitive Christianity" than to the influence of Paul. He also found in Paul's and Jesus' portrayals of God as "Father" a genuine point of contact. Harnack, however, claimed that "the Gospel, as Jesus preached it, has to do with the Father and not with the Son" and that Paul introduced the "speculative idea that not only was God in Christ, but that Christ himself was possessed of a peculiar nature of a heavenly kind."[5]

It was Wrede (writing in 1904), however, who drove the sharpest and deepest wedge between Paul and Jesus. He said Paul was no disciple of Jesus but held an independent notion of a celestial being, a divine Christ, before he believed in Jesus. On Damascus Road Paul identified Jesus with this glorious figure and transferred his ideas to him. Wrede famously declared Paul to be the "second founder of Christianity" who, "compared with the first, exercised beyond all doubt the stronger — not the better — influence."[6]

Bultmann (writing after World War I) stands apart from many others because he regards the historical Jesus as irrelevant to the kerygma of the risen Lord whom Paul proclaimed. Bultmann understood 2 Corinthians 5:16 ("even though we once knew Christ *kata sarka,* we know him thus no longer") to mean that Paul chose not to employ his knowledge of the historical Jesus kerygmatically, a view with which Bultmann agreed.[7] Accordingly, the influential scholar of Marburg declared Paul to be "the founder of Christian theology."[8]

Like Wrede, various Jewish scholars have considered Paul to be the true founder of Christianity. Broadly speaking, scholars from an earlier era like Klausner, Baeck, Buber, and Schoeps have tended to view Jesus as a true Jew, whereas Paul is seen as a renegade, influenced by Hellenistic ideas or other notions extraneous to the faith of Israel.[9]

More recently the tendency toward the appreciation of Jesus by Jewish writers was intensified, for example, by G. Vermes, who considered Jesus to be a "just man . . . zaddik . . . venerated by his intimates and less committed admirers alike as prophet, lord and son of God."[10] Implicit throughout

---

5. Quoted in Fraser, *Jesus and Paul,* 12.

6. ET, W. Wrede, *Paul* (Boston: American Unitarian Association, 1908), 148, 151.

7. See C. Wolf, "True Apostolic Knowledge of Christ: Exegetical Reflections on 2 Corinthians 4:14ff.," in *Paul and Jesus,* 84.

8. Quoted in Furnish, "The Jesus-Paul Debate," 49.

9. Summarized in Fraser, *Jesus and Paul,* 22.

10. G. Vermes, *Jesus the Jew* (Glasgow: Collins, 1973), 225.

Vermes' *Jesus the Jew* is the problem of identifying this Jewish Jesus with the Christ of the Nicene Creed quoted at the beginning of his book. Also implicit throughout is the inference that the early church in general and Paul in particular were responsible for this refashioning of Jesus.[11]

Rather more emphatic in tone is H. Maccoby, *The Mythmaker: Paul and the Invention of Christianity,*[12] whose title leaves little for the imagination. Maccoby doubts that Paul was a Pharisee or even a Jew!

These generally negative views of Paul (in contrast to generally positive view of Jesus) can also be found among many intellectuals outside the specialist forums of the NT academy. Nietzsche called Paul "the genius of hatred" who made Jesus "a God who died for our sins; redemption by faith; resurrection after death — all these things are falsifications of true Christianity."[13]

In the movie *The Last Temptation of Christ,* based on Nikos Kazantzakis's novel, there is a fantasy scene where Jesus hears Paul preaching the crucifixion and resurrection.

> JESUS: I'm a man like everyone else. Why are you spreading these lies?
>
> PAUL: I'm glad I met you. Now I'm rid of you. . . . I've created truth out of longing and faith. . . . If it's necessary to crucify you, then I'll crucify you — and I'll resurrect you, like it or not. The enemy is death and I'll defeat death by resurrecting you — Jesus of Nazareth, Son of God, Messiah.

Kazantzakis is echoing the outlook of Nietzsche that, in turn, is consistent with the views of the Continental giants of biblical scholarship.

Members of mainline conservative churches are generally unaffected by these attitudes toward Jesus and Paul. S. G. Wilson was doubtless correct in 1984 in asserting that "The traditional and implicit view of most major forms of Christianity has been to maintain a close connection between the historical Jesus and the Christ of faith, usually taking the gospel

---

11. In Vermes' later work *The Religion of Jesus the Jew* (London: SCM, 1993), he asks (212): "Is it an exaggeration to suggest that oceans separate Paul's Christian Gospel from the religion of Jesus the Jew?"

12. H. Maccoby, *The Mythmaker: Paul and the Invention of Christianity* (London: Weidenfeld and Nicholson, 1986).

13. Quoted in Fraser, *Jesus and Paul,* 9.

narratives at their face value and thus supposing that Jesus anticipated in all essentials the beliefs of the early church."[14]

Nonetheless, the views of the titans of the academy and skeptical intellectual philosophers and authors tend to be known among the elites in the Western world, widening further the chasm between the intelligentsia and the churches.

Was There a Wall?

How can we account for this imagined "wall" between Paul and the historical Jesus, and is such a wall justified? Is it a real or an imaginary wall?

To begin, we note that few scholars address the issue of the chronological closeness of Paul to Jesus. Where Paul's Damascus experience is conceived of as somewhat distant in time from Jesus, the idea of separation between the two figures seems cogent. Is this true to the facts?

The truth is, when Jesus first came up to Jerusalem as a public figure, Paul had been living in the city for more than a decade.[15] The student rabbi enrolled in the school of the famous Gamaliel could hardly have been unaware of the currents of thought in the Holy City, including those initiated by the prophet from the north.

Related to this is the brief time separating Paul's conversion/call from Jesus. By any reckoning, Paul's "Damascus event" must have occurred soon after the crucifixion, regardless whether one opts for A.D. 30 or 33 as the date for the execution of Jesus. It likely occurred about a year after the life span of Jesus of Nazareth ended in crucifixion and resurrection,[16] a contention

14. Wilson, "From Jesus to Paul," 18.

15. See chapter 3.

16. Calculations are based on (a) Paul's arrival in Corinth in A.D. 50 as a firm datum, and (b) the assumption that it took Paul two years to reach Corinth after his second visit to Jerusalem (Gal 2:1). There appear to be four options:

  i. Where A.D. 30 is the date of the crucifixion and fourteen years separate Paul's Damascus event and his second visit to Jerusalem (Gal 2:1; cf. 1:18), we conclude that Paul was converted/called in 34 (about four years after the crucifixion).

  ii. Where A.D. 30 is the date of the crucifixion and seventeen years separate Paul's Damascus event and his second visit to Jerusalem (Gal 2:1; cf. 1:18), we conclude that Paul was converted/called in 31 (about a year after the crucifixion).

  iii. Where A.D. 33 is the date of the crucifixion and fourteen years separate Paul's

that is consistent with Paul's bracketing of himself with those others to whom the risen Christ appeared at the first Easter (1 Cor 15:4-7).

In short, the years of Jesus' public ministry (ca. 29-33) occurred when Paul was under training in Jerusalem, and his Damascus experience occurred within a year of the first Easter. While Paul's words in 2 Corinthians 5:16 ("we once knew Christ *kata sarka*") do not mean that he knew the historical Christ, there are sound reasons based on chronology and proximity to assert that Paul would have at least *heard about* Jesus. On that basis the notional "wall" between the two is harder to maintain.

A second reason for thinking that Paul was "walled off" from Jesus is the belief that Paul was significantly influenced in a Hellenistic rather than a Palestinian milieu.[17] This hypothesis was advanced by the so-called history-of-religions school, notably by Bultmann.[18] According to this view, some of the Hellenist Jewish disciples who appear in the early Acts passages remigrated to Antioch in the 30s following Paul's persecutions; there they began to see Jesus in terms of the "lords" and demigods of Greco-Syrian religions. When Paul came to Antioch in the 40s, he adopted this Hellenistic theology and made it his own in his kerygma, as reflected in his letters. Bultmann's existential understanding of "faith" in an ahistorical Jesus found this Hellenistic Christ-myth explanation quite congenial.[19]

This reconstruction, however, is quite speculative.[20] There is no evidence that the returning Hellenists were subject to such religious influence in Antioch[21] or that they adopted it. It must not be forgotten that the Hel-

---

Damascus event and his second visit to Jerusalem (Gal 2:1; cf. 1:18), we conclude that Paul was converted/called in 34 (about a year after the crucifixion).

iv. Where A.D. 33 is the date of the crucifixion and seventeen years separate Paul's Damascus event and his second visit to Jerusalem (Gal 2:1; cf. 1:18), we conclude that Paul was converted/called in 33 (some months after the crucifixion). Our preferred option is (iii); see *BC* 22-26.

17. See chapter 6.

18. Bultmann's teacher, Heitmüller, advanced this view in 1912 (see Furnish, "The Jesus-Paul Debate," 32).

19. Bultmann rejected the *historische* (historical) Jesus for the *geschichtliche* ("historic" or "interpreted") Jesus.

20. See the classical critique of this view in M. Hengel, *Between Jesus and Paul* (London: SCM, 1983), 30-47. This chapter first appeared as a separate article in 1972.

21. See M. Hengel and A. M. Schwemer, *Paul between Damascus and Antioch* (Louisville: Westminster John Knox, 1997), 21-23, where the authors (depending on F. Millar, *The*

lenists were Jews and, like other Jews originating in the Diaspora, were quite aware of Gentile ideas and pressures. Why is it assumed that either these Hellenistic Jews or Paul the ex-Pharisee became Greco-Oriental syncretists?

In any case, Paul's first three years as a believer were spent near or in Palestine. In Damascus he was baptized by Ananias, who is called "a devout man according to the law" (*anēr eulabēs kata ton nomon* — Acts 22:12), that is, a conservative Jew. Within three years Paul was back in Jerusalem, where he stayed with Cephas for several weeks and also met James, brother of Jesus (Gal 1:18-20). True, Paul most likely heard and was influenced by Stephen and other Hellenists whom he persecuted. Their impact on Paul during this brief exposure appears to have been considerable regarding the supersession of the temple and the law/Moses (see later, 51-53). Yet there is no reason to ascribe pagan syncretistic ideas to the Jerusalem Hellenists, and even less reason to believe that Paul the ex-Pharisee and persecutor would have been impressed by those ideas. The influences on Paul point to Jerusalem as their source.

In other words, any notion of Hellenistic ideology as a "wall" between Paul and Jesus is conjectural and lacks a historical basis.

A more substantial reason for supposing that Paul was separated from Jesus is the apostle's relative silence about the details of Jesus' life and the apparent relative infrequency of his reference to the teachings of Jesus. To these questions we now turn.

Did Paul Know the Details of Jesus' Life?

Did Paul know about Jesus? Few deny that Paul's (undisputed) letters reveal some knowledge of Jesus. Those who supply a list of items usually point to the general sparsity of information and to critical omissions (e.g., details of Jesus' birth, his baptism by John, his miracles, his teaching in parables, his transfiguration, his clearing of the temple, his betrayal by Judas).[22]

In the list given below we find rather more information than we might expect to glean from a general reading of Paul's letters. Be that as it

---

Roman Near East, 31 BC–AD *337* [Cambridge: Harvard University Press, 1993]) point out how little we know about Syria in NT times.

22. See, e.g., Furnish, "The Jesus-Paul Debate," 43.

may, the consideration that is not always explored is the *access* Paul had to information about Jesus. Upon careful analysis, Paul's information about Jesus proves to be quite extensive.

It is certain that Paul had the opportunity to be well informed about the details of Jesus' life. First, so far as we know, Paul lived in Jerusalem throughout the span of Jesus' ministry; he had moved to that city years earlier (see chapter 3). Second, his participation in the trial and stoning of Stephen and his assault on both "Hebrew" and "Hellenist" believers in Jerusalem must have brought the raw facts about Jesus to his attention. Third, his association in Damascus with Ananias and with fugitive believers from Jerusalem would also have contributed to his knowledge about Jesus. Fourth, Paul himself states that within three years of the Damascus event he spent two weeks with Peter in Jerusalem, where he also met James, brother of Jesus (Gal 1:18-20). This evidence from Paul's own hand shows that he had opportunity for extensive knowledge about Jesus' early life (from James) and about Jesus' ministry and teaching (from Peter). Fifth, his lengthy association with Barnabas, an early disciple in Jerusalem, afforded opportunity for further (indirect) information.

In short, due to Paul's historical and geographical proximity to Jesus and considerable access to reliable second- and thirdhand information about him, we are not surprised at the extent and nature of the details reflected in Paul's writings.

Information about Jesus in Paul's Letters[23]

1. Jesus was a descendant of Abraham the patriarch (Gal 3:16).
2. Jesus was a direct descendant of King David. This is critical to the belief that he was the Christ, the Messiah of Israel (Rom 1:3; 9:5; 15:8; cf. 1 Cor 15:3).
3. The mention of Jesus being "born of a woman" (Gal 4:4-5) suggests that Paul knew of and confirmed the virginal conception of Jesus.[24]

---

23. See, e.g., F. F. Bruce, *Paul, Apostle of the Free Spirit* (Exeter: Paternoster, 1977), 95-112; J. D. G. Dunn, "Jesus Tradition in Paul," in *Studying the Historical Jesus*, ed. B. Chilton and C. A. Evans (Leiden: Brill, 1994), 155-78.

24. Paul's words in Gal 4:4-6 appear to be connected in some way with material in the early chapters of the Gospel of Luke: "The time had fully come . . . to redeem"/"[God] has visited and redeemed his people . . . as he spoke by the mouth of his holy prophets" (Luke

Paul's words are in agreement with Matthew's: "Mary, *of whom* Jesus was born, who is called Christ" (Matt 1:16). Jesus was born of the woman, Mary, not of her husband Joseph.

4. Jesus was born and lived in "poverty" (2 Cor 8:9).
5. Jesus was "born under" and lived under Jewish law (Gal 4:4).
6. Jesus had a brother named James and other brothers, unnamed (Gal 1:19; cf. 1 Cor 9:5).
7. Jesus had twelve disciples, to whom the risen Lord "appeared" (1 Cor 15:5; cf. Mark 3:14 pars.).[25]
8. Peter was the spokesman of the Twelve (e.g., Mark 8:27-30 pars.), a role that developed, postresurrection, into his leadership of the mission *(apostolē)* to the circumcised in Israel (Gal 2:7-8).[26]
9. Jesus' manner was one of humility and meekness, agreeing with his words recorded in the Gospel, "I am gentle and lowly in heart" (2 Cor 10:1; Matt 11:29).
10. He was externally "transfigured" on a mountain (Mark 9:2; Matt 17:2), as Paul expects believers to be "transformed" inwardly (2 Cor 3:18; cf. Rom 12:2).[27]
11. Jesus called God "abba" (Gal 4:6; cf. Rom 8:15).
12. He ministered primarily to Israel/Jews (Rom 15:8).
13. He instituted a memorial meal on the night he was betrayed (1 Cor 11:23-25).
14. He was cruelly treated at that time (Rom 15:3).
15. He was killed by the Jews of Judea (1 Thess 2:14-15).
16. He testified before Pontius Pilate (1 Tim 6:13).[28]
17. His "death on a cross" (Phil 2:8) implies execution at *Roman* hands for treason (cf. Gal 3:1; 6:17).
18. He was buried (1 Cor 15:4).

1:68-70); "God sent forth his Son"/"He . . . will be called the Son of the Most High" (Luke 1:32); "born of woman"/"Jesus . . . the son (as was supposed) of Joseph" (Luke 3:23); "born under the law"/"as according to [the] custom [of the Law]" (Luke 2:42). Was Paul familiar with a source that Luke subsequently incorporated in his Gospel?

25. See Wenham, *Paul,* 200-205.

26. See Wenham, *Paul,* 200-205.

27. The unusual verb *metamorphoō* occurs in the NT only in these references. For argument that Paul knew about the transfiguration of Jesus, see Wenham, *Paul,* 357-63.

28. It could be argued that in this late writing Paul was dependent on later rather than earlier Gospel traditions.

19. He was raised on the third day and was seen alive on a number of occasions by many witnesses, most of whom were still alive, able to confirm this (1 Cor 15:5-7).

Observations about Paul's Information

First, we notice that the information Paul uses about Jesus falls into two classes, liturgical and nonliturgical.

From preformed and likely pre-Pauline passages we find information about Jesus' Davidic lineage (Rom 1:1-4), his incarnation into a life of poverty (2 Cor 8:9), his birth to a woman, his life under the law and address to God as "abba" (Gal 4:4-6), his institution of the Lord's Supper (1 Cor 11:23-25), and his death, burial, resurrection, and risen appearances (1 Cor 15:3-5).

The remaining texts about Jesus in Paul's letters do not appear to have been liturgically preformed.

Whether Paul's texts are liturgical or nonliturgical references, Paul does not appear to be introducing new information about Jesus to his readers. Rather, his comments implicitly assume that the churches already knew whatever he chose to mention.

From this observation we draw the important conclusion that Paul knew this information before he arrived at the constituent churches and that, in the context of his primary ministry, he passed it on to his readers. It can scarcely have been otherwise since his original hearers must have had many questions about the crucified and risen redeemer who was the focus of Paul's preaching. As M. Hengel observed: "It was simply impossible in the antiquities to proclaim a man crucified a few years ago, as Kyrios, Son of God and Redeemer, without saying something about who this man was, what he taught and did, and why he died."[29]

Second, we cannot help noticing that Paul's spread of Jesus references, broadly speaking, can be arranged chronologically (as above) and that the sequence more or less coincides with the sequence in the Gospels. In other words, Paul was aware overall of the span of Jesus' life and ministry.

---

29. Cited in S. Kim, *Paul and the New Perspective: Second Thoughts on the Origin of Paul's Gospel* (Grand Rapids: Eerdmans, 2002), 281. Cf. also J. D. G. Dunn, *The Theology of Paul the Apostle* (Grand Rapids: Eerdmans, 1998), 185-89.

What, then, of the facts about Jesus that Paul omits? Here there are several possibilities. One is that he simply did not know (for example) that Jesus performed miracles. The other, more likely possibility is that he did know and teach about the miracles but that the issue was never raised in the churches so as to call for some comment. His reference to the "signs and wonders" that Christ "wrought in [Paul]" is consistent with the likelihood that Paul knew of his Master's "signs and wonders" (Rom 15:18-19).

Neither possibility detracts from the observation that Paul had extensive knowledge about Jesus and that it followed the broad sequence of the outline of the Gospels.

Third, it is worth remembering that Paul does not claim to have known the historical Jesus directly. He may indeed have seen and heard Jesus, but that must rest on conjecture. His claim to have "seen" the risen Lord (1 Cor 9:1) refers to the Damascus Christophany. His confession that he knew Christ according to the flesh (2 Cor 5:16) points back to his days as a persecutor when he had formed a "worldly" *(kata sarka)* misconception of Christ (which his recently arrived rivals in Corinth still have — 2 Cor 11:1-4). Had Paul seen and heard the historical Jesus, it would have been with the same "worldly" perceptions.

Did Paul Know Jesus' Teachings?

A significant body of literature has been devoted to this question. It is a complex question, however, due to the problem of deciding whether Paul is *quoting* Jesus, *echoing* Jesus, or *adapting* Jesus' teaching.[30] Among the many who have addressed this question, the estimates of Pauline usage of Jesus' teaching vary greatly, from just a few references to many hundreds.[31]

Yet it is evident from his echoes of them that Paul was aware of various teachings of Jesus that were then in circulation[32] and that he appealed

30. Furnish, "The Jesus-Paul Debate," 47-48, helpfully lists five distinguishable positions regarding Paul's use of Jesus' teachings: (1) Mair et al.: Paul confirms the teachings of Jesus; (2) Wellhausen, Harnack, Deissmann: Paul reasonably interprets the teaching of Jesus; (3) Wrede, Goguel: Paul develops the teaching of Jesus illegitimately; (4) Weiss, Beare: Paul develops the teaching of Jesus legitimately; (5) Bultmann: Paul has no interest in the teaching of Jesus.

31. See Thompson, *Clothed with Christ*, 15-17, for a review of a range of opinions.

32. See Barnett, *BC*, 111-49.

to various words or commands of the Lord (cf. 1 Thess 4:2, 15; 1 Cor 9:14; 10; 11:23; 12). In short, we can say that Paul was aware of various teachings of the Lord even if we are uncertain about the extent of that awareness.

Conclusion

While the giants of NT scholarship erected a wall separating Paul from Jesus, it may be observed that equally capable but for the most part less famous historians have demolished it. Because of their labors we are confident that Saul of Jerusalem was a contemporary of the historical Jesus, that his Damascus experience occurred months, not years, after the first Easter, and that within three years of the Damascus event Paul the apostle had extensive discussions in Jerusalem with both Peter the leading disciple and James the brother of the Lord, affording him detailed knowledge about Jesus.

Within historically reasonable limits it is clear that Paul's letters reflect an extensive global and sequential knowledge of Jesus' life details. Likewise do his letters to a significant degree quote, echo, and adapt the words of Jesus, even though we cannot know how much material was accessible to Paul when he wrote.

In short, there is no wall between Jesus and Paul, but only level ground between them. We are now able to proceed toward our objective in analyzing one aspect of the continuity between Jesus and Paul, that is, the continuity between Jesus' mission and Paul's mission.

THREE

Saul of Jerusalem:
A Pharisee Who Wrote Greek

He is a chosen instrument of mine to carry my name before the Gentiles
and kings and the sons of Israel.

Acts 9:15

Who was this man whose mission changed the face of Christianity and the course of world history? What can be known of his early life, and how might this have influenced his mission?

As we trace Paul's early life, we gain a better understanding of his later life as a man "in Christ." Paul was a Jew, born in Tarsus in the Diaspora, who came as a "youth" to live in Roman-occupied Jerusalem where he became a Pharisee through his membership in the school of the noted rabbi Gamaliel. His letters, written later, reveal an assured fluency in koine Greek and a mastery of the Greek Bible (Septuagint).

Importance of Chronology

Fundamental to historical discipline is the need to locate the subject under discussion *chronologically*. While it is not possible to date Paul's life exactly, the range of possibilities is not great. The parts of the NT on which we depend for Paul's chronology were written during or shortly after his life span. Paul's letters are (of course) contemporary with him, while the book of Acts may have been written soon after its narrative concluded, while Paul was still alive.[1]

Paul's Age

Paul does not reveal his age in his letters. All that mattered to him, apparently, was that his life fell into two parts, before and after he was a man "in Christ."[2]

There are two points where we are able to calculate Paul's age. One is in the book of Acts, which says he was "a young man" (*neanias* — 7:58) when he was persecuting the church in Jerusalem, that is, circa 33/34.[3]

The other clue is Paul's description of himself in a letter to his friend Philemon in about 55 as "an old man"[4] (*presbytēs* — Philem 9).[5] The Mishnah may cast some light on these references by observing that "one is fit . . . at thirty for authority . . . at sixty to be an elder" (*m. Avot* 5:21).[6] A degree of "authority" implying someone thirty years of age may be inferred by Paul's close involvement with the witnesses who stoned Stephen and his leadership in the persecutions that followed (Acts 7:58; 22:20). At the other extreme, Paul's reference to himself as *presbytēs* approximates to (but is less than) the Mishnah's "elder" as a sixty-year-old man. Perhaps by referring to himself as *presbytēs* Paul is not so much being precise about age as he is pointing to a sense of debility through imprisonment.

---

1. This is a conservative view. Many scholars argue that Acts was written in the 80s or 90s.

2. In Rom 16:7 he speaks of Andronicus and Junia as being "in Christ before" him.

3. See Barnett, *BC,* 22-26, for further discussion. R. Riesner, *Paul's Early Period: Chronology, Mission Strategy, Theology* (Grand Rapids: Eerdmans, 1998), provides detailed and thorough chronological discussion of the first twenty years of Paul's ministry. Riesner, however, argues for A.D. 30 as the date of the crucifixion.

4. Some dispute the meaning, contending rather that *presbytēs* means "ambassador," as indeed it does in some contexts.

5. Many think Paul wrote to Philemon from Rome, that is, in the early 60s. For two reasons, however, Ephesus is the more likely provenance for the letter: (1) it is far less likely that the slave of Paul's friend Philemon met Paul in prison in Rome than that he met him during a time of captivity in Ephesus; and (2) Paul's expectation of visiting Colossae is imaginable from Ephesus but less so from Rome. See also appendix B.

6. Gentile authorities also divided a man's life into its various ages. Hippocrates, for example, referred to the seventh "season" of life, between forty-nine and fifty-six (Philo, *On the Creation of the World* 105, quoting Hippocrates the physician).

In short, lack of firm data drives us to speculate broadly about Paul's age. In that spirit I estimate Paul's age as a "young man" circa 34 to have been about *thirty years* and his age as an "old man" circa 55 as *early to middle fifties.* On this basis Paul was born circa A.D. 5.

Tarsus and Jerusalem (ca. 5-34)

Paul famously summarizes his life before he was a man "in Christ."

> If any other man thinks he has reason for confidence in the flesh, I have more:
>> circumcised on the eighth day,
>> of the people of Israel,
>> of the tribe of Benjamin,
>> a Hebrew of Hebrews;
>> as to the law a Pharisee,
>> as to zeal a persecutor of the church,
>> as to righteousness under the law blameless.

Most likely this is not a random list. Rather, we notice a certain chronology, beginning with his origins, where he gives his tribal roots ("the tribe of Benjamin") and his prescribed circumcision ("on the eighth day"). From Acts we learn that he was called "Saul,"[7] doubtless in honor of the distinguished antecedent Benjamite who was the first king of Israel. The next elements in the list appear to apply to Jerusalem, from the years of his youth ("righteousness under the law") into his adult life ("a Pharisee . . . a persecutor").

If we base our assessment only on his letters, we would assume that Jerusalem had always been Paul's home (see, e.g., "from *Jerusalem* and as far round as Illyricum I have fulfilled the gospel of Christ" — Rom 15:19). Only from the book of Acts do we learn that he was born in "Tarsus in Cilicia" (Acts 22:3; cf. 9:11; 21:39), a place to which he returned many years after his life in Palestine (Acts 9:30; 11:25).

It is also from the book of Acts that we discover Paul's relationships with these two cities, Tarsus and Jerusalem.

---

7. Acts refers to him by his Hebrew name Saoul (9:4, 17; 13:21; 22:7, 13; 26:14) and by its Hellenized version Saulos (7:58–13:9 passim). See appendix A.

a. Following his arrest in Jerusalem circa 57, Paul declared: "I am a Jew, born *(gegennēmenos)* at Tarsus in Cilicia, but brought up *(anatethrammenos)* in this city, at the feet of Gamaliel, educated *(pepaideumenos)* according to the strict manner of the law of our fathers" (Acts 22:3).

b. Some years later Paul defended himself to Agrippa II: "My manner of life from my youth *(ek neotētos),* spent from the beginning among my own nation and at Jerusalem, is known by all the Jews" (Acts 26:4).

While Paul's birth in Tarsus is accepted, the time of his "upbringing" *(anatethrammenos)* and "education" *(pepaideumenos)* in Jerusalem is under debate. Everything depends on the meaning of (i) "brought up" (Acts 22:3), and (ii) whether "from . . . [his] youth" he "spent" his time in Jerusalem or (only) "from . . . [his] youth" he was "known" in Jerusalem.

In regards to (i), van Unnik has argued that "brought up" means "from birth" so that Paul had no exposure to the Hellenistic world of Tarsus, but was raised in Jerusalem by his parents from early childhood.[8] Regarding (ii), the same scholar contends that Acts 26:4 should be understood to mean that Paul was *well-known* in Jerusalem from his "youth."

In van Unnik's reconstruction Paul grew up in Jerusalem in a thoroughly Hebraized manner, speaking only Aramaic, knowing only a few Greek words, and that he gained his proficiency in koine Greek and in the Septuagint when living in Cilicia and Syria in the 30s and 40s.

This cogent argument presents several problems.[9] First, Paul's ease of writing koine and his mastery of the Septuagint (so evident from his letters) seem unlikely to have been acquired only in his later life in Tarsus in the decade or so before his first letters begin appearing.[10] Secondly, Acts 26:4 is open to another interpretation: that Paul had lived in Jerusalem from his "youth" and that *from that time* he had been well-known there.

If this interpretation is permitted, it would mean that Paul came (more likely, "was brought") to Jerusalem in his "youth," that is, in his preteen years. The same words "from my youth" in the mouth of the rich man replying to Jesus likely meant from the time of his early teens when he for-

8. In his critical study W. C. van Unnik, "Tarsus or Jerusalem, the City of Paul's Youth?" in *Sparsa Collecta* 1: *Evangelia — Paulina,* Acts NTSupp 29 (Leiden: Brill, 1973), 259-320, argues that Paul was brought from Tarsus to Jerusalem as a small child: so, too, M. Hengel, *The Pre-Christian Paul* (London: SCM, 1991), 22-23.

9. Hengel, *The Pre-Christian Paul,* 34.

10. Hengel, *The Pre-Christian Paul,* 35.

mally embraced the Torah as a way of life (Mark 10:20).[11] Accordingly, if Paul was brought to Jerusalem aged about twelve years, it would mean that he had lived in the Holy City from circa A.D. 17.[12]

This view has the advantage of explaining Paul's two-sided nature. His early years in Tarsus secured a basic (primary?) education in koine Greek while his attendance at the synagogue at least acquainted him with the Septuagint. On the other hand, the formative period in Jerusalem "from his youth" satisfies his insistence about his achievements as a Pharisee. His *expertise* in the Septuagint, however, suggests that he pursued these studies while living in Jerusalem.

In short, it seems that the pre-Damascus Paul spent his first dozen or so years in Tarsus in Cilicia and the next sixteen or so years in Jerusalem. It appears, then, that the years in Jerusalem would have been of profound importance in shaping the life and attitudes of Paul.

Tarsus: The Early Years (ca. 5-17)

Paul's Family in Tarsus

The most important detail about Saul's family in Tarsus was their strict adherence to the tenets of Judaism. We have only limited knowledge of the attitudes and practices of Diaspora Jews, but his own references suggest a rigorous upbringing as Jew.

The combined references in his letters reveal him to have been "a Hebrew of Hebrews," "an Israelite," "a descendant of Abraham," "a member of the tribe of Benjamin" who had been "circumcised on the eighth day" (Phil 3:5; Rom 11:1; cf. 2 Cor 11:22). It appears that his family were not merely conservative and strict Jews of the Diaspora in their observance of Judaism. Even more, as a "youth" his parents (likely) brought him to Jerusalem, a likely further indication of their commitment to the covenant of Israel (Acts 26:4).

11. "At five years old one is fit for the scripture . . . at thirteen for the fulfilling of the commandments" (*m. Avot* 5:21). We cannot be certain when the practice of bar mitzvah was begun.

12. Acts makes a curious reference to "the son of Paul's sister," who effectively saved Paul's life in Jerusalem circa 57 (Acts 23:16). This may support the view that Paul's parents had transferred their entire family to Jerusalem.

This family would have kept a careful distance from the cultural expressions of Hellenism in a city like Tarsus. Wealthy Jews often became assimilated into Hellenist ways, but not the family of Saul in Tarsus.

Nonetheless, Saul's was a prominent family in Tarsus. Paul later reveals that he was "a *citizen (politēs)*" of Tarsus (Acts 21:39), a citizenship he would have inherited from his father. Substantial wealth, property worth 500 drachmae (equivalent to two years' wages), was fixed as a qualification for enrollment as a citizen of Tarsus.[13]

More significantly, however, Saul was a *Roman* citizen, a highly privileged status into which he was "born" (Acts 22:28). This means his father must have been a Roman citizen. Principal routes to Roman citizenship were by *emancipation* from the servitude of a distinguished patron or as a *reward* for significant services rendered to a noted Roman leader. In regards the latter, some have pointed to Paul's trade as a leather worker/ tentmaker as a clue to the nature of a family business that, it is argued, had brought them wealth and influence.[14] (It is possible, however, that Paul learned this trade following his apostolic call, as a means of support.) Both the emancipation and the reward views have been canvassed,[15] though the resolution remains elusive.

Whatever the family circumstances had been, the Jew Saul, like his father before him, had been privileged as a citizen of the Greek city of Tar-

13. Dio Chrysostom, *Orations* 34.23. Tarsus appears to have been unusual in this regard. Full citizenship on an individual basis was typically disallowed to Jews living in Greek cities; Jews enjoyed concessions only on a corporate basis, in order freely to practice their ancestral religion. However, citizenship of a Gentile city typically involved participation in idolatrous sacrifices. It has been plausibly suggested, but without proof, that Jewish citizens of Tarsus formed a discrete group (*phylē*, or "tribe") who were relieved of religious obligations that would otherwise have applied. In Rom 16:7-21 Paul refers by name to six fellow believers he calls "kinsmen." These are unlikely to be blood relatives of Paul; we do not know of the conversion of family members. They were more probably fellow tribe members from Tarsus who may have enjoyed citizenship in the city as Jews following Augustus's benefactions after 42 B.C.; so W. M. Ramsay, *The Cities of St. Paul* (London: Hodder and Stoughton, 1907), 176-78.

14. Tents were then made of leather. "Tentmakers" also worked in all manner of leather goods. See Barnett, "Tent Making," in *Dictionary of Paul and His Letters* (Downers Grove, Ill.: InterVarsity, 1993), 925-27.

15. The reward view is classically expounded by Mommsen but is opposed by Hengel, *The Pre-Christian Paul*, 5, 14-15, who argues, but without substantial evidence, that Paul's antecedents were former slaves (following Pompey's invasion of Palestine) who, upon emancipation, were granted Roman citizenship.

sus and of the Roman Empire. Saul therefore belonged to the social elite of Cilicia, even if his family kept their distance from the life of the city.

During his mission years Paul occasionally reveals the mind of a Roman citizen. The believers' citizenship *(politeuma)*, he observed to the people of the Roman colony of Philippi, is in heaven (Phil 3:20). His geographical references dotted throughout his letters are not to generalized regions but to *Roman provinces* — Judea, Syria-Cilicia, Galatia, Macedonia, Achaia, Illyricum. He appears to have favored Roman colonies as centers for ministry, for example, Tarsus, Antioch in Pisidia, Iconium, Lystra, Troas, and Philippi, as well as capitals of Roman provinces like Antioch on the Orontes, Thessalonica, Corinth, and Ephesus. His objective to preach the gospel in Rome and lay the apostolic foundation there is quite understandable in one who was a Roman citizen (Rom 1:10-13; 15:23-24; Acts 19:21).

Life in Tarsus

Tarsus's long history as a Hellenistic city with a strong rhetorical tradition makes it likely that Saul had received a basic education in Greek language. Although his Jewish home life would have shielded him from overtly Hellenistic thought and practice, his early years in such a city would have ensured a working knowledge of Greek speech and reading. This remains true despite the probability of such Greek education being confined to the elementary level, which may have been home-based in a domestic *paidagōgos* (cf. Gal 3:24-25), and restricted to forms acceptable to a Jew. His writings have no echoes of Homer or Plato and betray little sophistication in those Greek rhetorical forms we would expect had he attended one of the philosophical schools in Tarsus. It is true enough that his letters have some allusions from the world of the Greeks, but Paul may have come across these in popularized forms in the course of his travels.[16] Rather, his writings are permeated with the language and ideas of the Greek Bible, the Septuagint mainly.

16. E.g., Paul's "Bad company corrupts good morals" (1 Cor 15:33) occurs in the poet Menander's play *Thais* (frag. 218). It may, however, have become a popular maxim. Luke's quotation of Paul's words "as even some of your poets have said, 'For we are indeed his offspring'" (Acts 17:28), appears to refer to works by Cleanthes of Assos and to Aratas of Soli; see M. Boring et al., *Hellenistic Commentary to the New Testament* (Nashville: Abingdon, 1995), #518, #520.

It is likely significant that Paul returned to Tarsus following his conversion to the Messiah Jesus (Gal 1:21; Acts 9:30). This was circa 37, more than twenty years after moving to Jerusalem. It appears there were family connections in Tarsus to give some support to Paul in his virtual exile from Israel (1 Thess 2:14-15 — "the Jews . . . drove us out").

Jerusalem: The Formative Years (ca. 17-34)

Here we make the important point that Paul was in Jerusalem for a lengthy period before the dramatic Damascus event. If we are right in thinking he arrived in Jerusalem as a prepubescent boy circa A.D. 17, he would have lived there for the next sixteen or so years. We reasonably assume these to have been highly formative years.

Two aspects of Paul's formation during those years emerge from the sources: (i) his eminence in the sect of the Pharisees; (ii) his expertise in the Greek texts of the scriptures. Before we address these apparently divergent aspects, we must reflect on the circumstances of life in Jerusalem during those critical years.

Living in Judea under Roman Rule

Paul's years in Jerusalem (ca. 17-34) belonged to that period beginning in A.D. 6 when Judea was for the first time permanently annexed as a province of Rome. Roman troops and their local "auxiliaries" were visible evidence that Judea was now "occupied" by a foreign power. Most critical of all was the requirement that individual Jews must pay personal tax to the emperor. Previously, under the indigenous client rulers (Archelaus the ethnarch and, before him, Herod the king), taxes were only indirectly passed on to the imperial treasury. Since A.D. 6, however, Judeans had to pay their own taxes directly to Caesar via *his* local officials.

To facilitate the introduction of this poll tax in the year 6, the Romans conducted a systematic registration of the people of Judea.[17] For Jews this

---

17. Whereas Luke refers only to the act of "registering" (*apographē* and *apographesthai* in Luke 2:1-5; *apographē* in Acts 5:37), Josephus's accounts suggest a further element in this process, that is, "assessment" (*apotimēsis* — *Ant* 18.4). These two aspects of taxation emerge

was highly objectionable since it was the Lord who commanded the numbering of the people (Num 1:2). Furthermore, to pay tax to Caesar was to treat him as a usurper of the rightful authority of the Lord over his people.

This census provoked a major uprising against the Roman authorities, led by Judas the Galilean (or Gaulanite), who was, according to Josephus, a *sophistēs* (likely a rabbi) whose associate was Saddok, "a Pharisee." Their slogan was "No master except God."[18] This left a deep imprint in the memories of Judeans. Luke quotes Gamaliel three decades later referring to "the days of the registration" (Acts 5:37), an event so well-known that nothing further needed to be said. The Pharisees' ominous question to Jesus about tax payment (Mark 12:13-17) was further evidence of the currency of the issue and the danger Jesus faced in answering it.

When the boy Paul came to Jerusalem, the events of A.D. 6-7 were a mere ten years in the past and, as we think likely, still a live issue.

By that time Judea had been a province under direct Roman rule for quite a brief period. Tiberius was the new *princeps* (14-37), under whom military governors (prefects) now served for a decade (unlike his predecessor, Augustus, who replaced them every three years). Tiberius's first prefect was Gratus (ca. 15-26), who was followed by Pontius Pilate (ca. 26-36). The capital of the Roman province of Judea was Caesarea.

From A.D. 6/7 when the Romans imposed their poll tax on the Jews until the arrival of Pilate in 26, life in Judea had been outwardly "quiet," as Tacitus declared.[19] That "quiet" was significantly disturbed when Pontius Pilate took up his appointment as prefect circa 26. It appears that the praetorian prefect L. Aelius Sejanus had been responsible for this rather than Tiberius, who was by then in virtual self-exile on Capri (from 26 to 31). Some authorities believe that Sejanus was a determined anti-Semite[20] and that he sent Pilate to Judea to destabilize the people.[21] While terror reigned

---

in Josephus's comment that "Judas . . . induced multitudes of Jews to refuse to enrol themselves *(mē poieisthai tas apographas),* when Quirinius was sent as censor *(timētēs)* to Judaea" *(JW 7.253).*

18. *JW* 2.118, 433; *Ant* 18.4-10, 23-25; cf. Acts 5:37.

19. We note Tacitus's famous laconic comment about Judea, that *sub Tiberio quies* (*Histories* 5.10). See P. Barnett, "Under Tiberius All Was Quiet," *NTS* 21 (1975): 564-71.

20. Philo, *Flaccus* 1.1; *Embassy to Gaius* 159-160. See E. M. Smallwood, "Some Notes on the Jews under Tiberius," *Latomus* 15 (1956): 325. It is possible that Sejanus harbored hopes of a personal cult (Tacitus, *Annals* 3.72; 4.2, 272; Suetonius, *Tiberius* 48, 65; Dio Cassius 58.2, 4; 5.7).

21. See A. D. Doyle, "Pilate's Career and the Date of the Crucifixion," *JTS* 42 (1941):

in Rome under Sejanus's treason trials, in faraway Judea his surrogate Pilate provoked incident after incident.[22] After Sejanus's death in 31, Tiberius issued a decree of toleration for Jewish people in the empire.[23]

In other words, while Jerusalem did not likely witness wholesale bloodshed during Paul's years there, there were at least two immensely important religious issues current: the hated poll tax symbolizing the kingship of Caesar over the covenant people and the series of crises arising from Pilate's attempts at subverting the laws of God. A young man like Paul who grew to maturity at that time and who was religiously intense could not have been unaffected by these circumstances.

In short, the era in which the young Tarsian Paul was living in Jerusalem was one of considerable religious and political tension. Paul the young Pharisee must have been deeply aware of the issues for his religion that Roman occupation created.

Paul the Pharisee

As noted earlier, Paul's autobiographical sketch in the Letter to the Philippians is broadly chronological and corresponds with his places of residence, Tarsus and Jerusalem.

circumcised on the eighth day,	Tarsus (ca. 4/5–17)
of the people of Israel,	
of the tribe of Benjamin,	
a Hebrew of Hebrews;	

---

as to the law a Pharisee,	Jerusalem (ca. 17-34)
as to zeal a persecutor of the church,	
as to righteousness under the law blameless. (Phil 3:5-6)	

190-93; P. L. Maier, "Sejanus, Pilate and the Date of the Crucifixion," *Church History* 37 (1968): 3-13; Maier, "The Episode of the Golden Roman Shields at Jerusalem," *HTR* 62 (1969): 109-21.

22. Josephus, *JW* 2.169-177; *Ant* 18.55-62; cf. Luke 13:1; Mark 15:7. For Philo's negative report on Pilate, see *Embassy to Gaius* 299, 302.

23. Philo, *Embassy to Gaius* 161.

Luke's account of Paul's witness to his pre-Damascus life is similar, though the vocabulary is different.

> I am a Jew, born at Tarsus in Cilicia, but brought up in this city at the feet of Gamaliel, educated according to the strict manner of the law of our fathers. (Acts 22:3)

> I am a Pharisee, a son of Pharisees. . . . (Acts 23:6)

> My manner of life from my youth, spent from the beginning among my own nation and at Jerusalem, is known by all the Jews. They have known for a long time, if they are willing to testify, that according to the strictest party (*hairēsis* — "sect") of our religion I have lived as a Pharisee. (Acts 26:4-5)

Using these sources, we gain some idea of the shape of Paul's career in Jerusalem from his preteen years to the point where, as a "young man," he participated in the stoning of Stephen.

i. Paul's self-reference in Philippians 3:5 as "a Hebrew of Hebrews" *(Hebraios ex Hebraiōn)* follows in a descending list of ever-tightening definition ("of the people of Israel"; but more than that, "of the tribe of Benjamin"; even more that that, "a Hebrew of Hebrews").[24]

It is unlikely, therefore, that in Paul's writings *Hebraios* denotes a linguistic preference for Aramaic over Greek.[25] On the contrary, *Hebraios ex Hebraiōn* points to a rigor and conservatism of Jewish belief and practice that he experienced first in Tarsus and that was reinforced and intensified in Jerusalem.

ii. In Philippians 3:5 Paul's most expansive statement, "a Hebrew of Hebrews," is followed directly by "as to the law a Pharisee." Clearly these two categories are close, so that the latter flows logically out of the former, but with an important difference. Becoming a Pharisee was a deliberate act that likely involved some process of enrollment in that faction.

"As to the law a Pharisee" points contrastively to other approaches to "the law," for example, the exegetical traditions of other known groups like

---

24. Paul's only other reference to "Hebrews" is in a reverse direction, where *Hebraioi* occurs first, to be followed by the ever-looser upward categories ("Hebrews," "Israelites," "seed of Abraham," 2 Cor 11:22).

25. In any case, there is little evidence as to the currency of Aramaic used by Jews of the Diaspora.

Sadducees and Essenes. It implies that the teenage Paul began to belong to a Pharisaic academy where he came to view the law according to the hermeneutical principles of the Pharisees.

Paul described himself as "a Pharisee, a *son* of Pharisees," implying that both father and son belonged to that sect (Acts 23:6). When did Paul (and his father?) join the "sect" of the Pharisees? To our knowledge, the Pharisees were not active before A.D. 70 in the Diaspora.[26] It appears, then, that father and son attached themselves to a Pharisaic academy in Jerusalem.

The book of Acts reveals the particular school of the Pharisees that Paul joined. It was the school of Gamaliel.

"At the Feet of Gamaliel"

In his midteens the young "Hebrew of Hebrews" became a "Pharisee," that is, enrolled in a sectarian academy. It was no ordinary rabbinic school, however, but the "house" of Gamaliel (Acts 22:3).

Gamaliel appears on one other occasion in the book of Acts, where the council of the Jews was about to execute the apostles. "But a Pharisee in the council named Gamaliel, a teacher of the law *(nomodidaskalos)*, held in honor by all the people, stood up and ordered the men to be put outside for a while" (Acts 5:34).

Here we learn that Gamaliel was (a) a member of the Sanhedrin, and (b) universally respected, so that (c) his (lenient)[27] verdict was heeded.[28]

Gamaliel is referred to many times within the Mishnaic tradition, but also, less frequently, within the talmudic tradition.[29] According to the Mishnaic tractate *Avot*, the two main interpreters of the law in the era

---

26. Hengel, *The Pre-Christian Paul*, 29-34.

27. Some authorities attribute this to the apologetic interests of the author of Acts. Gamaliel's reported judgment, however, is consistent with the Mishnaic tradition, viz.: "Any assembling together that is for the sake of heaven shall in the end be established, but any that is not for the sake of heaven shall not in the end be established" (*m. Avot* 4:11). Moreover, it is to be noted that whereas the Sadducees were in favor of the death penalty, the Pharisees were not (see K. Haacker, "Paul's Life," in *St. Paul*, ed. J. D. G. Dunn [Cambridge: Cambridge University Press, 2003], 22).

28. See B. D. Chilton and J. Neusner, "Paul and Gamaliel," *BBR* 14, no. 1 (2004): 1-43. Chilton and Neusner support the historicity of the Acts account (38), in contrast to Chilton's rather more skeptical argument in "Gamaliel," in *ABD* 2 (1992), 903-6.

29. Chilton and Neusner, "Paul and Gamaliel," 1-43.

prior to Jesus were the notable sages Hillel and Shammai.[30] Hillel, in particular, was viewed as especially significant as the repository of the divine wisdom God gave initially to Moses at Mount Sinai and which culminated in the Mishnah.[31]

Gamaliel was the son (or grandson) of Hillel, and his successor in that line of scholarship.[32] He flourished in the first third of the first century, and was the most prominent interpreter of the law in his generation. In observing the consequences of the deaths of various sages, none is accorded greater praise than Gamaliel. "When Rabban Gamaliel died," declared the Mishnah, "the glory of the Torah ceased, and purity and 'separateness' died" (*m. Sotah* 9:15).

Accordingly, to belong to Gamaliel's school, as Paul did, was no small thing. The Talmud claims that Gamaliel had 500 young men in his "house" who studied the Torah and 500 who studied Greek wisdom (*b. Bava Qamma* 83a). Even the lateness of the reference and its romantic tone do not blur the impression of a large academy, with its unexpected interest in the wisdom of the Greeks. Here is a window into two seemingly impossible groups of scholars, one studying the Torah in Hebrew and the other studying the classical texts of the Greeks in their language.

The Mishnah reports a number of brief life settings (the so-called *Ma'asim*) about which Gamaliel offers his verdicts and wisdom.[33] So scattered are they, however, that it is not possible to recover the "historical" Gamaliel with any confidence. One persistent impression, however, is that Gamaliel traveled beyond the borders of Eretz Israel and that he had various contacts with Gentiles.

---

30. K. Haacker has argued that the pre-Damascus Paul was a man of "zeal" (in the manner of the original Maccabees), whose aggressive attitudes to traitors to the covenant (like the first Christians) cast him as a follower of Shammai, rather than of Hillel-Gamaliel. Haacker's argument is sympathetically rehearsed by S. Y. Kim, *Origin of Paul's Gospel* (Grand Rapids: Eerdmans, 1982), 41-44, who argues that Paul as persecutor belonged to the more strident school of Shammai. J. Neusner, *The Rabbinic Traditions about the Pharisees before 70*, vol. 1, *The Masters* (Leiden: Brill, 1971), 341-76, was inclined to view Gamaliel as a Shammaite, an opinion he now has abandoned in Chilton and Neusner, "Paul and Gamaliel," 1-3.

31. So, Chilton and Neusner, "Paul and Gamaliel," 3.

32. Cf. F. F. Bruce, *Acts* (1997), 175, who thinks Gamaliel may have been quite independent of the Hillel tradition. Hengel, *The Pre-Christian Paul*, 28, doubts the prominence ascribed to Gamaliel by Chilton and Neusner, "Paul and Gamaliel," 1-43.

33. Helpfully analyzed at length by Chilton and Neusner, "Paul and Gamaliel," 9-30.

In one striking incident Gamaliel is in Akko (of all places) in a bath-house dedicated to Aphrodite! When challenged, Gamaliel answered that "they do not say, 'Let us make a bath for Aphrodite,' but 'Let us make an Aphrodite for an adornment for the bath.'" Gamaliel added, "what one treats as a god is prohibited, but that which one treats not as a god is permitted" (*m. Avodah Zarah* 3:4). Do we hear echoes of this view in Paul's words about idols in an idol house (1 Cor 8:4, 10)?

Given the Mishnah's topical rather than biographical arrangement of the sages' teachings, it is not possible to reconstruct a coherent and overall view of Gamaliel's attitude to the law. One thing that seems secure — and this is our point — is that Gamaliel was indeed eminent in his generation. Accordingly, the younger Paul was a disciple of the most prominent rabbi of that era. Nonetheless, Paul himself is not referred to in the Mishnah or Talmud.[34]

Did the Pre-Damascus Paul "Preach Circumcision"?

> I have confidence in the Lord that you will take no other view than mine; and he who is troubling you will bear his judgment, whoever he is. But if I, brethren, still preach circumcision, why am I still persecuted? In that case the stumbling block of the cross has been removed. (Gal 5:10-11)

At the time he was writing to the Galatians, Paul's circumcision-free gospel was being challenged (by the "agitators") because, it was alleged, he did "*still* preach circumcision."

Paul does not deny the accusation directly, but asks rhetorically *if* he *still* preached circumcision, why was he *still* being persecuted? It seems, then, that Paul did preach circumcision. So we must ask *when?*

Most likely the agitators' charge applied to the pre-Damascus Paul, implying that they knew about the pre-Damascus Paul and his reputation as one noted for preaching circumcision. This they are able to exploit against him since, they say, he was (inconsistently) "*still* preaching circumcision" when he claimed now only to "preach the cross."

---

34. F. F. Bruce, *New Testament History* (London: Oliphants, 1969), 225, quotes a talmudic reference to an unnamed disciple of Gamaliel who displayed "impudence in matters of learning" (*b. Shabbat* 30b).

Our difficulty is that we can only guess at the meaning of Paul's *former* and *present* preaching of circumcision. In regard to Paul's current exposure to the charge of "still" preaching circumcision, the most likely explanation is to be found in Paul's neutral attitude to the matter ("neither circumcision counts for anything, nor uncircumcision" — 6:15; cf. 1 Cor 9:19-23). Later, by the same principle of indifference and for pragmatic reasons, Paul was to circumcise Timothy, a member of the Galatian churches (Acts 16:1-3)! Perhaps this attitude left Paul open to the charge that he still *required* circumcision of a Gentile despite his protestations to the contrary.

In regard to the Pharisee Paul's *former* preaching of circumcision, it appears from Galatians 5:11 that he did indeed do so. But how are we to understand this? Was there a Jewish mission[35] to the Gentiles in the NT era whose objective was the circumcision of converts? Here there are two main options. One is that in "preaching circumcision" Paul was actively engaged in such a mission to win Gentile proselytes for the covenant people of Israel.[36] The other is that he did so defensively, as it were, to prevent a too-easy access for Gentile Godfearers to become members of the covenant people.[37]

Two problems for the former option are: (a) arriving at a definition[38] of such a mission (was it active and intentional or passive and haphazard?), and (b) the uncertain nature of the evidence. It appears that the evidence for such a mission from the NT,[39] Josephus,[40] and the Roman sources[41] is limited and ambiguous.[42]

True, significant numbers of Gentiles were attracted to Judaism, whether as Jewish sympathizers (the so-called Godfearers) periodically attending the synagogue, or (less frequently) as fully fledged circumcised

35. For a review of opinions see J. C. Paget, "Jewish Proselytism at the Time of Christian Origins: Chimera or Reality?" *JSNT* 62 (1996): 65-103.

36. See J. P. Dickson, *Mission-Commitment in Ancient Judaism and the Pauline Communities*, WUNT 159 (Tübingen: Mohr Siebeck, 2003), 1-85.

37. See P. W. Barnett, "Jewish Mission in the Era of the New Testament and the Apostle Paul," in *The Gospel for the Nations*, ed. P. Bolt and M. Thompson (Leicester: Apollos, 2000), 263-82.

38. See Paget, "Jewish Proselytism," 76.

39. Matt 10:5-6; 23:15; John 7:35.

40. *Ant* 18.81; 20.41-49.

41. Dio Cassius, *Roman History* 57.18.5a; Horace, *Satires* 1.4.138-142; cf. 1.9.68-72; Tacitus, *Histories* 5.5.

42. Barnett, "Jewish Mission," 271-75.

proselytes.[43] Jews did indeed see themselves as a "light" to the Gentiles (Rom 2:19), and a writer like Josephus engaged in apologetic discourse in his *Jewish Antiquities* and *Against Apion* to influence Gentiles to appreciate Judaism. Yet even those who support the notion of a Gentile mission are forced to use qualifying terms like "informal" and "sporadic."[44] It appears, then, that there was not an earlier Jewish mission to the Gentiles that provided a pattern for Paul's later *intentional* mission to the Gentiles, as from circa 47.[45]

The second option, that Paul "preached circumcision" *defensively,* is to be preferred. Here the example of Izates, king of Adiabene, is instructive. Influenced by his mother Helena's conversion to Judaism, Izates decided to follow her example but received conflicting advice. Ananias, a Jewish merchant, said one could be converted to Judaism without circumcision, whereas another Jew, Eleazar, convinced Izates it was necessary to be circumcised, a view the narrator Josephus implicitly supports.[46] Josephus's comment that Eleazar had "a reputation for being extremely strict when it came to the ancestral laws"[47] makes him sound like Paul, that is, a Pharisee. Eleazar was not opposed to a Gentile becoming a Jew, but he raised the bar high even for a king to jump over. It appears that Paul the Pharisee was known as a "preacher of circumcision" with an outlook similar to Eleazar's.

In short, Paul's disclosure that he formerly "preached circumcision" is consistent with his assertion that he "advanced in Judaism beyond many of my own age" (Gal 1:14). In turn, as we shall argue, these self-revelations are consistent with one who attempted to destroy the church of God and its faith.[48]

---

43. Three obstacles barred the way for Jews becoming proselytes: (1) the widespread unpopularity of Jews among the Greeks and Romans; (2) the severe synagogue punishments a wayward proselyte might face as a Jew; (3) the pain and medical danger associated with adult circumcision. See further Barnett, "Jewish Mission," 266.

44. So Dickson, *Mission-Commitment,* 48.

45. See chapter 8.

46. *Ant* 20.44-49.

47. *Ant* 20.43.

48. See later, chapter 5.

The Pre-Damascus Paul and the Law

In two passages Paul reflects on his former life as a man "under law." But do his words articulate his feelings pre-Damascus or later, as a man "in Christ"?

A Prisoner under Law

Paul employs negative and connected images of a *custodian* and a *pedagogue* for his former life "under law."

> 22But the scripture *shut up* all under sin that the promise from faith in/ of Jesus Christ might be given to all who believe. 23Before faith came we were *guarded* under law, shut up until the faith that was to come was revealed. 24So the law was our pedagogue until Christ came, that we might be justified by faith. 25But when faith came we were no longer *under a pedagogue.* (Gal 3:22-25, author's translation)

Law as a custodian "shut up" Paul "under sin" (v. 22) and "guarded" him "under law" (v. 23). Likewise, law was a "pedagogue" (i.e., a harsh home-based child's attendant),[49] that is, "until Christ/faith came" (vv. 24, 25; cf. Gal 4:1-2).

In this contrasting eschatological "before and after" statement, Paul writes both about Israel ("until Christ came" — v. 24) and *about himself* ("when faith came" — v. 25). Paul skillfully writes both representatively and personally. His major thrust, however, is to say that as a man "under law" he was "under sin," locked up (under a custodian) and subject to a harsh regime (under a pedagogue).

Is Paul describing the imprisonment "under sin" and "under law" that he felt back then, or is this an understanding he came to have retrospectively, post-Damascus, as a man "in Christ"? We will address this question shortly, after reviewing Romans 7:22-25.

---

49. C. Spicq, *Theological Lexicon of the New Testament* (Peabody, Mass.: Hendrickson, 1994), 2:1-2.

Slain by the Law?

Paul's self-disclosure in Romans 7:7-24 about his inner life is a famous battleground for interpreters.[50]

> I *(egō)* was alive *(ezōn)* apart from the law formerly *(pote)*. But when the commandment came *(elthousēs)*, sin sprang to life *(anezēsen)* and I *(egō)* died *(apethanon)*. And the commandment that was intended to give life proved to be *(heuthethē)* for death for me *(moi)*. (Rom 7:9-10, author's translation)

Paul's first-person singular pronouns "I" and "me" suggest that he is writing a spiritual autobiography.[51] Two questions (among many others!) must be addressed. The first is, to which phase of his life is Paul pointing? Those who argue that Paul is describing his *postconversion* experience point to his use of the present tense in 7:14-25.[52] With greater probability, however, the above reference to the "coming" of the "commandment" points to a time of sharp awareness of the demands of God's law, most likely as a prepubescent boy when he attained the status of bar mitzvah.[53]

The other question is: Was Paul reflecting about his pre-Damascus life as he regarded it then or as he came to regard it retrospectively, post-

---

50. For a review of various opinions see J. Lambrecht, *The Wretched "I" and Its Liberation: Paul in Romans 7 and 8* (Louvain: Theological and Pastoral Monographs, 1992).

51. The repeated singular pronouns *egō* and [*e*]*moi* in verses 7-14 suggest that Paul is speaking about himself (as he does in Phil 3:3-5) rather than representatively of (for example) Adam (Käsemann) or Israel (Stauffer). Objection against a *personal* interpretation of this passage was raised by W. G. Kümmel in 1929, restated in *Römer 7 und das Bild des Menschen in Neuen Testament: Zwei Studien* (Munich: Chr. Kaiser, 1974), 52-53. A contrary view was expressed by R. H. Gundry, "The Moral Frustration of Paul before His Conversion: Sexual Lust in Romans 7:7-25," in *Pauline Studies: Essays Presented to Professor F. F. Bruce on His Seventieth Birthday*, ed. D. A. Hagner and M. J. Harris (Grand Rapids: Eerdmans, 1970), who wrote: "we may call the passage the biography of Everyman if we like, but here Everyman's biography is the autobiography of Paul" (229). Nonetheless, Gundry's observation that Paul's bar mitzvah coincided with the time of puberty and sexual temptation is speculative (232).

52. Appeal to the present tense as evidence of present experience is not sustainable; in Phil 3:3-6 Paul uses the present tense to describe his preconversion *past*.

53. While the *ceremony* of bar mitzvah has medieval origins, the recognition of the responsibility of the prepubescent boy was recognized in *m. Avot* 5:21; cf. *Encyclopaedia Judaica*, 16 vols. (Jerusalem, 1971-72), 4:243-44.

Damascus? Most likely Paul is revealing his thinking circa 57 about the reality of earlier "unrecognized sin"[54] in his preconverted life.

Summary

These expressions of spiritual bondage (Gal 3:22-25) and of moral death (Rom 7:7-24) are striking. Did they arise before or after Paul was a man "in Christ"? There is significant force to the argument that Paul was writing as a man "in Christ" when the Spirit gave him a deeper sense of the power and ineradicable nature of sin that he did not recognize pre-Damascus. Nonetheless, on exegetical grounds it seems likely that Paul also felt this way beforehand, however dimly, even if he did not identify these feelings then so clearly as he would do retrospectively in the passages quoted above.

Paul, the man "in Christ," declared that he had "received mercy" (2 Cor 4:1; 1 Tim 1:13) and that "now" the "love of Christ controlled [him]" (2 Cor 5:14). Two things, at least, formed the background to these emotions in the pre-Damascus Paul, however imperfectly. If one was the shame of the persecutor, the other was the sense of sin due to his inability to fulfill the law.[55] It was in retrospect, however, that he came to feel the full force of his own moral failure, past and present.

Paul, a Pharisee Who Is Master of the Greek Bible

Paul according to Luke

Luke's account of Paul in Jerusalem in the late 50s portrays Paul as fluent in both Greek and Aramaic speech. "The tribune said [to Paul], 'Do you

---

54. I owe this helpful reference to S. Chester, *Conversion at Corinth* (Edinburgh: T. & T. Clark, 2003), 147.

55. Unhelpful are the stark alternatives "plight to solution" (Lutheran) and "solution to plight" ("New Perspective"). While the latter is truer than the former, it is unlikely to be absolutely true and the former is unlikely to be absolutely untrue. Paul the "zealot" persecutor was no psychopath but a man who knew about "conscience" and that the Torah commanded "Thou shalt not kill." Common sense suggests that while the post-Damascus Paul looked back on his preconverted life with shame (as persecutor) and guilt (as lawbreaker), those sentiments were not altogether lacking beforehand. Most likely, the critical element in Paul's post-Damascus perspective on himself was that beforehand he had been utterly unable to recognize the tenacity of sin or to deal with sin by the power of law.

know *Greek (hellēnisti)?'* . . . Paul . . . spoke to them in the *Hebrew* language *(tē Hebraidi dialektō)"* (Acts 21:37, 40; cf. 22:2).

This cultural Greek-Aramaic duality is consistent with Paul being a citizen of Tarsus growing up in Jerusalem. Luke wants his readers to recognize Paul as bilingual and bicultural.

Our understanding of Paul's history accounts for his bilingualism. He lived first (i) in Greek-speaking Tarsus (until a preteen), then (ii) in (primarily?) Aramaic-speaking Jerusalem (until about age thirty), then (iii) in regions where both Aramaic and Greek were spoken (for a decade and a half), before entering his final phase (iv) where Greek would have been exclusively in use (a decade). Paul's ability to speak Aramaic and Greek should come as no surprise.

Paul's Greek Scholarship Revealed in His Letters

What does surprise us is that (a) this ex-Pharisee writes Greek so fluently, and (b) he is a master of the Greek versions of the sacred Scriptures.

Regarding (a), Hengel states that while Paul uses Greek idiosyncratically, he does so with "such a masterly control" that "he is hardly likely to have learned it as a second language."[56] This evident competence, while attributable to Greek education in his early years in Tarsus, also demands that Paul continued to use Greek during the sixteen or so years between his arrival in Jerusalem and the Damascus encounter.[57]

Furthermore, his earliest extant letters (whether Galatians or 1 Thessalonians) reveal general linguistic competence as well as familiarity with the epistolary format.[58]

At the same time, Paul's letters are characterized by elements from Jewish Palestine, whether the forensic categories of the Pharisees (e.g., "justification") or the apocalypticism of the Essenes (e.g., messianism and dualism).[59]

In short, Paul's writings reveal competence in Greek language, while the idiom expressed is frequently Palestinian in character.

Regarding (b), Hengel comments further that Paul's "treatment of

56. Hengel, *The Pre-Christian Paul,* 35.
57. For evidence of the currency of Greek language in Jerusalem, a cosmopolitan city, see Hengel, *The Pre-Christian Paul,* 54-57.
58. See Barnett, *BC,* 44-45.
59. Hengel, *The Pre-Christian Paul,* 46-53.

the texts of the Greek Bible is also so sovereign that we may assume that he grew up with it."[60]

This "sovereign" ease with the Septuagint and other Greek texts, however, cannot be explained by early exposure in the synagogue of Tarsus alone. Rather, several other factors come into play. One is that Jerusalem must have been a place of scholarship of Greek texts of the sacred Scriptures as well as of various edifying writings. The other is that the techniques and rhetoric in Paul's letters reveal a prior background as a synagogue instructor of the indigenous Greek-speaking Jews in Jerusalem as well as of the visiting Jews and Godfearers from the Diaspora.[61]

Paul, Greek-Speaking "Hebrew of Hebrews"

Paul's missionary achievements, his leadership of numerous coworkers, and his writings mark him as a man of remarkable vision, energy, and intellectual capacity. For all that, however, there is evidence of others who, like Paul, belonged to the Greek-speaking synagogues of Jerusalem (and who were likely bilingual). The "Hellenists" were Greek-speaking Jews from the Diaspora, whether disciples of Jesus (Acts 6:9) or opponents of Paul (Acts 9:29). Like Paul, they were likely able to speak Aramaic as well, at least to some degree.

Paul's newly arrived opponents in Corinth in the mid-50s[62] probably originated from the Diaspora synagogues of Jerusalem. They were (a) "Hebrews," (b) fluent Greek-speakers, (c) skilled textual exegetes, who (d) traveled to the Diaspora (to Corinth to overturn Paul's work there). They provide further indication of conservative Jews in Jerusalem ("Hebrews") who were Greek-speaking (2 Cor 11:4-6, 22).

Conclusion

There is nothing written in this chapter that has not been observed many times before. Yet often these aspects of Paul are expressed retrospectively from the viewpoint of his later missions and letters.

60. Hengel, *The Pre-Christian Paul*, 35.
61. Hengel, *The Pre-Christian Paul*, 57-61.
62. See chapter 9.

To trace the life of the pre-Damascus Paul diachronically as we have attempted to do helps us better to understand the man upon whom the Damascus event made such an impact, an impact that marked the beginning of the mission that would dominate the remainder of his life and change the course of history.

Paul was many things. He was from an aristocratic Diaspora family and a Roman citizen by birth, yet conservatively Jewish in nurture (in Tarsus) and education (in Jerusalem); he was an eminent younger Pharisee, yet bilingual and an accomplished scholar of the Greek Bible. The risen Lord called him "my chosen instrument," and for good reason.

FOUR

Why Paul Persecuted the Church

"Benjamin is a devouring wolf. In the morning, he will devour his prey, and at night he will apportion the food" (cf. Gen 49:27). This thoroughly fits Paul, who was from the tribe of Benjamin. For when he was young, he was a ravaging wolf. However, when he believed, he "apportioned the food."

Hippolytus, *Refutation of All Heresies* 5.168

The book of Acts raises a question that it only implicitly answers. That answer, when you stumble across it, provides a critical link back to Jesus, explaining why Paul set out on his world mission.

The Question

The question is: Why did Paul begin to persecute[1] the disciples of the Lord when his teacher Gamaliel, who was "held in honor by all the people," advised that they should not be executed but released (Acts 5:33-39)? This was weighty advice from the most prominent scholar of the law of his generation.

---

1. For references to Paul's persecutions, see 1 Cor 15:9; Gal 1:13, 23; Phil 3:6; 1 Tim 1:13; Acts 8:1; 9:4-5; 22:4, 7-8; 26:9-15. For a review of possible reasons for Paul's persecutions, see E. Schnabel, *Early Christian Mission* (Downers Grove, Ill.: InterVarsity, 2004), 927-28.

That advice had the effect of moderating the hostility of the temple authorities to the "Sect of the Nazarenes." In any case, that hostility had not been extreme, certainly not as extreme as it would become.

The question why Paul departed from his teacher's counsel is likely connected with another question: Why did the earlier moderate hostility of the authorities soon become the violent hostility against Stephen that initiated Paul's pogrom against the church?

Did Paul Depart from Gamaliel?

It is often assumed that Gamaliel stood in the moderate tradition of Hillel (his father or grandfather) rather than in the more radical tradition of Shammai, Hillel's contemporary.[2] As noted earlier, identifying Gamaliel with the Hillel tradition appears to be a sound judgment because it is consistent with his "wait and see" advice about the disciples of the Nazarene in Jerusalem.

Our first glimpse of Paul, which comes sometime after Gamaliel's advice to the Sanhedrin, is that this "young man" was "consenting to [Stephen's] death" (Acts 8:1).

This must mean one of two things: Paul, despite his attachment to Gamaliel, was not actually a Hillelite but a Shammaite (as some have argued);[3] or something had happened to change Paul's mind from the earlier attitude of his esteemed teacher. In our view, the book of Acts hints that it was the latter explanation. Most likely, Paul changed his mind. But why?

Hebrews and Hellenists

In Paul's writings the church in Jerusalem that he persecuted is undifferentiated; it is merely "the church of God" or "the church" (1 Cor 15:9; Gal 1:13; Phil 3:6). It is otherwise in the book of Acts where, uniquely, we meet two groups of disciples, "Hebrews" and "Hellenists" (*Hebraioi* and *Hellēnistai* — Acts 6:1).[4] The "Hebrews" are the Galilean disciples of Jesus whose pri-

2. See earlier, 34-36.
3. See 35n.30.
4. M. Hengel, *Between Jesus and Paul* (London: SCM, 1983), 4 (following Harnack),

mary language was Aramaic, whereas the "Hellenists" were Greek-speaking disciples in Jerusalem from various synagogue congregations of Jews from the Diaspora (cf. 6:9).[5]

The book of Acts indicates that the ingathering of disciples in Jerusalem was solely due to the initiative of the Galilean apostles, led by Peter and John (cf. 3:1; 4:1-4, 13). Those "added" to the original cohort from Galilee included Aramaic-speaking Jews from Jerusalem, Greek-speaking pilgrims from the Diaspora,[6] and Greek-speaking Jews in Jerusalem (Hellenists). The large number of disciples in Jerusalem (4:4) suggests that the local Hellenists may have been greater in number than the Hebrews from Galilee. In other words, the original leaders were soon in the *minority*.

The author of Acts allows us to see the *Hebraioi* and *Hellēnistai* together only once, but already there is tension between them, over the quota of food allocated daily to the Hellenist widows (6:1). Nonetheless, the fact of the tension is instructive since it suggests that hitherto the *Hebraioi* and *Hellēnistai* had been one "body of disciples" led by the apostles (6:2).

Most likely this means that they held joint meetings for instruction and worship (5:12 — "they were all together in Solomon's Portico"). Plenary gatherings independent of the apostles' leadership are difficult to imagine, such was their status as original disciples of the Lord and witnesses to his resurrection. It is, however, likely that various "house" meetings were linguistically defined, according to their "Hebrew" (Aramaic-speaking) or "Hellenist" (Greek-speaking) membership.

Surely, though, their linguistic differences necessitated separate global meetings. Against this we note that a practical bilingualism was likely a mark of both groups. The "Hebrews" lived in a Hellenistic milieu in Galilee and the "Hellenists" of Jerusalem inhabited an Aramaic metropolis, and each had to be accommodating linguistically within their respective milieux. This likely bilingualism made joint meetings of Hebrews and Hellenists possible. Once more, however, we emphasize the absolute hier-

---

supports a theory of an "Antiochene" source for sections of the book of Acts, which began with references to "Hebrews" and "Hellenists."

5. See Hengel, *Between Jesus and Paul*, 4-11, for a convincing definition of these groups along linguistic lines. Hengel, however, likely goes too far in asserting that language became the basis of their differences and that only the "Hellenists" were forced from the Holy City by Paul's persecutions (13-17).

6. Acts 2:41; 4:4. The Theodotus Inscription provides a window into a Diaspora synagogue in Jerusalem (see Barnett, *BC*, 19-20).

archical dominance of the Twelve, led by Peter, over all the disciples, including the Hellenists (cf. 6:2, 6).

Catalyst

Peter's hierarchical leadership over the disciples coincided with the earliest phase of the history of the church in Jerusalem, when external opposition against it was moderate.

Acts 6 marks the beginning of Peter's loss of that authority and the beginning of division of the earlier community into two groups, Hebrews and Hellenists. It also marks the end of moderate opposition from the temple leaders and the beginning of hostile and violent opposition.

The dispute over equal distribution to the widows was not the catalyst. The choice of seven Hellenist almoners solved that problem. Indeed, Luke mentions that issue only to bring the seven "deacons"[7] into his narrative, in particular to introduce Stephen (and Philip) for the critical roles they will play in the unfolding drama.

In reality the catalyst, as stated by Luke, was as follows: "And the word of God increased; and the number of the disciples multiplied greatly in Jerusalem, and *a great many of the priests* were obedient to the faith" (Acts 6:7).

The catalyst was the influx of "a great many" temple priests into the community of believers.

We must note the onrushing sequence of Luke's narrative marked by "And" (6:5), "And" (6:7), and "And" (6:8).[8] *First,* he gives the name of the seven Hellenist almoners, led by Stephen (6:5). *Next* he brings the numerous priests into the church (6:7). *Next* he relates the deeds of Stephen and his disputes in the Hellenist synagogues (6:8-11). *Then* immediately he narrates the accusations against Stephen in the council, that he spoke against the *holy place* and *the law* (6:13).

Luke wants us to see a connection between the entry of the numerous priests into the church *and* Stephen's forthright preaching and dis-

---

7. Luke notes that these men were appointed "to serve" (*diakonein* — Acts 6:2); the noun "deacon"/*diakonos* does not appear in Acts 6.

8. Luke makes frequent use of "And" *(Kai)* to commence sentences, including at points where the narrative is moving in significant new directions.

puting *and* the radical new level of opposition from the temple authorities.[9] The entry into the church of priests of the temple appears to have provoked Stephen to vigorous preaching and disputing in the Hellenist synagogues.

That is not all. Following the stoning of Stephen, Luke writes, "*And* Saul was consenting to his death. *And* on that day a great persecution arose against the church in Jerusalem. . . . Saul was ravaging the church" (8:1, 3). Luke's distinctive use of "And" from Acts 6:5 to Acts 8:3 joins one event to the next. The sequence began with the new prominence of Stephen, continued with the influx of the priests, and ended with the beginning of the great persecution led by Paul.

Luke only formally brings Saul into his narrative at the point where Stephen is stoned (7:58). Yet with his earlier mention of the synagogue "of those from Cilicia" (6:9), which is later picked up in Paul's reference to himself as "from Tarsus in Cilicia" (21:39; 22:3; cf. 9:11 — "a man of Tarsus"), Luke most likely wants us to understand that Paul had been in that synagogue when Stephen preached, that he had instigated the accusers, and that he had brought news of these radical views to the temple authorities.

Paul the Hillelite

By this reconstruction we conclude that originally Paul would have shared the moderate views of his teacher, the eminent Gamaliel, regarding the earliest community led by Peter. When, however, sacrificing priests joined the church, everything changed. Stephen the Hellenist leader radically attacked the temple in the hearing of Paul, whose violent reaction led to the stoning of Stephen and the beginning of the great persecution. According to this reconstruction, Gamaliel would likely also have reacted against Stephen for attacking the temple.

Was Paul a Shammaite? Most likely he was a Hillelite, following the tradition of Gamaliel. Accordingly he may have felt an uneasy toleration toward the sect of the Nazarenes in its earliest months. All that changed, however, when a new factional leader (was said to have) attacked the pillars of the covenant faith, the temple and the law.

---

9. Contra Hengel, *Between Jesus and Paul,* 23, who argues that the opposition to Stephen was due to his "spirit-inspired preaching."

Profile of Paul

A profile of Paul emerges from Luke's unfolding narrative. Clearly he had been present during the Sanhedrin trial of Stephen and went with the council members and the accusers outside the city for the stoning of the guilty man. The accusers who heard Stephen in the synagogue of the Cilicians and who brought the charges against him now execute him by stoning (Acts 6:11; 7:58).[10] Significantly they leave their clothes (outer garments?) in the safekeeping of Paul, the "young man" (7:58; 22:20) who was "consenting to his death" (8:1). This suggests that Paul had played a part in instigating the arrest and trial of Stephen. This is confirmed by his new role as leader of the persecution that now ensued, and further confirmed by the authority he received to go to Damascus to extradite fugitive disciples there.

Luke's account of Paul broadly coincides with Paul's own version of himself.

Paul the Persecutor

Paul informed the Galatians of his "advance" in Judaism. "For you have heard of my former life in Judaism, how I persecuted the church of God violently and tried to destroy it; and I advanced in Judaism beyond many of my own age among my people, so extremely zealous was I for the traditions of my fathers" (Gal 1:13-14).

In Galatians Paul is opposing those Jewish Christians who were attempting to circumcise the Galatian Gentile males, that is, bring them under "Judaism," the "Judaism" under which he belonged in his *former* life. Paul amplifies his "former life in Judaism" by saying "I was advancing[11] in Judaism," which he further amplifies by saying he was "extremely zealous"[12] "for the traditions of my fathers."[13] That is to say, Paul's growing

10. The man to be stoned was naked; see F. F. Bruce, *The Acts of the Apostles* (Grand Rapids: Eerdmans, 1990), 212.

11. The verb *proekopton* is an imperfect tense used with a durative meaning, "was advancing."

12. Paul's "zeal" was also expressed as "a persecutor of the church" (Phil 3:6). Paul's "zeal" for God doubtless expressed itself both in his scholarship and then in his persecution of, as he saw it, the dangerous lawbreaking sect associated with Jesus.

13. Josephus makes a similar claim about his education as a boy (*Life,* 8 — "I made great progress in my education").

progress "in Judaism" was evident in his zealous scholarship in the oral traditions from earlier generations of sages.[14]

This academic "advance," however, had been within the cloisters of Gamaliel's academy.[15] His persecution of the disciples made him a public figure in a way that he had not been previously. In short, his significant "advance in Judaism" was achieved in scholarly privacy but was revealed at large in Jerusalem by his attempt to "destroy"[16] both the church and its "faith" (Gal 1:23).

Paul's claim to preeminence among his generation "in Judaism," from which he had been dramatically converted (Gal 1:15-16), is offered to the Galatians as the reason they must not be swayed by the current attempts of the Jewish Christians to impose "Judaism" on them.

The Hellenists, Paul, and World Mission

Our argument, then, is that the addition of many priests (who offered *sacrifices* in the temple) proved to be the catalyst that cast Stephen and the "Hellenist" disciples into opposition with Peter and the "Hebrew" disciples.

Luke does not tell us Stephen's motivations. Was he influenced by Jesus' expulsion of the vendors from the temple? Did he grasp the vision of Jesus' death as the true sacrifice and high priest that effectively spelled the end of the role of the temple (in the manner of the Letter to the Hebrews)? As a Jew from the Diaspora, did he have a natural affinity for the people of the Diaspora, both Jews and Gentiles? These are real possibilities.

Whatever his reasons, Stephen was charged with having preached against both temple and law/Moses in the Hellenist synagogues (Acts 6:9-15). In his defense to the Sanhedrin Stephen[17] argued that historically the

14. Cf. Josephus, *Ant* 13.297.

15. Luke's report of Paul's words to Agrippa confirms Paul's own account: "My manner of life from my youth, spent from the beginning among my own nation and at Jerusalem, is known by all the Jews. They have known for a long time, if they are willing to testify, that according to the strictest party of our religion I have lived as a Pharisee" (Acts 26:4-5).

16. Both Paul and the author of Acts use the word "destroy" *(portheō)* of Paul's persecutions (Gal 1:13, 23; Acts 9:21). Most likely Paul attempted to destroy the church by isolating its members from the synagogues, as happened to Stephen (cf. *aposynagōgos/*"expelled from the synagogue" in John 9:22; 12:42; 16:2). See further, Schnabel, *Early Christian Mission*, 927.

17. Contra Hengel, *Between Jesus and Paul*, 19, who disputes the historicity of the details of Stephen's words as reported by Luke.

people of Israel resisted Moses (7:23-44), to whom God gave his "living oracles" at Mount Sinai and who made a "*tent* of witness" according to the directions and pattern God gave him (7:44). Joshua brought this "tent of witness" into the land; it remained until the days of David, "who found favor in the sight of God" (7:45-47). It was Solomon, however, who later built *the temple,* contrary to everything God had directed Moses to do (7:47-51). In sum, Stephen defended himself against the charge that he was opposed to Moses and the law but effectively accepted the charge that he spoke against the temple.

Implicit in Stephen's criticism of the temple was a rejection of the eschatological centrality of Jerusalem. For him the mission of God for the gathering of the nations was not centripetal (pulling in to the center) but centrifugal (driving out from the center). That is to say, Stephen's antitemple polemic reversed the direction of the prophetic expectations, which saw God "pulling in" the nations to Jerusalem/the temple as the center of God's end-time plan for Israel and the nations.[18]

This interpretation is made more likely when we consider Philip, the second of the seven Hellenist leaders, who evangelized the Samaritans (in Sebaste?), a Godfearer (?) from Ethiopia, and the Hellenized city-states from Azotus to Caesarea (8:4-13, 26-40). It is reasonable to assume that Philip shared Stephen's views, as outlined above. When Paul's assaults fell on the church of Jerusalem, that is, upon both the Hebrews and the Hellenists, all the disciples were forced from the city.[19] Luke, however, pointedly excludes the apostles, who steadfastly remained in Jerusalem (8:1). The author gives no reason for this, but it is likely that the Twelve saw themselves remaining in Jerusalem because it was to be the center of God's end-time universe.

Philip, when scattered from Jerusalem, took the gospel of Messiah-Jesus away from Jerusalem — to Samaritans, to an Ethiopian, and to the Hellenized coastal strip from Azotus to Caesarea, and likely northward to the cities of Tyre and Sidon (27:3, 7).[20] For good reason Philip becomes known as "the evangelist" (21:8). This was not merely because he was a passionate preacher, but also because he understood that God's purposes were *outward from* Jerusalem and not inward, into Jerusalem.

18. See, e.g., Isa 60:1-18; 65:18-21; Zech 8:20-23.
19. Many scholars suggest that only the Hellenists were driven out. Acts 8:1, however, states that "all were scattered" (cf. 9:31).
20. Contra Hengel, *Between Jesus and Paul,* 24, who suggests that Philip's motivation (in part) was due to Hellenists themselves being marginalized in Jerusalem.

The notion of Jerusalem as centrifugal and not centripetal in God's mission to the nations, which became so much associated with Paul, had its seeds in the vision of Stephen and the activities of Philip.

Conclusion

Why did Paul violently oppose the church of God, contrary to the quietist approach of his great teacher Gamaliel (who was himself a member of the Sanhedrin)? Disciples of great rabbis usually followed the views of their masters. Why did Paul set off in a different direction? Was he, after all, a Shammaite at heart whose true sympathies emerged in his assault upon the followers of the Way?

It is more likely that *something* external to Paul occurred that changed Paul's previously held laissez-faire attitude toward the disciples, and likely also changed Gamaliel's attitude. That something was the new radical teaching of Stephen, leader of the Hellenists.

That teaching was precipitated by the influx of large numbers of sacrificing priests into the community of believers. Stephen likely disagreed with the apostles over these new priestly members. Their presence represented a denial of Jesus' purification of the temple and the effects of his propitiatory death that superseded the temple, its priests, and its sacrifices.

Accordingly Stephen began attacking the very existence of the temple. Most likely Paul himself heard this preaching in the Diaspora/Hellenist synagogues in Jerusalem and, in response, initiated a series of actions that led to the eventual stoning of Stephen and to Paul's own assault on the disciples in the Holy City and beyond to the cities of the Diaspora nearest to the land of Israel.

At heart Stephen believed that the mission of God to the nations must go out *from* Jerusalem and its temple, rather than in the opposite direction. Philip's mission to Samaria, his approach to the Ethiopian, and his evangelism to the Hellenistic coastal cities gave practical expression to Stephen's views.

The Hellenists' radical assault on the temple provoked Paul's violent opposition, which in turn initiated Philip's mission to Samaritans and Godfearers. At Damascus Road the vision of Stephen and Philip to the "outsiders" captured Paul's own heart, and it became his life's work.

FIVE

The Damascus Event (ca. 34): Was Paul Called or Converted?

God . . . shone in our hearts.

2 Corinthians 4:6

Paul: Called or Converted?

Since the Reformation Paul's Damascus experience has been viewed as a template for the conversion and justification of the sinner. Honest introspection addressing a guilty conscience is seen as a necessary precondition to claiming Christ in faith as the resolution of one's moral crisis. Paul was seen as the great example of one who had been struggling beforehand with a tortured conscience over his failure to observe the law of God.[1]

In 1963 Krister Stendahl famously challenged this paradigm, arguing that the preconversion moral struggles of such icons as Augustine and Luther had wrongly influenced Western perception of the moral plight of the pre-Damascus Paul.[2] In fact, said Stendahl, Paul had not been "plagued by

1. See, e.g., P. Gardner, *The Religious Experience of St. Paul* (London: Williams and Norgate, 1911), 20-39.

2. K. Stendahl, "The Apostle Paul and the Introspective Conscience of the West," *HTR* 50 (1963): 199-215. In his review article B. Corley, "Interpreting Paul's Conversion — Then and Now," in *The Road from Damascus*, ed. R. N. Longenecker (Grand Rapids: Eerdmans, 1997), demonstrates that the moral struggles of both Augustine and Paul were subsequent to, not prior to, their conversions (1-17). For a rebuttal of Stendahl's thesis see P. T. O'Brien, "Was

guilt" beforehand as a precursor to his conversion and "justification by faith" on Damascus Road.[3] Rather he was "called" to his apostolate there; Damascus Road for Paul was not about his conversion but about his new vocation to become apostle to the Gentiles.[4]

Stendahl argued that because Paul did not change his religion, he was not "converted." Serving one and the same God, Paul merely received a new and special calling in God's service.[5]

Given Stendahl's challenge, how are we to understand what happened to Paul in the Damascus event? Was he "converted," or "called," or both "converted and called"? In this chapter we investigate the evidence, first from the book of Acts, and then from Paul's own writings.

Damascus Road according to Acts

Since Paul is the main character in the book of Acts, it is no surprise that Luke narrates this life-changing event outside Damascus no fewer than three times (Acts 9:1-19; 22:4-16; 26:9-20). The first is a third-person report while the other two are given in Paul's own words.[6]

There is a story line common to all three: (i) Paul the persecutor of the church in Jerusalem sets out[7] for Damascus;[8] (ii) approaching Damas-

---

Paul Converted?" in *Justification and Variegated Nomism*, vol. 2, *The Paradoxes of Paul*, ed. D. A. Carson, P. T. O'Brien, and M. A. Seifrid (Tübingen: Mohr Siebeck, 2004), 360-91.

3. Fundamental to the "new perspective" on Paul are the views: (1) the Judaism of Paul's day was not a legalistic system based on "works of the law" that provoked individual guilt, and (2) Paul's teaching on "justification" did not criticize the law but rather provided a means of entry for Gentiles to the covenant of God.

4. Corley observes that Stendahl's critique "has become a programmatic feature of the 'new perspective' on Paul that emphasizes the apostle's call, rather than his conversion, and his mission to the Gentiles, rather than justification by faith" ("Interpreting Paul's Conversion," 3).

5. K. Stendahl, *Paul among the Jews and Gentiles* (Philadelphia: Fortress, 1976), 7. For the contrary view written from a Jewish perspective, see A. Segal, *Paul the Convert* (New Haven: Yale University Press, 1990), 6.

6. See C. W. Hedrick, "Paul's Conversion/Call: A Comparative Analysis of the Three Reports," *JBL* 100 (1981): 415-32.

7. The shorter route was via a crossing of the Jordan at Bethany, then proceeding north through Perea and Batanea, a journey of about 140 miles and taking about a week; see J. Polhill, *Paul and His Letters* (Nashville: Broadman and Holman, 1999), 46-47.

8. It may be asked, Why Damascus? If, as seems likely, the Jewish "Hellenist" disciples

cus, he is struck down; (iii) in Damascus he is baptized (but not in the third account).

As we compare these narratives, it is clear that Luke is emphasizing three elements:

a. Luke is contrasting the ravaging persecutor in Jerusalem with the sorry blinded figure on the road outside Damascus who is then led into the city and humbled in baptism.

b. In each account Luke brings out the following dialogue: the Lord asks: "Saul, Saul, why do you persecute me?" to which Paul responds by asking: "Who are you, Lord?" to which the Lord declares, "I am Jesus [of Nazareth] whom you are persecuting." Only in the third account does Jesus say to Paul, "It hurts you to kick against the goads."

c. Significantly, each narrative gives the Lord's commission to Paul to take his message to the Gentiles. In the first two accounts it is given obliquely to Paul through Ananias[9] (inside Damascus) in the context of the baptism of Paul.[10] In the third the commission is given directly and at length to Paul, but on the road outside Damascus (with no description of Paul's arrival in the city or his baptism there). Historically speaking, the likely correct sequence is found in the first and second accounts; the third is a consolidated version appropriate to the specific context of an audience with King Agrippa II.

Put simply, Luke is telling us that the Lord intercepted and humbled the furious persecutor, in a word, "converted" him. Jesus' words ("It hurts you to kick against the goads" — Acts 26:14) suggest that Paul had been "plagued" in conscience beforehand, though not as guilt-ridden law-breaker but as a persecutor inwardly affected by his assaults on innocent and good people, the disciples of the Lord. At the same time, Luke is showing how the Lord "called" this now "converted" former persecutor so that he became a preacher to the Gentiles.

The traditions Luke uses for these accounts can have come from only one source, Paul himself. Of course, they are now told in Luke's words and in the direction of his literary apologetic for his hero, Paul.

---

were the chief objects of his persecution, their line of escape would have been to a city outside the land of Israel. Damascus was the closest such city, just beyond the border, and moreover, one that had a large number of Godfearers (so Josephus, *JW* 2.559-561).

9. Jesus addresses both Saul and Ananias by name. Unlike Saul, who asks "Who are you, Lord?" Ananias replies "Here I am" (Acts 9:10).

10. The book of Acts does not say explicitly that Ananias baptized Paul.

Luke's account will not allow us to explain the encounter outside Damascus in subjective or psychological terms, as a mere vision. True, Paul saw a blinding light (Acts 9:3; 22:6; 26:13; cf. 2 Cor 4:6), but equally he *saw* the Just One and *heard* the voice from his mouth (Acts 22:14; cf. 1 Cor 9:1); "the Lord Jesus . . . *appeared* to [Paul] on the road" (Acts 9:17; cf. 1 Cor 15:8).

To anticipate, when we come to analyze Paul's own account of the Damascus event, we will notice a number of similarities with the book of Acts. Both versions stress a "before and after" motif with Damascus as the "turning point." Paul the Pharisee, who persecuted the church of God, saw the Lord and a bright light at Damascus, whereupon he became God's messenger to the Gentiles.

Luke's accounts of Paul's "conversion" and "call" are a quite straightforward set of narratives; God humbled this fierce persecutor and made him a tireless missionary to the Gentiles. Paul's own accounts of the impact of the Damascus event, however, are more personally and theologically complex (as we shall soon notice).

Damascus Road according to Paul

The overwhelming evidence from his letters leaves no doubt that Paul's life and his life's direction changed at Damascus. Paul approached Damascus as a persecutor, but once there he became a preacher of the message he had attempted to destroy.

There are two kinds of evidence in Paul's letters for his amazing turnaround at Damascus, specific references and identifiable allusions. The latter are usually signaled in context by contrasting verb tenses. Although they do not directly refer to Damascus, they are clearly identifiable in that setting. Paul must have explained his Damascus experience beforehand in the churches, which explains why he needs only to allude to it in passing, to establish some other point.

Paul's Direct References

Galatians

To the Galatians Paul contrasted his "former life in Judaism" as a persecutor of the church with his present life as a preacher of the faith he had previously attempted to destroy (Gal 1:13-14, 23). He explains how this radical volte-face occurred.

> 13 For you have heard of my former life in Judaism, how I persecuted the church of God violently and tried to destroy it; 14 and I advanced in Judaism beyond many of my own age among my people, so extremely zealous was I for the traditions of my fathers. 15 But when he who had set me apart before I was born, and had called me through his grace, 16 was pleased to reveal his Son to me, in order that I might preach him among the Gentiles, I did not confer with flesh and blood, 17 nor did I go up to Jerusalem to those who were apostles before me, but I went away into Arabia; and again I returned to *Damascus.* 18 Then after three years I went up to Jerusalem. (Gal 1:13-18)

The before-and-after motif emerges clearly. In Jerusalem the eminent younger Pharisee attempted to destroy the church of God. At Damascus, however, God "called" Paul to "preach [his Son] among the Gentiles," after which he "went away into Arabia" before "again" coming to Damascus. At Damascus and in Arabia the persecutor became the preacher of the faith he had sought to destroy and a member of the community he had sought to destroy.

Philippians

Paul also made a sharp contrast to the Philippians between his former life and his present life.

> 4 Though I myself have reason for confidence in the flesh also. If any other man thinks he has reason for confidence in the flesh, I have more: 5 circumcised on the eighth day, of the people of Israel, of the tribe of Benjamin, a Hebrew born of Hebrews; as to the law a Pharisee, 6 as to zeal a persecutor of the church, as to righteousness under the law blameless. 7 But whatever gain I had, I counted as loss for the sake of Christ. 8 Indeed I count everything as loss because of the surpassing worth of knowing Christ Jesus my Lord. For his sake I have suffered the loss of all things, and count them as refuse, in order that I may gain Christ. (Phil 3:4-8)

This list shows that Paul had more reason than others at that time for "confidence in the flesh" (where "flesh" is shorthand for self-achievement and for Paul's prideful preconverted life). He summarizes this former "confidence" about his *status* ("circumcised on the eighth day . . .") and his *achievements* ("a Pharisee, . . . a persecutor of the church"). Yet from his post-Damascus perspective he counted those confidence-boosting items of his previous life "under the law" as "refuse" in contrast with the incomparable value in the *present* of "knowing Christ Jesus," despite having lost everything on his account. In short, Paul is contrasting his perception *then* of his preconversion past (as "blameless") with his perception of it through his *now*-converted eyes (as "refuse").

This radical "then-now" change of attitude occurred *at a specific time* when, as he said, "I was seized by Christ" (*katelēmphthēn hupo Christou* — Phil 3:12). True, Paul does not mention Damascus, but there is little doubt that by this picture of his dramatic "capture by Christ" he is referring to the Damascus event. At that time all his life values changed.

It must not pass unnoticed that Paul wrote these words almost thirty years after arriving in Damascus. He speaks of a total change of dependence in respect of the righteousness of God. Formerly, his confidence rested in his status and achievements as a "Hebrew," "under law," whereas now that confidence depended instead on being found "in Christ." For Paul Christ had replaced the Torah as the source of his right standing with God. This radical shift in confidence occurred at and subsequent to the occurrences near and at Damascus.[11]

Identifiable Allusions

Romans

The key text in Romans is the assertion of his apostleship to the Gentiles: "Now I am speaking to you Gentiles. Inasmuch as I am an apostle to the Gentiles, I magnify my ministry" (Rom 11:13).

Paul's present "ministry" had a beginning. This is evident from his use of verb tenses in associated references in Romans. He was "*set apart* for the gospel of God" (1:1); he "*received* grace and apostleship" (1:5), "grace *given* . . . by God" in order for Paul to be "a minister of Christ"

---

11. See M. Hengel and A. M. Schwemer, *Paul between Damascus and Antioch* (Louisville: Westminster John Knox, 1997), 13.

(15:15-16).[12] Paul expects his readers to know that his ministry of apostleship *began* at a specific moment.

True, Paul does not mention Damascus by name. Nonetheless, his references to *preaching to the Gentiles* (Gal 1:16) and *apostleship to the Gentiles* (Rom 1:13) connect the passages and point to Damascus as the place where that ministry to Gentiles began. In any case, Paul must have informed the churches where his persecutions ended and his preaching began.

1 Corinthians

The "before and after" motif is clearly enunciated in this letter. The persecutor (15:9) "saw" Jesus the Lord (9:1; 15:8), whereupon he was "entrusted with a stewardship" (9:17), which he then began to exercise by preaching the gospel that he continues to do (free of charge — 9:18).

Paul "Entrusted" with a Commission (9:16-19)   Verb tense contrasts in the following passage are instructive.

> 16 For if I preach the gospel, that gives me no ground for boasting. For necessity is laid upon *(epikeitai)* me. Woe to me if I do not preach the gospel! 17 For if I do this of my own will, I have a reward; but if not of my own will, I am entrusted *(pepisteumai)* with a commission. 18 What then is my reward? Just this: that in my preaching I may make the gospel free of charge, not making full use of my right in the gospel.

Paul preaches because "necessity is laid upon" him. This, in turn, is because he has been "entrusted with a stewardship" *(oikonomian pepisteumai)*,[13] almost certainly a reference to the Damascus "call." In short, his present and ongoing "necessity" to "preach" had its origin in the Damascus event.

Resurrection Appearances (9:1; 15:8-9)   Two passages in 1 Corinthians are connected and are to be read together.

---

12. *Aphōrismenos* (1:1) is perfect tense, and both *elabon* (1:5) and *dotheisan* (15:15) are aorist.

13. The perfect tense, passive voice tells us that Paul *had been entrusted* and was *still entrusted* for this vocation *by God*.

Have I not seen Jesus our Lord? (9:1)

Last of all, as to one untimely born *(hōsperei tō ektrōmati),* he appeared also to me. For I am the least of the apostles, unfit to be called an apostle, because I persecuted the church of God. (15:8-9)

It is clear that Paul's "Have I not *seen* Jesus our Lord?" and "[Christ] *appeared* also to me" are two ways of referring to the one event.[14] Both verbs "seen" and "appeared" and the unusual expression "untimely" birth point to a *past* moment when Paul "saw" the now-risen Lord.[15]

Furthermore, Paul implies a sequence of events: *first* he persecuted the church of God; *then* he saw the risen Lord; *then* he became *and is* the apostle who, along with other apostles, preaches the crucified, buried, and raised-up Christ (cf. 15:11).

Once more, we note that Damascus was Paul's "change point" from persecutor to preacher, although that city is not mentioned by name.

2 Corinthians

Nowhere is the "before" and "after" pattern plainer than in 2 Corinthians. Although Paul makes no mention of Damascus by name, or the persecutions beforehand, both are presupposed. This is because he is emphasizing his present ministry, which he must defend in Corinth.[16] Yet he does this assuming his readers know about the prior Jerusalem-based persecutions and the Damascus event where his ministry began.

Paul's Representative Autobiography (5:15-17) Paul displays considerable skill in writing both autobiographically and representatively.

> 15 And he died for all, that those who live might live no longer for themselves but for him who for their sake died and was raised. 16 From now on, therefore, we regard no one from a human point of view; even though we once regarded Christ from a human point of view, we regard him thus no longer. 17 Therefore, if any one is in Christ, he is a new creation; the old has passed away, behold, the new has come.

14. The verb "seen" *(heōraka)* is perfect tense and "appeared" *(ōphthē)* is aorist.

15. This observation does not depend on a particular interpretation of the unusual term *hōsperei tō ektrōmati* ("untimely born").

16. See chapter 10.

Once Paul (or "any one") is "in Christ," he "no longer" lives for himself nor comprehends Christ "according to the flesh" (i.e., in a superficial, worldly way). Rather, "now" that he (or "any one") is "in Christ," he "lives for" Christ and comprehends Christ (by inference) "according to the Spirit." These radical changes he sums up as being a "new creation" in which "the old has passed" and "the new has come."

This is Paul's Damascus story, which is also his own proclaimed gospel message.

Having "This Ministry" (4:1, 5, 6)   In this passage (2 Cor 4:1-6) Paul is defending his integrity against current criticisms in Corinth. His apologetic is embedded in reflections about his present ministry in relationship to its beginnings.

> 1 We have this ministry even as we have received mercy. . . . 5 We preach . . . Jesus Christ as Lord. . . . 6 God . . . has shone in our hearts to give the light of the knowledge of the glory of God in the face of Christ. (RSV adapted)

Once again we note that Paul does not specifically mention his persecutions or Damascus. Most likely this indicates that his churches had learned his story on his original visit. Accordingly he is able to allude to it, understanding that his readers know what he means.

The words "we have received mercy" (v. 1) are expressed in a single Greek word *(eleēthēmen)* whose aorist tense and passive voice point to a past moment when Paul *received mercy from God.* As in other references, Paul writes personally and also inclusively. In respect of himself it is certain that he refers to the mercy God gave to him in Damascus in regards his recent persecutions in Jerusalem (cf. 1 Tim 1:13 — "formerly I was a . . . persecutor . . . but *I received mercy*" [author's translation]).

Significantly, at that same moment God shone in Paul's heart (v. 6). This was to expel the inner darkness of an Israelite like Paul, from whom the true and glorious "end" *(telos)* of the law (i.e., Christ) was "veiled" (3:12-13). When Paul "turned" to the Lord Christ (at Damascus), the "veil" covering the "end" of the law was removed (3:16).[17]

At that moment God shone in Paul's heart, for a *purpose (pros* — cf.

17. See chapter 8.

Gal 1:16 — God revealed "his Son to me, *in order that* [*hina*] I might preach him among the Gentiles"). The now-sighted recipient of divine mercy was "to give" to others "the light of the knowledge of the glory of God in the face of Christ" that he had received at Damascus (2 Cor 4:6).

Thus 2 Corinthians 4:1, 6 refer to two aspects of the one event on the Damascus Road. In that single moment Paul (a) "received mercy from God" and (b) God "shone" in his heart. Both aspects express the *end* to corresponding aspects of Paul's former life (i.e., as a persecutor *and* spiritually blind), and both express the *beginning* of his new life (as now sighted, and as a preacher of the gospel of Christ giving light to others).

"Made Sufficient" for Ministry of the New Covenant (3:6) In 2:17–3:6 Paul makes an elaborate contrast between "those who peddle the word of God" and himself.[18] They have a letter of commendation written in ink, but his "letter" is written *in the Spirit of the living God;* their ministry is written on tablets of stone, but his — the now-converted Corinthians — is written on tablets *of human hearts.* These peddlers are preaching a gospel that commits the people to "tablets of stone," that is, to Moses and the old covenant (see vv. 12-14).

In this regard, then, this comment (v. 6) is quite pointed: "God . . . has made us sufficient (*hikanōsen*) as ministers of a new covenant, not in the letter,[19] but in the Spirit. For the letter kills, but the Spirit gives life" (author's translation).

That point becomes clear in the light of Exodus 4:10 where Moses says, "I have not been sufficient (*ouk hikanos*) in former times. . . . I am weak in speech and slow-tongued" (author's translation). Paul is saying that Moses (as advocated by the peddlers) was not sufficient for the ministry of the old covenant (which is now ended anyway), whereas the new covenant as prophesied (Jer 31:31-34; Ezek 36:24-27) has now come and God has made Paul "sufficient" for its ministry. Moses is a negative "type" anticipating Paul the positive "antitype."

Once again the grammar is important. Paul's verb tense "made suffi-

---

18. See chapter 9.

19. By "letter" (*gramma*), Paul means the law *itself*, not a legalistic and Pharisaic interpretation of it (as in "letter of the law"); see Rom 3:29; 7:6. For Paul "letter"/"law" is the now-superseded "old covenant" whose "end" is Christ (Rom 10:4).

cient"[20] indicates a specific moment when God fulfilled this in him. It was at Damascus that God appointed Paul a minister of the new covenant.

Given to Paul: The Ministry of Reconciliation (5:18-20)   As in other passages in this letter, Paul distinguishes between the *beginning* and the *continuation* of his activities. This he does by contrasting use of aorist and present verb tenses.

> 18 All this is from God, who through Christ reconciled us to himself and gave us the ministry of reconciliation; 19 that is, in Christ God was reconciling the world to himself, not counting their trespasses against them, and entrusting to us the message of reconciliation. 20 So we are ambassadors for Christ, God making his appeal through us. We beseech you on behalf of Christ, be reconciled to God.

Paul's vocation was "from God," who at a defined moment "gave" him "the ministry of reconciliation" (v. 18) and "entrusted" in him "the word of reconciliation" (v. 19).[21] Clearly, his Damascus "call" was the moment Paul began to exercise that ministry and proclaim that word.

In the twenty or so years since, Paul has been engaged in this ministry. He *is* an ambassador (or apostle) of Christ, who comes in his name and on his behalf *(hyper Christou)*, through whom God *is making* his appeal, "be reconciled to God." From this passage, then, we are able to trace Paul's current ambassadorial/apostolic ministry back to its source, at Damascus.

Given the Lord's Authority (10:8; 13:10)   Twice Paul writes of the authority (*exousia*/"delegated authority") the Lord gave him for positive rather than negative purposes. The wording differs only slightly.

> our authority, which the Lord gave for building you up and not for destroying you. (10:8)

> the authority which the Lord has given me for building up and not for tearing down. (13:10)

---

20. Aorist tense.

21. Both verbs are aorist participles. Also an aorist participle is "reconciled," prompting the question whether this also applies primarily to Paul (as "gave" and "entrusted" do). For the argument that Paul makes this a referent to himself as a former enemy of God, see S. Kim, "God Reconciled His Enemy to Himself: The Origin of Paul's Concept of Reconciliation," in *The Road from Damascus*, 102-24.

The verb tense (aorist) points to a particular moment when the Lord "gave" his authority to Paul, which, we conclude, was at the Damascus event, which he is currently exercising in the churches, in person and by letter.

The Limits God Assigned to Paul (10:13)   Paul is objecting that in coming to Corinth these Jewish "ministers of Christ" (11:22-23) have trespassed into "the limits God has apportioned" to Paul. "But we will not boast beyond limit, but will keep to the limits God has apportioned us, to reach even to you."

Paul is engaging in wordplay. His newly arrived opponents are boasting "beyond measure" *(ta ametra),* whereas Paul will boast according to the measure *(to metron)* of the field *(to kanōn)* that was measured out *(emerisen)* for him.

The verb tense (aorist) points to a particular moment that God "apportioned" to Paul his sphere of ministry, that is, to the Gentiles (as in Corinth). At one level Paul is likely appealing to the missionary accord forged between the Jerusalem "pillars" and the Antioch delegates, Barnabas and Paul (Gal 2:7-9). More fundamentally, however, Paul is not pointing the Corinthians to that moment in Jerusalem but rather to an event prior to that, at Damascus when God assigned to Paul his "field" of ministry among the Gentiles.

Galatians

Entrusted with the Gospel for the Gentiles (2:2, 7, 9)   Paul reports to the Galatians his meeting with three "pillars" of the church in Jerusalem.

> 2 I laid before them . . . the gospel which I preach among the Gentiles. . . . 7 When they saw that I had been entrusted with the gospel to the uncircumcised . . . 9 James and Cephas and John . . . gave to me and Barnabas the right hand of fellowship, that we should go to the Gentiles.

James, Peter, and John recognized that Paul had been "entrusted with the gospel to the uncircumcised." Here once more the verb use (perfect tense, passive voice) points to a past moment when God "entrusted" Paul with the message for the Gentiles and which these leaders endorsed, with their encouragement to "go" with that message to the Gentiles. The message Paul had been "entrusted" to preach he *continues* (v. 7 — present tense) to preach.

When was Paul "entrusted" (by God) with this message for the Gentiles? Clearly it was at the Damascus event.

Accursed on a Tree (3:10-13) Does Paul's assertion "Cursed be every one who hangs on a tree" (Gal 3:13, quoting Deut 21:23) reflect his pre-Damascus or his post-Damascus understanding?

> 10 For all who rely on works of the law are under a curse; for it is written, "Cursed be every one who does not abide by all things written in the book of the law, and do them." 11 Now it is evident that no man is justified before God by the law; for "He who through faith is righteous shall live"; 12 but the law does not rest on faith, for "He who does them shall live by them." 13 Christ redeemed us from the curse of the law, having become a curse for us — for it is written, "Cursed be every one who hangs on a tree" — 14 that in Christ Jesus the blessing of Abraham might come upon the Gentiles, that we might receive the promise of the Spirit through faith.

True, the passage exhibits a well-developed argument, buttressed by OT citations (Deut 27:26; Hab 2:4; Lev 18:5; Deut 21:23), and points to mature reflection, likely based on mission debates in the synagogues. Paul concludes that life "under law" was "accursed [by God]" due to the impossibility of fulfilling its demands, but that the crucified one had "become a curse for us." The lawbreaker cannot be "justified before God by the law," but only "in Christ" crucified, by faith.[22]

Nonetheless, despite the comprehensive construction in this passage, it is possible to detect a pre-Damascus perception by Paul that the crucified Jesus was "accursed" (by God). When Paul knew of the messianic claims the disciples were making about Jesus, he must have immediately reached an opposite conclusion, that he was a false messiah. After all, the Pharisee scribe must have known Deuteronomy 21:23 and decided that the impaled Jesus was "accursed" by God and that his followers must be destroyed. As noted earlier, however, Stephen's attack on the temple was the catalyst for Paul's assault on the church.

---

22. See S. Y. Kim, *The Origin of Paul's Gospel* (Grand Rapids: Eerdmans, 1982), 274.

When "Faith" Came (Gal 3:23-26)   As already noted, Paul occasionally writes both autobiographically and representatively for other believers. He is a paradigm for others and his story is also his gospel message (see 175-79). In the next passage he writes autobiographically but also representatively, so as to tell the now-fulfilled salvation history of Israel. In the latter sense Israel was "confined under the law, kept under restraint until faith [i.e., Christ] 'came'/'was revealed,'" after which, however, they are "all sons of God, through faith." Paul, however, is also speaking about himself.

> 23 Now before faith came, we were confined under the law, kept under restraint until faith should be revealed. 24 So that the law was our pedagogue until Christ came, that we might be justified by faith. 25 But now that faith has come, we are no longer under a pedagogue; 26 for in Christ Jesus you are all sons of God, through faith. (RSV adapted)

When we understand that Paul is speaking about himself, we notice another before-and-after pattern. The turning point was when "faith came/was revealed," which must refer to the single and unique Damascus event. Before that, however, Paul was "kept under law" by a (harsh) "pedagogue." This is parallel with previously having been "shut up under sin" (3:22). Clearly to be "under law" necessarily means to be "shut up under sin," that is, in a form of bondage. After the Damascus event, however, Paul is redeemed/free (4:5) and is a son of God, "justified by faith."[23] For Paul after Damascus, the way to God was through Christ, no longer through law.

As discussed earlier,[24] this passage must be read alongside Romans 7:9-11. As to the perennial question about which stage of Paul's life this is, it seems that Paul is reflecting on a sense of unease he felt pre-Damascus but that he realized acutely afterward. In neither passage, however, do we have the sense that the pre-Damascus Paul was tortured with guilt as a lawbreaker.

---

23. According to J. Dupont, "The Conversion of Paul, and Its Influence on His Understanding of Salvation by Faith," in *Apostolic History and the Gospel*, ed. W. W. Gasque and R. P. Martin (Exeter: Paternoster, 1970): "In rejecting entirely and without reserve the notion of a righteousness and a salvation which may be secured by observance of the law, he came to grasp with greater penetration and to express with greater clarity what it was that constituted the novelty and originality of Christian soteriology, viz. that salvation is given only by and in Christ to those who are joined to him by faith" (194).

24. 39-41.

Nonetheless, in this passage Paul traces his "justification by faith" and divine Sonship to the Damascus event. In other words, it is not correct to argue that Paul devised "justification by faith" for the sake of the inclusion of the Gentiles into the covenant.[25] "Justification by faith" is equally applicable to Jews like Paul and to the Gentiles he preached to, since both are "under sin" (*huph' hamartian* — Rom 3:9).

Ephesians: "Grace That Was Given"

In this passage, more than any other, Paul discloses the origins of his ministry to the Gentiles.[26]

> 2 assuming that you have heard of the stewardship of God's grace that was given to me for you, 3 how the mystery was made known to me by revelation, as I have written briefly. 4 When you read this you can perceive my insight into the mystery of Christ, 5 which was not made known to the sons of men in other generations as it has now been revealed to his holy apostles and prophets by the Spirit; 6 that is, how the Gentiles are fellow heirs, members of the same body, and partakers of the promise in Christ Jesus through the gospel. 7 Of this gospel I was made a minister according to the gift of God's grace which was given me by the working of his power. 8 To me, though I am the very least of all the saints, this grace was given, to preach to the Gentiles the unsearchable riches of Christ. (Eph 3:2-8)

There is a striking accumulation of verb tense uses that points to the converging past moment when to Paul *"was given"* the stewardship of God's grace (v. 2; cf. vv. 7, 8); when the mystery of Christ was *"made known"* (v. 3) and was revealed to him (v. 5); when Paul "was *made* a minister . . . to preach to the Gentiles" (vv. 7-8).

Once again, Paul is pointing back allusively to the Damascus event.

---

25. E.g., as stated by J. D. G. Dunn, "'Justification by faith' was Paul's answer to the question: How is it that Gentiles can be equally acceptable to God as Jews?" in *The Theology of Paul the Apostle* (Edinburgh: T. & T. Clark, 1998), 340.

26. Those who regard Ephesians as deutero-Pauline nonetheless recognize genuine Pauline concepts in the letter, including his sense of apostleship to the Gentiles. Ideas like these in Ephesians are confirmed in Paul's undisputed letters (cf. Rom 1:1, 5; 11:3; Gal 1:16-17; 2:7-9). See appendix B.

Tabulation of Paul's References, Explicit and Implicit

From our survey of relevant passages in Paul's letters, we notice a before-and-after pattern hinging on the Damascus event.

	Before	Damascus	Afterward
Gal 1:13-17	persecuted the church	God called Paul	to preach his Son among the Gentiles
Gal 2:2, 7, 8		Paul entrusted with the gospel to the circumcised	Paul preached the gospel among the Gentiles
Gal 3:22; 3:23-26	shut up under sin under a pedagogue under law	faith came faith was revealed	justified by faith a son of God redeemed/free
1 Cor 9:16-18		entrusted with a stewardship	under necessity to preach the gospel
1 Cor 9:1; 15:8; 15:11	Paul persecuted church	Paul saw Jesus the Lord Christ appeared to Paul	I am an apostle, preaching Christ
Gal 3:11	crucified Jesus "accursed"	Jesus spoke from the heavenly light	justification not by law but in the "accursed" one
2 Cor 3:6		made "sufficient"	as minister in new covenant
2 Cor 4:1, 5, 6	[persecutor] veiled to *telos* of Moses	received mercy from God God shone in Paul's heart	to give light (to others)
2 Cor 5:15, 16, 17	lived for himself knew Christ *kata sarka*	"in Christ"	now lives for Christ [knows Christ *kata pneuma*] "a new creation"
2 Cor 5:18, 19		God gave ministry of reconciliation God gave word of reconciliation	an ambassador for Christ, God appealing through him
2 Cor 10:8; 13:10		Lord gave Paul his authority	for building up the churches
Rom 1:1, 5; 11:13; 15:15		set apart for the gospel Paul received grace grace was given	apostle to the Gentiles
2 Cor 10:13		the limits God assigned to us	keeping within them

	Before	Damascus	Afterward
Eph 3:2-8	mystery of Christ not known	mystery of Christ made known by revelation	Paul a minister to preach to the Gentiles
Col 1:25		Paul became a minister	to make the word of God known
Phil 3:4-7	as to zeal, a perse-cutor of church	"seized by Christ Jesus"	the loss of all things

Our analysis allows us to make some comment about the mind of the pre-Damascus Paul and how the Damascus event changed him.

The Pre-Damascus Paul

It is important at the outset to recognize that we know the mind of the pre-Damascus Paul only from his postconversion perspective; this is the only perspective available to us. The Damascus event and subsequent develop-ments and circumstances affecting him suggest that we should exercise some caution in assessing Paul's views before he became a man "in Christ."

Nonetheless, three long-term connected attitudes of the pre-Damascus Paul may be discerned. Two of these are "global" relating to Is-rael, and the other is personal to Paul.

First, Paul assumed that the law (referred to as "Moses" in 2 Cor 3:12-15) was permanent (never to be "abolished" — 3:7, 11, 13, 16) and that it had no glorious "end" (the Christ who was to come) that was lying concealed within (3:13). When Paul "turned to the Lord [Christ]," that "veil" was "abolished" (3:14, 16) and God "shone" in Paul's heart, dispelling the "veil" of darkness (4:6). Paul preached Christ so that Israelites could "turn" to Christ for the "veil" to be removed so they could understand the tempo-rary and anticipatory nature of the law ("Moses"). Christ was the "end" of the law (Rom 10:4).

Second (and related to the first), Paul had not anticipated the inclu-sion of the Gentiles in the covenantal people *through the ministry and ac-tivity of the Messiah* (Eph 3:2-8; Rom 16:25-27). Before Damascus this had been a "mystery" to him. God's call to Paul as "apostle to the Gentiles" who was called to preach God's Son to the Gentiles (Gal 1:15-16; Rom 1:1, 5; 11:13; 15:15-16; Eph 3:2-8) likely came as a complete surprise.

Third, from his new position "in Christ," Paul recognized that prior to Damascus he had been "under law" (as if "under" a harsh "pedagogue"), and therefore, that he had been "under sin," that is, subjected to moral defeat in relationship with the law. The pre-Damascus Paul likely felt only a partial awareness of this failure. In general the preconverted Paul passed a favorable verdict upon himself, as those around him would have done, that he was "blameless" as far as the law was concerned (Phil 3:6).

As a man "in Christ," however, who was now morally sensitized (through the Holy Spirit and the shame he likely felt retrospectively as a violent persecutor),[27] Paul was now more aware of the depths of that moral debility. One does not have the impression that the pre-Damascus Paul was a man of plagued conscience. Paradoxically, Paul becomes fully aware that he was "in Adam" (a sinner subject to death) only when he became a man "in Christ." Prior to Damascus Paul likely believed that redemption from Adam's "fall" was attainable through law.[28] The glory of the Damascus Christophany opened his eyes to Jesus' true identity as the *Kyrios* and to the undeniable truths of Stephen's claims.

In short, the mind of the pre-Damascus Paul was dominated by his sense of the absolute and permanent nature of the law and, therefore, of the *exclusion* of the Gentiles from the Mosaic covenant, rooted in the law as it was. As noted earlier, it was not the apostles' assertion of Jesus' messiahship per se that aroused Paul's anger; like his mentor Gamaliel, Paul could afford to wait and see about this.[29] Rather, Paul was stirred into violent persecution by the Hellenists' claim that Jesus as Messiah had so fulfilled the law and abrogated the temple that the Gentiles were now potentially included *in him* in the historic covenant people.

---

27. So S. Chester, *Conversion at Corinth* (Edinburgh: T. & T. Clark, 2003), 164-72.

28. While the pre-Damascus Paul would have subscribed to a belief in Adam's "fall" (as in: "O Adam, what have you done? When you sinned your fall occurred not only for you, but for your descendants" — 4 Ezra 7:118), he likely also believed in redemption *through law* (as in: "We have nothing now besides the Almighty and his law. If we prepare our hearts and make ourselves ready, in this way we shall again acquire everything which we have lost and much better things than we had lost" — 2 Bar 85:3-4; cf. Hillel's dictum "Much Torah, much life" — *m. Avot* 2:7).

29. See earlier, chapter 4.

The Post-Damascus Paul

Those scholars are correct who reject Stendahl's claim that Paul was "called" but not "converted."[30] In the Damascus event God changed Paul's relationship with Christ *and* gave him a new vocation.[31]

Relationally, at Damascus Paul "saw the Lord" (1 Cor 9:1; cf. 15:8) and became a man "in Christ" who "received mercy" (in respect to his persecutions — 2 Cor 4:1), to whom "faith came"/"was revealed" by which he was "justified" and became a "son of God" (Gal 3:23-26). As a result he now "knew Christ," not as he had known him before, "according to the flesh" *(kata sarka),* but by implication "according to the Spirit" *(kata pneuma),* so that "from now on" out of Christ's love for him Paul lived for him and no longer for himself (2 Cor 5:15-16). In regard to Paul's radical relational change to Christ and the accompanying reorientation of his values, we may refer to Paul as "converted."

Integrally connected was Paul's *new vocation.*[32] At Damascus God called Paul to be his apostle to the Gentiles (Gal 1:15-16; Rom 1:5; 11:13; 15:15-16; Eph 3:2-8), preaching his Son to them and having "authority" to build up the churches (2 Cor 10:8; 13:10). At the same time, God made Paul "sufficient" to become a "minister of the new covenant" of righteousness and Spirit, long prophesied by Jeremiah and Ezekiel. As a herald of Christ, Paul was his ambassador and apostle, through whom God made his appeals.

The Damascus Event

Why speak of the "Damascus event"[33] rather than the "Damascus *Road* event"? It is because the baptism of the persecutor in Damascus somehow

---

30. See O'Brien, "Was Paul Converted?" 360-91.

31. For a view that argues for a minimal influence from a Damascus conversion and a maximum influence in the subsequent exposure to the church, see P. Fredriksen, "Paul and Augustine: Conversion Narratives, Orthodox Traditions and the Retrospective Self," *JTS* 37, no. 1 (1986): 3-34.

32. Many times Paul refers to his missionary vocation, though without alluding to Damascus as the point of its origin (see, e.g., 1 Cor 3:5-15; 9:19-23; 2 Cor 2:14-16; 4:7-15; Rom 10:14-21; 15:15-21; Col 1:24-29). For analysis of these texts see E. Schnabel, *Early Christian Mission* (Downers Grove, Ill.: InterVarsity, 2004), 945-82.

33. Chapter 3 in Kim, *The Origin of Paul's Gospel,* is titled "The Damascus Event."

completes the Lord's encounter with Paul on the road approaching the city. This is evident from Ananias's words to Paul in the first and second of the three narratives in the book of Acts.

> "Brother Saul, the Lord Jesus who appeared to you on the road . . . has sent me that you may . . . be filled with the Holy Spirit." . . . Then he rose and was baptized. (Acts 9:17-18)

> Brother Saul . . . the God of our fathers appointed you to know his will, to see the Just One and to hear a voice from his mouth; and you will be a witness for him to all men of what you have seen and heard. And now why do you wait? Rise and be baptized, and wash away your sins, calling on his name. (Acts 22:13-16).

Ananias was critical to Paul (i) in first receiving and then mediating God's missionary call to Paul (Acts 9:15; 22:14-15); (ii) in instructing Paul about baptism, the "washing away of sins" and being "filled with the Holy Spirit"; and (iii) for (likely) bringing Paul into the fellowship of the disciples in Damascus, after which he began preaching in the local synagogues (9:19b-21).

Soon enough, however, the young convert "confounded the Jews who lived in Damascus" (9:22). By the time he was forced to leave the city sometime later, he appears to have become the leader of the disciples in Damascus (cf. "*his* disciples" — 9:25).

Clearly, therefore, we must include all that happened *in* Damascus in the following days with the Lord's interception of Paul on the road approaching the city.

The comprehensive nature of the Damascus event, with its likely lengthy period of time preaching in the city, raises the question of the extent of Paul's knowledge about "the faith" he acquired in Damascus that he had previously "attempted to destroy," and which he now vigorously proclaimed (cf. Gal 1:23).

There are several catechetical and liturgical echoes in Paul's letters that point to Damascus as the place of Paul's initial instruction as a disciple of the Lord.

First, in Romans 6 when speaking about baptism, Paul writes in the first-person plural: "*all of us* who have been baptized . . . *we* were buried . . . with him by baptism" (vv. 3-4). Later in that passage he refers to believers having been handed over to a "standard of teaching" (v. 17; cf. 16:17).

Clearly, baptism was related to this standard of teaching, both Paul's baptism and his Roman readers' baptisms.[34]

Which teaching? The sonorous creedlike opening lines of Romans focused on the son of David who is the resurrected Son of God are significantly similar to Paul's preaching in the synagogues of Damascus (which doubtless included Gentile Godfearers).[35] There the newly baptized Paul preached Jesus as "the Son of God," "proving that Jesus was the Christ" (i.e., son of David) (Acts 9:20, 22). This is strikingly confirmed by Paul's own words about God's Damascus "call" to "preach [his Son] among the Gentiles" (Gal 1:16-17). My contention is that Paul's subsequent and frequent proclamation of Jesus as the Son of God in Damascus (including to the Gentile Godfearers) had its beginnings in his baptismal instruction in Damascus (cf. 1 Thess 1:9-10; 2 Cor 1:19).[36]

Another catechetical echo is found in 1 Corinthians 15:1-7 where Paul cites the "received" tradition of the expiatory death of Christ, his burial and resurrection, which the other apostles also preach (15:11). Where did Paul "receive" this tradition? There are three main options — Damascus in the early 30s, Jerusalem in the mid-30s, and Antioch in the 40s. The third is unlikely,[37] the second is possible,[38] but the first is probable.[39] In my view, this critical catechesis was formulated under the apostles in Jerusalem and "handed over" to Paul in the nascent community in Damascus.[40]

When Paul's letters begin to appear — whether with Galatians in the

---

34. See chapter 11.

35. M. Hengel, "The Stance of the Apostle Paul toward the Law in the Unknown Years between Damascus and Antioch," in *The Paradoxes of Paul*, 81-83.

36. See Barnett, *BC*, 88-94; P. W. Barnett, "Romans and the Origin of Paul's Christology," in *History and Exegesis*, ed. San-Won (Aaron) Son, Festschrift for E. E. Ellis (Edinburgh: T. & T. Clark, 2006), 90-103.

37. For a critique of Antioch as the source of Paul's Christology as favored by the history-of-religions school, see M. Hengel, *Between Jesus and Paul* (London: SCM, 1983), 30-47; Barnett, *BC*, 55-85.

38. In support of Jerusalem as the source of Paul's *paradosis*, see F. F. Bruce, *Paul, Apostle of the Free Spirit* (Exeter: Paternoster, 1977), 83-94; Hengel and Schwemer, *Between Damascus and Antioch*, 147.

39. See Barnett, *BC*, 87-88.

40. Christ as "raised on the third day" is an unusual grammatical construction and is found only in the preformed text cited by Paul (1 Cor 15:4) and in Luke's summary of Peter's kerygma to Cornelius's household (Acts 10:40). See further, Barnett, *BC*, 87-88.

late 40s (as I argue)[41] or 1 Thessalonians circa 50 — the apostle's doctrine of the expiatory death of Christ *(hyper hamartiōn/hēmōn)* and his resurrection is firmly established and confidently asserted (see, e.g., Gal 1:1, 4; 1 Thess 5:10). The same is true of Paul's early assertions of the divine Sonship of Jesus, the son of David (and therefore the Christ), in those earliest letters (see, e.g., Gal 4:4; 1 Thess 1:10). Accordingly we concur with the judgment of M. Hengel, that "it is impossible to demonstrate a *fundamental* change in the center of the Pauline message [Christology] from the time of his conversion or from the beginning of his missionary activity as an apostle."[42] In short, the core elements of Paul's doctrines that he was to preach were formed in Damascus.

Conclusion

Was Paul "converted" as well as "called"? The weight of the evidence from the book of Acts and the specific references, and the identifiable allusions in Paul's letters, leaves no doubt that the Damascus event represented a complete relational and moral turnabout that was accompanied by a radical new vocation as one commissioned to preach to the Gentiles to bring them into the divine covenant.

The direction and trajectory of Paul's life and movement from Damascus onward are written on every page of Paul's letters and are the engine that drives the narrative of the Acts of the Apostles. To deny this is to deny the evidence of history.

This, however, does not in itself resolve the presenting and underlying question that this book addresses. Did Paul's message and ministry genuinely continue the emphasis and trajectory of the message and ministry of Jesus? The answer to this question must await further discussion (see chapter 7).

---

41. See Barnett *BC,* 206-10.
42. Hengel, "The Stance," 85.

Paul's Levantine Years (ca. 34-47): Damascus, Arabia, Judea, and Syria-Cilicia

We confront important questions when we consider Paul's ministry between the Damascus event (ca. 34) and the first of his westward missions (ca. 47).[1] It is only during those later missions that we have letters from Paul and a detailed understanding of his movements. For this reason the period from 34 to 47 has been called Paul's "unknown years."[2] Nothing from his pen survives from those fourteen years, and the book of Acts passes over them in only sixteen verses.

The questions are these. Did Paul come to his view of Christ and of the mission to the Gentiles at Damascus, or were these ideas formed later at Antioch? Why did Paul wait fourteen years to seriously begin his apostolate to the Gentiles, and what prompted him finally to begin his major westward missions? Underlying these questions is the possibility that the real change in Paul's thinking and action did not occur at Damascus at the beginning but in Syria-Cilicia a dozen or more years later.

---

1. My chronological assumptions are: the first Easter (33), the Damascus event (34), Paul's first return visit to Jerusalem (36/37), Paul in Tarsus/Cilicia (37-45), Paul in Antioch (45-47), second Jerusalem visit (47), mission to Cyprus and South Galatia (47-48). See further, Barnett, *BC*, 22-26.

2. The classical study for this period is M. Hengel and A. M. Schwemer, *Paul between Damascus and Antioch: The Unknown Years* (London: SCM, 1977); see also M. Hengel, "The Stance of the Apostle Paul toward the Law in the Unknown Years between Damascus and Antioch," in *Justification and Variegated Nomism*, vol. 2, *The Paradoxes of Paul*, ed. D. A. Carson, P. T. O'Brien, and M. A. Seifrid (Tübingen: Mohr Siebeck, 2004), 75-103.

Unknown Years?

We must qualify the notion that Paul's Levantine years are *unknown*. First, we notice that we are able to reconstruct the sequence and likely dates of Paul's movements and activities during these years. We are fortunate that our sources, Paul and Luke, are in broad agreement regarding Paul's movements from Damascus to Antioch.

Paul provides us with that sequence in one letter, his personal narrative to the Galatians, covering the decade and a half from his persecutions in Jerusalem through to his preaching of Christ crucified in Galatia (Gal 1:13–3:1). When we set Paul's narrative alongside Luke's narrative in the book of Acts, we note significant agreement of sequence.

Paul's Sequence	Acts Sequence
Damascus	Damascus
Arabia	
Damascus	
Jerusalem	Jerusalem
Syria-Cilicia	Tarsus
[Antioch][3]	Antioch
Jerusalem	Jerusalem
[South] Galatia[4]	Pisidia/Lycaonia

The major difference between the two versions is that the book of Acts makes no reference to Paul's ministry in Arabia followed by his return to Damascus. Otherwise the two versions are in agreement.

The identifiable common thread discernible in the narratives of Paul and Luke calls into question the contention that Paul's ministry during these years is in fact "lost" to historical research. The details are not extensive, yet the agreement in sequence is noteworthy.

Furthermore, it would not be true to infer that Paul became completely cut off from the Jerusalem church. Its leadership "sent" him to Tarsus and later "sent" Barnabas to Antioch, who in turn "brought" Paul from Tarsus to Antioch (Acts 9:30; 11:22, 26). The leaders of the church in Jerusa-

---

3. Gal 2:1 does not indicate specifically that Paul and Barnabas came to Jerusalem from Antioch, though this is a reasonable assumption.

4. See Barnett, *BC*, 206-10.

lem appear to have been aware of Paul's presence in Tarsus/Cilicia and of his ministry there.

Again, Paul's writings do not leave the impression of a "blank" space for these years. Paul sees the Levantine period as of a piece with his later westward missions in Galatia, Macedonia, Achaia, and Asia. In about 57 he declares retrospectively to the Romans that he has fulfilled the gospel "in a circle" *(en kuklō)* from Jerusalem around as far as Illyricum (Rom 15:19). His preaching in Damascus, Arabia, Judea, and Syria-Cilicia belonged to that circular gospel sweep.

Accordingly, Paul makes no distinction between his ministry during the Levantine years and the following decade of the westward missions in the Roman provinces of Anatolia and Greece. His list of major sufferings (or "peristasis") in 2 Corinthians (11:1–12:13) provides a global review of his entire ministry period, including the decade and a half between Damascus and Antioch. In Paul's mind his whole ministry began at Damascus and was thereafter a single entity.

His escape from Damascus "down" the wall when the gates of Damascus were guarded by Aretas's ethnarch/consul precedes his experience when he was caught "up" to paradise, which must have occurred when he was in Cilicia some years later (2 Cor 11:32-33; 12:3). Both events belong to the earliest period of his ministry, in the Levant.

Likewise, his "five times I have received at the hands of the Jews the forty lashes less one" (2 Cor 11:24), which finds no echo in the book of Acts, likely relates to the Levantine span of years. Those floggings were a reaction against his preaching of the Messiah Jesus in the synagogues (cf. 1 Cor 1:23); the former persecutor is now the persecuted.

Nor is Luke, for all his apparent minimal interest in Paul at this time, entirely silent. He gives clear hints that Paul established churches with Gentile members during Paul's years in Tarsus/Cilicia. James's decree from the Jerusalem Council was addressed to "the brethren who are of the Gentiles in Antioch and *Syria and Cilicia*" (Acts 15:23). Upon leaving Antioch Paul and Silvanus delivered the letter to these Syrian and Cilician churches (Acts 15:41; 16:4). Luke allows us to understand that Paul's years in Cilicia were not years of idleness.

Paul in the Levant

It is worth surveying briefly Paul's ministry in sequence during the Levantine years. While details are lacking in some cases, we have a general impression of sustained ministry by Paul throughout these years.[5]

Damascus (ca. 34)

It made sense that the young zealot should have gone to Damascus[6] for further action against the disciples of the Lord. Most likely they were Hellenist Jews from Jerusalem seeking refuge in the city closest to the borders of Eretz Israel that Paul sought to bring back to the Holy City (Acts 9:2; 22:5).

According to Josephus, there was a large Jewish community in Damascus that was most likely Greek speaking.[7] The book of Acts refers to multiple synagogues (9:2, 20). Josephus reports that the wider population of Damascenes disliked and feared the Jews in their midst. One likely reason, he says, is that a majority of Gentile women in Damascus had converted to the Jewish religion.[8] Though likely an overstatement, there must have been some truth in it.

Doubtless aware of the number of Gentile Godfearers attending the local synagogues, the persecutor may have journeyed to Damascus because he was alarmed at the prospect of the fugitive Hellenist believers from Jerusalem making disciples within these synagogues.

If it made sense for Paul the persecutor to go to Damascus, it made sense also for him to have been converted there and to have commenced his new vocation there. There was a ready-made nurturing community of disciples in the city. And there were also many Jews and, as we have noted, many Gentile Godfearers also.

---

5. For argument that throughout this period Paul was engaged in ministry rather than, for example, in some kind of meditative preparation for his major missions, see E. J. Schnabel, *Early Christian Mission* (Downers Grove, Ill.: InterVarsity, 2002), 1035-36.

6. By NT times Damascus was a Hellenistic city, laid out on a Hippodamian street grid (cf. the street called "straight") and with Greek institutions (theater, gymnasium).

7. At the outbreak of the war between the Jews and the Romans in A.D. 66, the people of Damascus captured and killed the entire Jewish population, 10,600 in all (Josephus, *JW* 2.559-560).

8. Josephus, *JW* 2.561.

It appears that (not for the last time) Paul would become a victim of his own success. The young scribal scholar began preaching to Jews and Godfearers that Jesus was "the Son of God," "proving" (from the Scriptures) that he was "the Christ" (Acts 9:20, 22; cf. Gal 1:16).

This provoked amazement in the synagogues that the persecutor of those who called on "this name" in Jerusalem and who had menacingly come to Damascus was now preaching that "name" (Acts 9:21). Herein lies the source of Paul's new but rapidly spreading reputation that, as from Damascus, he was "preaching the faith he once tried to destroy" (Gal 1:23). Inevitably the synagogue authorities would have to remove this dangerous subversive, and so they plotted to kill him (Acts 9:23).[9] After no more than a few months he, the former persecutor, becomes the persecuted, and must himself flee — "into Arabia" (Gal 1:17).[10]

"Into Arabia" (ca. 34/35)[11]

But why did Paul go "into Arabia" and not elsewhere, for example, north to Palmyra, south to the Hellenistic cities of the Decapolis, or west to the Hellenized coastal cities of Phoenicia? The answer, most likely, is that "Arabia" or "Nabatea" was a major kingdom near Eretz Israel and home to a people who, as descendants of Ishmael, were a kindred tribe to the descendants of Isaac. At the same time, the Nabateans/Arabs were "Gentiles" and a part of Paul's newly mandated missionary vocation.[12]

9. Paul had to leave Damascus twice, once on account of "the Jews" (Acts 9:24), later on account of the Nabatean ethnarch/consul following his preaching in "Arabia" (Gal 1:17-18; 2 Cor 11:32). Luke has combined Paul's two flights from Damascus into one. Most likely Paul escaped through the city wall only once, following his return visit to Damascus.

10. Luke omits Paul's foray "into Arabia," even though it likely occupied two years, but proceeds to narrate Paul's brief and turbulent return to Jerusalem, from which he had to flee to Tarsus (Acts 9:28-30), where he remained in obscurity. Luke likely has two reasons for his emphases and omissions: (i) to focus attention on Peter's ministry in Israel as a prelude to the ingathering of Gentile Godfearer Cornelius before reintroducing Paul; (ii) to dramatize the beginning of Paul's westward missions (in Acts 13), which become the sole focus of his narrative. Luke ignores Paul's ministry in "Arabia" and minimizes his work in his own native "Syria and Cilicia" because these were not immediate stepping-stones to the apostle's great movement toward Rome, world capital of the Gentiles.

11. See Hengel and Schwemer, Paul, 106-26.

12. The desert kingdom of Nabatea is located on the Arabian plateau to the east of

Paul does not indicate where he traveled in Arabia/Nabatea or whom he addressed.[13] We reasonably assume that once more he went to synagogues to argue from the Scriptures that the long-awaited Christ had now come in the person of the crucified and risen Jesus, where he sought to influence *Gentile* Godfearers as well as Jews.[14] It is no coincidence that upon being intercepted by God near Damascus and called to proclaim "his Son . . . to the Gentiles," he went first to Damascus, then upon expulsion, "into Arabia." Paul intends his readers to understand that he preached to Gentiles in Arabia as well as in Damascus.

It appears that Paul was as unwelcome in "Arabia" as he had been in Damascus, though for a different reason. Paul arrived in Arabia-Nabatea at a singularly inopportune time. Some years earlier Aretas IV had given a daughter in marriage to Herod Antipas, doubtless to help secure friendly border relationships. During the late 20s, however, Antipas committed adultery with Herodias, prompting the Nabatean princess to flee.[15] Hostilities were reaching a boiling point at the very time Paul the Jew was preaching in the synagogues in Arabia-Nabatea.

The only light thrown on this period in Paul's life is his own comment that Aretas's ethnarch/consul in Damascus sought to seize him when he returned to the city (2 Cor 11:32). This suggests that Paul's preaching in Nabatea had come adversely to the attention of the king, though further

---

Perea and the Dead Sea. In the previous century the former nomads of this region learned how to dam, channel, and even mine water, and they established a series of settlements, notably their capital, the rock-city necropolis Petra, to the south. Like the people of Israel and the Idumeans, the Nabateans had become deeply influenced by Hellenism, though they retained their native tongue (now transcribed in Greek script).

13. Schnabel, *Early Christian Mission,* 1038 (following Murphy-O'Connor), argues that Paul confined his ministry to northern Nabatea, including the cities of the Decapolis east of the Jordan (1043). Hengel and Schwemer, *Paul,* 184, contend that Paul traveled as far south as the capital, Petra. In reality, we do not have sufficient evidence to do more than guess where Paul went in Arabia!

14. Cf. Hengel and Schwemer, *Paul,* 113.

15. The Nabateans had dynastic connections with the Idumean Herods: (i) Herod's mother Cypros was from an aristocratic Nabatean family in Petra; (ii) Herod Antipas, tetrarch of Galilee and Perea from 4 B.C., son of Herod the king, married the daughter of Aretas IV, Nabatea's most famous king (9 B.C.–A.D. 40). Antipas's shabby treatment of the Nabatean princess provoked the implacable hatred of her father, who bided his time to inflict vengeance. Various clashes circa 34-36 erupted into open war in 37 when the Nabateans decimated the army of the tetrarch of Galilee and Perea.

details are lacking. Once more, therefore, Paul must flee, and so he returned to Damascus.

Back to Damascus (ca. 35/36)

We know from Paul's initial time in Damascus that there were Jewish disciples in the city, indigenous Damascenes like Ananias as well as fugitive Hellenist Jewish disciples from Jerusalem. These would have continued to be members of the synagogues, as well as meeting separately with fellow believers. We may reasonably assume that, forced from Arabia, Paul returned to Damascus to encourage the disciples in Damascus.

However, it was not possible to stay long in Damascus, as Paul himself explains. "At Damascus, the [ethnarch] under King Aretas guarded the city of Damascus in order to seize me, but I was let down in a basket through a window in the wall, and escaped his hands" (2 Cor 11:32-33).

In the previous century, until the end of the reign of Aretas III (ca. 85-72 B.C.), Damascus had been part of the Nabatean kingdom, but from Pompey's coming in 63 B.C. Damascus appears to have been an independent city-state (one of the cities of the Decapolis?).[16] This is obliquely confirmed by Paul's words "I returned [from Arabia] to Damascus" (Gal 1:17), and to his reference, as above, to "the *city* of Damascus," implying a city-state.

How, then, do we explain an ethnarch of Aretas king of the Nabateans in a city that was not part of his realm? At that time it was not uncommon for concentrations of nationals in cities foreign to them to have an "ethnarch" or consul appointed as a leader of their community, as for example over the large Jewish community in Alexandria.[17]

Since Paul had been "away in Arabia," it is reasonable to suppose that the orders to seize him came from Aretas, king of the Nabateans. To that

16. F. Millar, *The Roman Near East, 31 BC–AD 337* (Cambridge: Harvard University Press, 1993), 56-57, argues that Damascus was under Nabatean control, whereas R. Riesner, *Paul's Early Period: Chronology, Mission Strategy, Theology* (Grand Rapids: Eerdmans, 1998), 70-79, believes it was an independent city-state.

17. Josephus, *Ant* 14.117. According to Strabo, an ethnarch "governs the nation, and distributes justice to them and takes care of their contracts and of laws pertaining to them, as if he were the ruler of a free republic" (*Geography* 17.798). By this understanding Aretas's "ethnarch" in Damascus would have had jurisdiction over Nabateans within the city and acted for his king in seeking to capture Paul.

end the gates of the city were effectively guarded, allowing no passage through them. Paul climbed through a window in the exterior of the city wall and was lowered in a flexible basket usually used for hauling up merchandise. The passive "lowered" points to fellow believers (Acts 9:25 — "his disciples") who helped Paul escape from the city.

So Paul's second stay in Damascus most probably ended as abruptly as had his first. We cannot overestimate the importance of these two visits to Damascus for the unfolding story of Paul's ministry.

At the first, Christ's interception of the persecutor outside the city was followed inside the city by the call to preach to the Gentiles mediated by Ananias, and by catechetical instruction, baptism, and the coming of the Spirit. From the nurturing community of disciples Paul began immediately to go out to preach the message about the Messiah, as commissioned by God. In short, that initial visit confirmed and consolidated Paul as a disciple of the Lord and as a preacher to Jews and — significantly — to Gentiles (i.e., Godfearers).

After his years missioning alone (as it appears) in Arabia/Nabatea, he came again to the comfort and fellowship of the disciples in Damascus. But now, once more forced to flee, he will go back to Jerusalem to meet the leaders of the church he had previously attempted to destroy.

Paul's First Return Visit to Jerusalem (ca. 36/37)

A return visit to Jerusalem was not an urgent priority. There were at least two earlier opportunities to go back to Jerusalem, his city of adoption. Had he wished to, Paul could have returned either after his first withdrawal from Damascus or when he decided to leave Nabatea.

We are fortunate to have two independent accounts of this return visit; however, they do not entirely agree.

> Then after three years I went up to Jerusalem to visit Cephas, and remained with him fifteen days. But I saw none of the other apostles except James the Lord's brother. (Gal 1:18-19)

> And when he had come to Jerusalem he attempted to join the disciples; and they were all afraid of him, for they did not believe that he was a disciple. But Barnabas took him, and brought him to the apostles, and

> [Paul] declared to them how on the road he had seen the Lord, who spoke to him. . . . (Acts 9:26-27)

Both accounts agree that on leaving Damascus he came to Jerusalem, where he met apostles. The difficulty is that Luke points to a meeting with "the apostles," implying *all* the apostles, whereas Paul himself declares on oath that he saw only Cephas and James. Can we resolve this apparently awkward disagreement in our sources?

Paul is unlikely to have arrived in Jerusalem and immediately presented himself to the Christian community there, which he had "tried to destroy" (Gal 1:13). It is more realistic to think that he slipped quietly into Jerusalem, perhaps staying at first with relatives there (we know of a nephew who later saved his life in Jerusalem — Acts 23:16-22). Only then would the former persecutor have likely approached the believers in the Holy City and been taken by Barnabas to tell the apostles of his encounter with the Lord on the way to Damascus and of his preaching in the city.

Perhaps it was subsequent to such a meeting that he was invited to stay with Cephas and when he also met James. The discrepancy between the two passages would be eased if it were allowed that a meeting with these leading apostles was in *private* and, therefore, of a different order to his meeting with the other apostles.[18] After all, Cephas was a leader of the Jerusalem church, and James appears to have been an emerging leader (in a conservative subgroup within the wider community?). These were the people Paul needed to meet.

Paul's meeting with Cephas circa 36/37 provided the former Pharisee with an opportunity to learn about the historical Jesus, his words and works. When Paul's letters come to be written, starting in the late forties, they are marked by references to "the word of the Lord [Jesus]" and to allusions to the character and teachings of Jesus.[19] From whom did Paul learn these, except from Peter and the other apostles in Jerusalem where the process of collecting these teachings had likely already begun?

We have already contended that he received the formal baptismal catechesis at Damascus from Ananias and the Hellenist fugitives from Jerusalem. Paul himself was to "deliver" to others the liturgical and creedal

---

18. See Hengel and Schwemer, *Paul*, 133-42.
19. See Barnett, *BC*, 111-49.

teaching he had "received" at that time, including to new disciples in Nabatea.[20] But it was probably in Jerusalem, from the lips of Cephas, that Paul was instructed in a more comprehensive way about Jesus and his ministry. Perhaps, too, Paul "received" the Last Supper/Lord's Supper "tradition" from the apostles in the Holy City at this time.

From James the brother of the Lord Paul had the matchless opportunity to learn about the story of Jesus' early life and how the formerly unbelieving James himself had become a disciple following the first Easter (cf. 1 Cor 15:7; John 7:5).

Luke states that Paul "went in and out among them at Jerusalem," that is, among the apostles. He "went in" among the apostles for fellowship and support, but he "went out," as the text of Acts proceeds to say, "preaching boldly in the name of the Lord." This is further elaborated: "he spoke and disputed against the Hellenists; but they were seeking to kill him" (Acts 9:28-29). Paul, the persecutor-become-preacher, now went to the synagogues of Greek-speaking Jews in Jerusalem, as Stephen had done (Acts 6:8-12). The former synagogue teacher, with Greek Bible in hand, preached the fulfillment of the promises of God in the Messiah, Jesus. Like Stephen, he aroused the dangerous hostility of his audience. Once again, though not for the last time, this preacher had to leave town for his own safety.

These "Hellenists" were Greek-speaking Jews, though, unlike those referred to as "disciples," they did not welcome the preaching of the Messiah Jesus. There was a significant community of such "Hellenists" in Jerusalem, only some of whom responded positively to the preaching. As a Jew whose letters reveal such competence in Greek and in the Septuagint, Paul himself most likely had been part of their community.[21] Doubtless Paul was well-known within this group in Jerusalem as a synagogue teacher.[22]

20. See 1 Cor 15:1-5 for the most comprehensive reference to the preformed "tradition" that Paul "received."

21. See earlier, 41-43.

22. Those who later dogged Paul's tracks among the Gentiles, and who sought to overturn his teachings, were probably drawn from this community of Greek-speaking Jews. Those Jews who came to Corinth in the middle 50s to overturn Paul's ministry must have been fluent in Greek, for they were superior rhetoricians (2 Cor 11:5-6; cf. 10:10). Jews whose first language was Aramaic would not have made themselves understood in the Greek world of Corinth.

There was likely more involved in this visit to Jerusalem than we would conclude from Galatians 1:18-19 and Acts 9:26-30. Twenty years later Paul testified to King Agrippa II that his recent ordeal in Jerusalem was due to his earlier preaching in Jerusalem and Judea: "I . . . declared first to those at Damascus, then *at Jerusalem and throughout all the country of Judea,* and also to the Gentiles, that they should repent and turn to God and perform deeds worthy of their repentance" (Acts 26:19-20).

This more comprehensive and extensive[23] character of Paul's ministry in Judea is also to be inferred from Paul's reflections to the Thessalonians: "For you, brethren, became imitators of the churches of God in Christ Jesus which are in Judea; for you suffered the same things from your own countrymen as they did from the Jews, who killed both the Lord Jesus and the prophets, and drove us out, and displease God and oppose all men" (1 Thess 2:14-15).

Paul is referring to a five- or six-year period of persecution from "the Jews" that was directed (i) to Jesus himself (ca. 29-33) and subsequently (ii) to the churches in Judea (from ca. 34), and (iii) to Paul himself (ca. 36/37).

Tarsus/Syria-Cilicia (ca. 37-45)

Paul now withdrew altogether from Palestine. Again, his own account may be put in parallel with that of the Acts of the Apostles.

> Then I went into the regions of Syria and Cilicia. (Gal 1:21)

> And when the brethren knew it [that the Hellenists were seeking to kill him], they brought him down to Caesarea, and sent him off to Tarsus. (Acts 9:30)

Although the account in Acts is longer, the two accounts agree on the facts of Paul's movements. Acts, however, hints at the reason for his journey. It was to get this stormy preacher away from danger — for his own sake, and perhaps also for the peace of his companions in Jerusalem. A logical place for him to go was his home province of Cilicia, to his city of ori-

---

23. Luke's use of imperfect verb tenses for Paul's ministry in Jerusalem (Acts 9:28-29) suggests a rather protracted period of time there.

gin, Tarsus, where he was a "citizen" (Acts 21:39). Possibly members of his family had remained in that city.[24]

24. Various descriptions of Tarsus have survived from those times. Paul himself described Tarsus as "no mean city" (Acts 21:39). Strabo wrote that "Tarsus lies in a plain . . . and it is intersected by the Cydnus River . . . [whose] source is not very far away and its stream passes through a deep ravine and then empties immediately into the city; its discharge is both cold and swift" (*Geography* 14.5.12-13). The fertile plain of Cilicia is hemmed in by the Mediterranean to the south and the Taurus Mountains on the north and west, where they come down to the sea. The trade route from the east crosses eastern Cilicia through Tarsus before striking north through the "Cilician Gates," the main access through the Tarsus range. The city of Tarsus is located about ten miles from the coast.

Originally Hittite but more recently Persian, Tarsus had been refounded as a Greek city following Alexander's conquests of that region; Alexander won the battle of Issus at the gateway to Syria in 333 B.C. Tarsus was among the cities that Alexander refounded as Greek cities. "Alexander established more than seventy cities among savage tribes and sowed all Asia with Grecian magistracies and thus overcame its uncivilized and brutish manner of living . . . for by the founding of cities in these places savagery was extinguished and the worst element gaining familiarity with the better, changed under its influence" (Plutarch, *Alexander* 328ff.).

As part of the Seleucid kingdom, whose capital was Antioch in Syria, Tarsus became a noted Hellenistic city with a reputation for scholarship. According to Strabo, Tarsus was famous for various schools of rhetoric, in particular for the teaching of Stoic philosophy (14.5.12-13). Later the Romans expanded their empire eastward under the leadership of Pompey. In 67 B.C. Cilicia was annexed as a province to Rome. Dio Chrysostom described the political significance of Tarsus as "the greatest of all the cities of Cilicia and a metropolis from the start" (*Orations* 37.7-8).

Circa 44 B.C. Augustus rewarded the city for supporting him against Cassius with tax exemptions, by enlarging its territory so it was a co-terminus with Cilicia itself, and by bestowing on it the status of "free city." These measures led to the city's burgeoning prosperity so that it soon was second only to Antioch of Syria in that region. In 25 B.C. eastern Cilicia was joined administratively to Syria as the province of Syria and Cilicia, the title by which Paul correctly refers to it (Gal 1:21).

From early in the second century B.C. large numbers of Jews settled in Cilicia, where they are known to have been powerful and influential. It is likely that the hostility Antiochus IV showed toward Jews in Judea was replicated in other parts of his empire, including toward the Jews in a region like Cilicia that was so close to Antioch. Numbers of Jews appear to have succumbed to syncretism under the pressure of Antiochus's aggressive Hellenism. Others were seduced by the gentle influences of Greek culture — the theater, the gymnasia, the games, and the philosophic academies. Therefore Jews like Paul's parents who retained intact their integrity under the covenant must have exercised considerable determination to do so. Paul's strict Jewish upbringing, as he described it, demands that his family was among those who retained their distinctive Jewishness against the powerful influence of Hellenism.

Since Paul traveled by sea from Caesarea up the coast of Syria to Tarsus, his coaster would have landed at various ports en route like Tyre and Sidon (cf. Acts 27:3). Since he had good friends in these Syrian cities (21:3; 27:3), the question arises whether he "stopped over" for short periods of evangelizing as he went up the coast.

The greater part of Paul's Levantine years was spent in Tarsus and Cilicia. He appears to have arrived in 36 or 37 and to have remained there until he went to Antioch in Syria in the early to mid-40s, that is, a period of seven or eight years. Our information is limited to incidental mention by Paul and in Acts. From these sources it is clear that Paul preached to *Gentiles*[25] during his lengthy sojourn in Cilicia.

Those Gentiles were likely the many "Godfearers" who had attached themselves to the synagogues of Cilicia at this time.[26] It is probable that Paul preached in the synagogues in Cilicia and that the Jewish members in general rejected his preaching of the Christ crucified and risen, but that numbers of Godfearers received his message. This was to be the pattern elsewhere, as recorded in Acts for Paul's missionary journeys through the provinces of Asia Minor and Greece. The various synagogue beatings already mentioned (78) probably occurred during these years of ministry in Tarsus and its surrounding towns (2 Cor 11:24).[27] Did the synagogue authorities punish Paul for drawing away Godfearers from their congregations?

Meanwhile Barnabas had not forgotten Paul. He had been sent to Antioch to superintend the new church that had emerged there. He went to Tarsus and brought Paul back with him to assist him in ministry to the congregation. Paul was being brought one stepping-stone nearer to the point of launching the great westward mission to win the Gentiles for the Christ of Israel.

---

25. (i) In his review of his fourteen-year apostolate Paul laid before the leaders of the church in Jerusalem "the gospel which I preach among the *Gentiles*" (Gal 2:2); (ii) Luke's reference is to James's letter from the Jerusalem Council circa 49 to "the brethren who are of the *Gentiles* in Antioch and *Syria* and *Cilicia*" (Acts 15:23). "Brethren" of "the Gentiles" from "Cilicia" doubtless owed their conversion to Paul from Tarsus; we know of no one else preaching in Cilicia at that time.

26. See further Hengel and Schwemer, *Paul,* 158-67.

27. See Schnabel, *Early Christian Mission,* 1054-69, for a comprehensive survey of possible cities and towns in Cilicia where Paul may have preached.

Antioch on the Orontes (ca. 45-47)

During the 30s and 40s a church was established in Antioch,[28] to which Paul was to attach himself as one of the leaders, and from which, with Barnabas, he would be sent westward toward the Roman world.

28. Antioch was a new city founded along Greek lines in 300 B.C., following Alexander's conquests. Located on the Orontes River about fifteen miles from the sea and in a large fertile plain, Antioch became the capital of the Seleucid empire, a city that at its height is estimated to have had a population of about 300,000 (Hengel and Schwemer, *Paul,* 186).

Pompey captured Antioch in 66 B.C., making it capital of the Province of Syria. So began Antioch's history as a great Roman city with considerable extension and beautification of the city from that time. Antioch became Rome's military sentinel guarding the eastern frontier against formidable enemies like the Parthians. Judea, too, came under the administrative supervision as well as the military protection of Antioch. After the death of Herod in 4 B.C. and at the outbreak of insurgency in A.D. 66, the legions were marched south from Antioch to restore peace to Judea. By NT times Antioch was the third-largest city in the empire, after Rome and Alexandria.

Greek-Jew relationships had a troubled history in Antioch from 175 B.C. when Antiochus IV attempted to Hellenize Jerusalem and Judea, leading to the outbreak of the Maccabean revolt and the eventual loss of Judea from the Greco-Syrian kingdom. From its inception Jews formed a significant proportion of its population; the numbers have been estimated as high as 50,000. There was an ongoing dispute with the Greek community over Jewish citizenship rights. The available evidence suggests that, as in most other places, Jews enjoyed a corporate but not an individual citizenship, allowing them to pursue their religion unhindered (Josephus, *JW* 7.43). However, Jews periodically agitated for individual citizenship rights, leading to serious tension between the two communities.

At the same time, Jews who upheld strict standards held a certain attraction to numbers of Gentiles, based on the monotheism of the covenant of Israel and the superior ethical and family values practiced by Jews. Josephus commented: "through their worship [the Jews] attracted a large number of Greeks and in a way made them part of themselves" (*JW* 7.45). These "Greeks" were Godfearers who had become part of the synagogue congregations. Others, however, became proselytes accepting baptism and circumcision as members of the covenant people. Nicolaus the "proselyte of Antioch" was one of the seven almoners chosen to serve the widows of the Hellenist community in Jerusalem (Acts 6:5). It is reasonable to believe that Nicolaus returned to Antioch following the scattering of the Hellenists during Paul's onslaught.

The immediate background to the rise of Christianity in Antioch was the turbulent principate of Caligula and the furor amongst Jews created by his policies that threatened to erupt into open war in the Greek cities of the eastern Mediterranean, including Antioch. Simmering hostility in Alexandria broke out into a bloody pogrom against Jews in 38. Significantly, Antioch held Caligula and his father Germanicus, who had died in the city, in particular honor. There are medieval accounts of a Greek assault of Jews in Antioch, including the burning of their major synagogue (see Hengel and Schwemer, *Paul,* 183-91).

Clearly, cities like Antioch in the late 30s and early 40s witnessed severe hostility by

According to Luke, the message of the Christ of Israel came to Antioch in two waves. First, there were Hellenists displaced by Paul's assaults who had remigrated to Antioch. There is no reason to doubt that this occurred from circa 34 as an immediate consequence to Paul's pogrom in Jerusalem. Some Hellenists went inland to Damascus, perhaps with the intention of returning later to Jerusalem. Others traveled north along the coast, some settling in Phoenicia, others going offshore to Cyprus, others still coming to rest in the great northern metropolis of Antioch (Acts 11:19). These, however, directed their preaching of the Christ to the Jews in the synagogues, possibly with quite limited response.

A second wave, also composed of unnamed men who came to Antioch, is more closely identified as "men of Cyprus and Cyrene." The date of their arrival is not known, but it may have been as early as the late 30s. These took the bold step of preaching the Christ to "Greeks," that is, to Gentiles, "a great number [of those] that believed turned to the Lord" (Acts 11:21). The question, however, is which "Greeks" — the Gentile Godfearers in the synagogues or rank outsiders? On balance, it is more likely that Luke intends to mean the Godfearers in the synagogues rather than those Gentiles who were outside the orbit of the synagogues.

Then, however, Luke makes an easily unnoticed but utterly critical first reference to "the church" in Antioch (Acts 11:26), provoking the question of *when* these disciples, "Jews" and "Greeks," withdrew from the synagogue into a distinctive "church" assembly. Most likely it was this new and different congregation that attracted the attention of the people of Antioch, causing them to call these people *Christianoi/*"Christians"[29] (Acts 11:26).

Did this dramatic development happen before or after Barnabas

---

Greeks against Jews (and by Jews against Greeks). It is against this background that we must understand how alarmed the Greeks and Romans of Antioch must have been to hear the reports that a Messiah/Christ of Israel was being proclaimed in the synagogues by recently arrived Jews. Jews everywhere might be united under this leader, who would even rival the emperor himself. This explains why these preachers and their supporters were called *Christianoi*, that is, adherents of the Christ. At the same time, we can only reflect on the turmoil fomented within the synagogues of Antioch because these preachers, fellow Jews as they were, were offering the salvation of the God of Israel *free* to *Greeks!* We may not easily imagine how explosive for Greeks and Romans and Jews the arrival in Antioch of these preachers of the Christ must have been.

29. This word, like *Hērōdianoi* (Mark 3:6; 12:13 pars.), is political in nature and points to those who were publicly-known followers of a noted leader.

arrived from Jerusalem? Again, on balance it seems that the establishment of a discrete church in Antioch occurred as the result of the preaching of these Cypriots and Cyreneans, that is, in the late 30s, and this was the new development that attracted the attention of the leaders in Jerusalem.

Critical Questions about Paul's Levantine Years

The extent of Paul's Levantine years, which however are recorded with sparse detail, prompts two important questions.

Where Was Paul's Christology Formed — Jerusalem or Antioch?

As noted, the sequence of Paul's movements between Damascus and Antioch (ca. 34-45) finds remarkable agreement in our sources, Paul's own writings (chiefly Galatians) and the book of Acts. Furthermore, we are able to date Paul's location in the various places — Damascus, Arabia, Damascus, Jerusalem/Judea, Tarsus/Cilicia, and Antioch — with reasonable confidence.

Our problem, however, is that no writings from Paul (if there were any)[30] have survived from the Levantine years. Our earliest written work by Paul — Galatians or 1 Thessalonians[31] — comes after these years.

The question, then, arises about the origin of Paul's theological understanding as revealed (for example) in 1 Thessalonians. Broadly speaking, there are two viewpoints as to when and where Paul's Christology was "formed" — Damascus in the early 30s and Antioch in the mid-40s.[32]

The latter view, famously associated with W. Bousset and R. Bultmann and the history-of-religions school, argued that Paul was fundamentally influenced by the "atmosphere" of Greco-Oriental religious

---

30. See Barnett, *BC,* 44-45, for the opinion that the accomplished nature of Paul's earliest extant letters suggests that there may have been earlier letters, now lost.

31. This is the preferred view of many NT scholars. For argument for the prior dating of Galatians, see Barnett, *BC,* 206-10.

32. For a magisterial review of this question, which emphatically argues for Damascus in the early 30s, see Hengel and Schwemer, *Paul,* 268-310.

syncretism (mystery cults and Gnostic circles) that characterized Antioch in Syria. This would help explain Paul's preoccupation with referring to Jesus as "Lord"/*Kyrios* and "Son"/*Huios* in 1 Thessalonians and, written soon afterward, 1 Corinthians, which expands in many ways on the earlier letter (see, e.g., 1 Thess 1:10; 1 Cor 1:9; 8:5).

So, do Paul's Christology and mission preaching originate from Damascus in the early 30s or from Syria in the mid-40s? In my view the evidence for the origin of Paul's normative Christian thought points conclusively to what has been called "the Damascus event," dated circa 34.

This is not, however, to insist that Paul's *expressions* of his Christology and mission preaching became rigidly fixed at Damascus. His letters are at some points dialectical, even emotional, such was his personal and pastoral sensitivity to the circumstances of the people and the churches of his mission (see, e.g., 2 Cor 6:11-13; 11:1–12:13; Gal 3:1). Nonetheless, his varying responses are anchored to critical core beliefs that he came to hold at the *beginning* of his years as apostle and minister.

A dominant reason for this conviction is the central place Damascus occupies in Paul's thinking, whether in regards "direct references" or "identifiable allusions," as discussed in chapter 5. Damascus was the hinge on which Paul's life turned, separating his "former life in Judaism" (as persecutor) from his new life "in Christ" (as preacher).

Damascus was the place — and his arrival there the time — that everything changed for Paul, whether in regards his relationship with God (as one now "justified" in Christ crucified and risen — Gal 3:24-25) or his new vocation (as apostle to the Gentiles — Rom 11:13; Gal 1:15-16). As noted previously, Paul frequently employs contrastive verb tenses to indicate the radical "before and after" nature of the various changes of his beliefs and life direction.

This fundamental Damascus hiatus appears consistently within Paul's writings. True, Paul had visions and revelations subsequent to Damascus (see, e.g., Acts 22:17; 2 Cor 12:1-4; Acts 16:9; 18:9; appendix C), but none of these is ever cast in terms of the sharp before-and-after life-changing contrasts that characterize the Damascus event.

Furthermore, critical to the question of Paul's christological "formation" is the central place Paul attributes to Jerusalem and the leaders of the Jerusalem church, especially seen in his letter to the Galatians. True, Paul insists that his Damascus "call" to preach the Son came from God (Gal 1:11, 15-17) and not men. Yet it is equally true that Paul looked to the *endorse-*

ment of the leading apostles in Jerusalem, at both his first and his second visits.[33]

Of special interest is Paul's meeting with the "pillar" apostles James, Peter, and John in Jerusalem that effectively concluded his Levantine years. Paul "laid before *(anethemēn)* them . . . the gospel which I preach among the Gentiles" (Gal 2:2), seeking the favorable verdict of these leaders. He asks rhetorically whether he had been "running in vain" all these fourteen years since his Damascus "call" when he abandoned his "former life in Judaism" to preach to the Gentiles "the faith he once tried to destroy" (Gal 1:12-13, 23). On the contrary, these leaders endorsed the message he had been preaching in Damascus, Arabia, and Syria-Cilicia and agreed to a further "going" with his circumcision-free message to the Gentiles (Gal 2:8-9).

Paul's vindication in Jerusalem, however, was not repeated in Antioch (Gal 2:11-13). When James's delegates arrived there, Peter, Barnabas, and "the rest of the Jews" took sides against Paul over the question of eating with Gentile believers. But Paul's insistence on the circumcision-free message to Gentiles was the underlying point of division. It appears that James, Peter, and Barnabas were retreating from their more liberal attitudes expressed earlier in Jerusalem. The new preoccupation with circumcision of Gentiles and Jewish table-fellowship with them and other matters related to Jewish ritual are, of themselves, indicative that the issue of syncretism from Antioch, as contended by the history-of-religions proponents, was of no concern whatsoever.

What part, then, in Galatians (and other writings) does Antioch play in Paul's disclosures about his "formation," or possible new departures in his view of Christ, or the direction of his ministry? The answer is: none at all. Antioch was merely the last phase of that fourteen-year span of his ministry in the Levant (Gal 2:1), and a brief one at that (Acts 11:26). Paul's Christology and mission preaching were well and truly formed, tried and tested, by the time he arrived in Antioch.

Moreover, and in any case, the presuppositions about the syncretistic "atmosphere" in Antioch, on which the history-of-religion school based its reconstructions, are without foundation in evidence.[34] It is true that

---

33. See J. D. G. Dunn, "The Relationship between Paul and Jerusalem according to Galatians 1 and 2," *NTS* 28, no. 4 (1982): 461-78.

34. Hengel and Schwemer, *Paul*, 279-86.

Antioch was a deeply pagan metropolis, and remained so for centuries into the Christian era. Yet little evidence of Antioch's religious life from the NT era survives, whether in literary, numismatic, or archaeological sources.[35] This is not to suggest that first-century Antioch was not pagan nor indeed syncretistic; it likely was.[36] But most of our evidence comes from later centuries.[37] This must drive history-of-religions advocates to the realm of conjecture, giving no basis for historical confidence.

In this regard, we must remember that the first disciples (from the mid-30s) in Antioch were Jews (Acts 11:21-22). They were remigrating Hellenist Jews from Jerusalem for whom pagan religious life in the Diaspora would have held few surprises. The elderly Paul, writing to the Philippians from Rome many years after his childhood in Tarsus, still remembered how conservatively Jewish his family life in the Diaspora had been (Phil 3:4-5). There is no reason to doubt that the original Jewish disciples in Antioch were as resistant to syncretism as Paul's parents had been. In turn, these Jewish disciples would have held in check any Gnostic or cultic tendencies in the Gentiles who began to belong to the emerging church. In any case, the majority of incoming Gentiles were likely Godfearers (Jewish "sympathizers") who had already turned their backs on pagan ways to belong to Diaspora synagogues.

Finally, the center point of Paul's worldview was Jerusalem and not Antioch. It was in Jerusalem (for the Twelve and "all the apostles") and in Damascus (for Paul) that God initiated the worldwide preaching of Christ crucified and risen (1 Cor 15:9-10). Whatever their differences of emphasis and emotion concerning circumcision of Gentiles, Paul and the Jerusalem leaders agreed about the message of the vicarious death and resurrection of Christ (15:11).

Jerusalem is the point of departure *from* which Paul's apostolate to the Gentiles "encircled" the eastern Mediterranean (Rom 15:19), and it was *to* Jerusalem that Paul returned with the collection from the Gentile provinces (15:25-31). In Paul's references Antioch is merely one dot among others in that "circle."

---

35. Hengel and Schwemer, *Paul*, 268-79.

36. According to R. Turcan, *The Cults of the Roman Empire* (Oxford: Blackwell, 1996), 131-32, the cults from Syria did not have the same impact on outsiders as those from Egypt. While this observation is made regarding the influence of expatriate Syrians, the comment likely applies also to the minimal impact of Syrian cults on Jews resident in Antioch.

37. Cf. Millar, *Roman Near East*, 460-67.

Why Did Paul Wait So Long before Commencing His Westward Missions?

We have been arguing that while Paul and Luke agree on the sequence of Paul's movements during the Levantine years (ca. 34-47), their perspectives of Paul's activities throughout those years are different. Luke treats those years with such brevity that some refer to them as Paul's "unknown years." Indeed, Luke may have unintentionally contributed to the impression that Paul was "unknown" throughout this lengthy period.

It is not that Luke's perspective is inaccurate. Initially as Paul's traveling companion and later as his chronicler, he enjoyed unparalleled access to the apostle's life story.[38] But Luke also wanted to acknowledge the prior contributions of Peter, Stephen, and Philip to bringing the gospel to the Gentiles. Only after doing that does he resume his interest in Paul, who then becomes the sole focus of his attention for the greater part of the rest of his narrative. Once Paul's precursors have run their respective courses, the spotlight falls on Paul alone (Acts 13–28).

Furthermore, Luke does intend for us to understand that Paul had been active during those years, implied by the reference to Gentiles in churches in Antioch and Syria and Cilicia (Acts 15:22, 41). The existence of those churches and their Gentile members must have been due to Paul's ministry in Tarsus/Syria-Cilicia during this sparsely documented period (ca. 37-45).

Paul's letters, however, give us a quite different perspective on his activities in the Levant. It is clear in Galatians that starting in Damascus and during the fourteen years that followed he preached God's Son to the Gentiles, and that the "pillars" of the Jerusalem church retrospectively recognized his God-given apostolate to the uncircumcised *throughout that period* (Gal 1:15-16; 2:8-9).

How, then, can we explain the length of time Paul stayed in the region of the Levant before beginning his missions to the Gentiles? Was he disobedient to the heavenly "call," or somehow undiscerning of its missionary intent?

One possible element limiting Paul's movements may have been the crisis in the cities of the eastern Mediterranean created during the principate of Caligula (37-41). A situation of near civil war between Greeks and Jews occurred in Alexandria, but also in Antioch (though the sources

---

38. See Barnett, *BC*, 190-93.

are inferior).[39] Did the turbulent state of affairs in Antioch keep Paul in Cilicia for the moment?

Greater weight, however, should be given to the view that Paul interpreted the Damascus "call" to preach to the Gentiles as already being fulfilled in his ministry to *the Godfearers in the synagogues* of the Levant. It seems unlikely initially that Paul thought he should seek Gentile converts outside the orbit of the synagogues. After all, as Hengel and Schwemer have demonstrated,[40] there were great numbers of the Gentile "sympathizers of Judaism" in the synagogues of the cities of the Levant visited by Paul during these years. As well, his five synagogue beatings (2 Cor 11:24) seem to have occurred during the Levantine years, suggesting a concentration on synagogue-based ministry to Godfearers.

I think, however, that it was in Antioch that Paul began to consider that God wanted him to seek out other Gentiles, that is, Gentiles *outside the synagogues.* On one hand, the large intake of Gentiles in Antioch (some of whom may not have been Godfearers) may have pointed toward a more intentional mission toward Gentiles who were outside the synagogues. On the other hand, however, Paul may have come to realize that an eschatological "hardening" of Israel had begun (their rejection of Christ was now demonstrable).[41]

As we will see, however, this radical new direction was to have onerous consequences for Paul. It provoked a vigorous Jerusalem-based countermission that was to seek to overturn Paul's circumcision-free basis of divine righteousness and covenantal equality. Effectively it created tension between Paul and the Jerusalem leadership and resulted in the end of Paul's working relationship with Barnabas, and the end of his formerly close associations with the church in Antioch. From that time forward Paul had to make new friends in new places, westward toward Rome.

Conclusion

Paul's Levantine years, beginning in Damascus, were of special importance for Paul. His fundamental convictions about Christ and the direction of

39. See Hengel and Schwemer, *Paul,* 183-91.
40. See Hengel and Schwemer, *Paul,* passim.
41. See chapter 9.

his future ministry were established in Damascus and expressed in his ministry in that city, then in Arabia, Jerusalem and Judea, Tarsus and Cilicia, and Antioch in Syria.

This initial decade and a half in the Levant is recorded only minimally by Paul and Luke in contrast with the next decade of Paul's apostolate (ca. 48-57) in the provinces of Anatolia and Greece, which is fully narrated in the book of Acts and illuminated by Paul's writings from that period.

How helpful, therefore, is it to refer to the Levantine years as "unknown"? Our argument has been that while these years are sparsely documented, it is not altogether accurate to describe them as "unknown." In fact, we have a clear idea of the sequence of Paul's movements from place to place and reasonable confidence in the dating of those movements. Moreover, there are snippets of information from both Paul's letters and the book of Acts that offer glimpses of Paul at work in his new vocation in various places.

When we compare Paul's narrative (in Galatians chiefly) with Luke's, we observe strikingly different perspectives. Luke introduces Paul in the book of Acts as persecutor in Jerusalem, then as convert in Damascus, with meager details for the period following until Paul's westward missions commence years later. Luke does little more than introduce his hero in those early chapters, leaving him in relative obscurity until his dramatic journey to Cyprus and then onward to Pisidia and Lycaonia. It is as if Luke does not see Paul really beginning his work and apostleship until then.

Paul's perspective is strikingly different. He sees his ministry as having begun at Damascus and continuing in an undifferentiated way until he reviews the progress of the gospel from Jerusalem to Illyricum in his letter to the Romans a quarter of a century later (15:19). His journey from Damascus to Antioch is merely the first part of a greater circle that will reach Illyricum.

Paul's ministry in the Levant prompts important questions. Did Paul's Christology undergo significant change in the latter part of these years, notably in Antioch (as the history-of-religions school contends)? On the contrary, Paul's basic theological convictions were formed in Damascus and underwent little change throughout the remainder of his life.

Did Paul's approach to the ingathering of Gentiles change during these years? The answer is, probably, yes. Most likely Paul initially thought he was fulfilling the heavenly "call" in reaching Gentiles by preaching to Godfearers within the synagogues. At some point, however (at Antioch?), he began to understand that it was God's purpose for him to preach to Gentiles wherever they were, inside or outside the synagogues.

SEVEN

Paul, True Missionary of Jesus

Paul's Mission . . . is nothing less than the outworking of Jesus' own mission.

J. R. Wagner[1]

We come now to the most critical question of all, one that inspired the writing of this book. We must ask: Was Paul's mission to the Gentiles according to the mind of Jesus and an authentic extension to his own ministry in Israel? Was Paul a true missionary of Jesus?

Much hangs on the historical answer to that question. If it could be shown that Paul set off independently on his mission to the nations, he would have been, indeed, as Wrede complained, the "second founder of Christianity"[2] and a more potent but less desirable one than Jesus.[3]

---

1. J. R. Wagner, "The Heralds of Isaiah and the Mission of Paul: An Investigation of Paul's Use of Isaiah 51–55 in Romans," in *Jesus and the Suffering Servant: Isaiah 53 and Christian Origins*, ed. W. H. Bellinger and W. R. Farmer (Harrisburg, Pa.: Trinity, 1998), 198.

2. See earlier, 13.

3. See D. H. Akenson, *Saint Saul* (Oxford: Oxford University Press, 2000), whose unlikely thesis is that while "Saul" is well-known and historically accessible, Jesus (though revered) is a shadowy and distant figure known only from sources that postdate the war of A.D. 66-70.

Christ's Mission to Israel and the Gentiles (Romans 15)

We are struck by Paul's sense of a two-stage mission, beginning with Israel and extending from Israel to the Gentile nations. This is clear, of course, in Paul's "the Jew first and also to the Greek" (= Gentile; Rom 1:16; 2:9).

Less obvious but equally important are his references in Romans 15 where he is addressing the separation of Gentile from Jewish believers that characterized Roman Christianity in the middle 50s. In this passage he writes of *Christ's* two-stage ministry, which had been directed first to Israel and was now being directed to the nations. The consequences of Christ's "welcome" to both Jews and Gentiles should have been their mutual "welcome" of one another, which, sadly, was not the practical reality.

This Israel-to-nations progression had deep roots in Israel's history, beginning with God's call and promise to Abraham, and was reiterated many times through the prophets.[4] All that had recently happened to Israel (in Christ's life, death, and resurrection) and was happening in the nations (through Paul's mission) was in fulfillment of the promises God made "beforehand in the Holy Scriptures" (cf. Rom 1:2).

Although this positive vision of the attachment of the nations to Israel was grounded in the Law and the Prophets, it is doubtful that Paul the Pharisee would have been seized by it. In fact, the early Paul would likely have regarded the Gentiles with moral condescension if not outright hostility.

According to J. Jeremias, "The attitude of late Judaism towards non-Jews was uncompromisingly severe. In addition to their abhorrence of idolatry, their attitude was largely developed by the oppression they had undergone at the hands of foreign nations, and by their fear of the increasing prevalence of mixed marriages."[5] Rabbi Eliezer ben Hyrcanus (ca. 90), a respected authority of the era, declared that "no Gentile will have a part in the world to come."[6] Most likely the pre-Damascus Paul regarded Gentiles like that. We must understand that God's "call" to Paul to preach to Gentiles meant that he underwent a conversion of attitude toward them. His tireless labors bringing the gospel to them and his passionate ad-

---

4. In particular, Gen 12:1-3; Isa 49:1-3, 6; Amos 9:11-12. But see also, e.g., Gen 17:4-6; 18; 22; 26:4; 35:11; Pss 2:8; 18:49; 22:27-28; 46:10; 57:9; 67:2, 4; 86:9; 96:3; 98:2; 102:15; 108:3; 111:6; 117:1; Isa 11:10, 12; 42:1, 6; 52:10; 60:3, 5, 11; 61:11; 62:2; 66:19-29; Jer 3:17; 4:2.

5. J. Jeremias, *Jesus' Promise to the Nations*, SBT 24 (London: SCM, 1958), 40.

6. Quoted in Jeremias, *Jesus' Promise*, 41.

vocacy of their access to God based on "grace alone" serve as testimony to the depth of that conversion.

Nowhere is this "conversion" in Paul more evident than in his injunction to Gentiles and Jews in Rome to "welcome one another . . . as Christ has welcomed you" (Rom 15:7), which is likely his key text in Romans.

Remarkably, however, in the pastoral circumstances of early Roman Christianity, it is the Gentiles who were to have the greater responsibility in welcoming. They, "the strong," must make the concessions to the dietary scruples of "the weak" (Rom 14:13-21). We might have expected that the natural "olive tree" would have been the chief welcoming party, but it was otherwise when Paul was writing to the Roman believers. It is the branches of the "wild olive" who are to "receive" the members of the historic trunk.

God achieves the first stage of his universal plan (to Israel) directly through the Messiah/Christ, Jesus. "Welcome one another . . . for the glory of God. For I tell you that Christ became a servant to the circumcised to show God's truthfulness, in order to confirm the promises given to the patriarchs, and in order that the Gentiles might glorify God for his mercy" (Rom 15:7-9a).

God's "truth" *(alētheia)*, expressed in his "promises" to "the fathers" (the patriarchs), was actualized in Christ's work as "servant" to the circumcised (Israel). This is the story the four Gospels were to tell, which Paul summarizes in one potent sentence.

For the moment Paul does not indicate how the mercy of God extended beyond the circumcised to the Gentiles. Yet such an extension to the nations is implied by his word "became" (whose verb tense points to a "lasting effect")[7] and his chain of cited OT texts that promised the (now realized) joy and praise of the Gentiles (vv. 9b-12).

How, then, is God fulfilling his promises in extending his mercy beyond Israel to the nations? Christ is as much the divine agent of the second stage of the divine plan as he had been in the first, except that now he does so *through an intermediary,* Paul himself.[8] The apostle writes of "the grace given me by God [i.e., at Damascus] to be *a minister of Christ Jesus to the Gentiles* in the priestly service of the gospel of God" (Rom 15:15-16). Paul

---

7. *gegenēsthai* is perfect infinitive.

8. For a discussion of the cultic language, Exodus terminology, and Servant language in Rom 15:14-33, see A. J. Köstenberger and P. T. O'Brien, *Salvation to the Ends of the Earth,* NSBT 11 (Downers Grove, Ill.: InterVarsity, 2001), 168-73.

adds, "In Christ Jesus . . . I have reason to be proud of my work for God. For I will not venture to speak of anything except what *Christ has wrought through me* to win obedience from the Gentiles, . . . so that from Jerusalem and as far round as Illyricum,[9] I have fulfilled[10] the gospel" (Rom 15:17-19).

Paul is Christ's "minister" *(leitourgos)* to the Gentiles "through" whom he has worked to win their obedience to God and his plan.

Christ, through Paul, has extended the mercy of God to the nations as the outworking of the "promises" according to the "truth of God." Remarkably, Paul sums up this divine initiative and activity as "the gospel" that he, Paul, is "fulfilling" (Rom 15:19). Those translations are incorrect that render this text as saying that Paul has *"fully preached* the gospel."

True, Paul's characteristic activity was preaching. That preaching, however, was the announcement that the global plan of God promised initially to the patriarchs and repeated by the prophets was being "fulfilled."[11] That is to say, God's promise of salvation to the descendants of Abraham and the ultimate inclusion of the Gentiles was becoming a reality. God's primary agent in this fulfillment was his "servant" Christ in his ministry to Israel, and *through his subsidiary* Paul to the nations.

Paul mentions the same Christ-centered two-stage process in another letter.[12] "[Christ Jesus] came and preached peace to you who were far off [i.e., Gentiles] and peace to those who were near [i.e., Israel]; for through him we both have access in one Spirit to the Father" (Eph 2:17-18).

Since historically speaking (so far as we know) Christ Jesus generally did not preach to the Gentiles, we must assume that (as in Rom 15:18 above) this text is declaring that Paul was the ascended Lord's intermediary in ministry to the Gentiles. Just as in the Romans passage, the overriding purpose of God stated in Ephesians 2:17-18 was to secure unity in the church between Jews and Gentiles in Christ, according to the predetermined plan of God.

9. For discussion of the geographical references "Jerusalem . . . Illyricum," see Köstenberger and O'Brien, *Salvation,* 170-73. Paul's reference to Jerusalem as the starting point for his missionary sweep is significant given the centrality of the Holy City as the gathering point for the nations (as in Isa 66:18, 20).

10. *peplērōkenai* = "fulfilled"; the verb "preached" does not appear in this text.

11. See Köstenberger and O'Brien, *Salvation,* 184, for comment on the practical meaning of "fulfilling the gospel."

12. Even those who regard Ephesians as deutero-Pauline tend to accept the presence of genuinely Pauline ideas in this letter. See appendix D.

Our argument, then, is that this divinely mandated Israel-to-nations staged ministry is clearly on view in Paul's texts. This, however, may have been Paul's own idiosyncratic scheme. Is there any reason to believe that the historical Jesus envisaged a ministry to Israel that would find extension in a ministry to the nations?

Jesus' Mission to Israel and His "Promise" to the Nations[13]

There is ample evidence from the Gospels to support the proposal that Jesus restricted his ministry and the ministry of the Twelve to the people of Israel[14] but that he had envisaged the extension of that ministry to the Gentiles.[15]

True, Jesus traveled outside the boundaries of Eretz Israel (as narrated in Mark 7:24–9:29), but he appears to have limited those journeys to regions inhabited by Jews and confined himself to a ministry to Jews. Nonetheless, there were exceptions to this limitation, for example, his preaching to the Samaritans (John 4:1-42), the healing of the centurion's attendant (Matt 8:5-13), the deliverance of the daughter of the Syrophoenician woman (Mark 7:24-30), and the healing of a Samaritan leper (Luke 17:17).

The Gospel of Mark

According to Mark's narrative, Jesus generally avoided public exposure in Herod Antipas's tetrarchy Galilee after the feeding of the 5,000.

Mark alone reports Jesus' extensive travels inside the borders of Tyre and Sidon; he records the conversation with the Syrophoenician woman (Mark 7:24-30; which Matt 15:21-28 reproduces, with important changes — see below). Embedded within this spirited exchange is a logion of Jesus whose offensive character demands its recognition as authentic. "Let the children first be fed, for it is not right to take the children's bread and throw it to the dogs" (Mark 7:27).

Jesus' use of the word "first" implies that the bread for the children

---

13. The section title is suggested by Jeremias, *Jesus' Promise to the Nations*.

14. See Jeremias, *Jesus' Promise*, 35.

15. For a detailed study of the mission theme in each of the Gospels, see Köstenberger and O'Brien, *Salvation*, 73-159 (Mark, Matthew, Luke-Acts), 203-26 (John).

(i.e., Israel)[16] will, in due course, be available for the "dogs" (i.e., most likely Gentiles).[17] By this understanding, a two-stage process (Israel first, then the nations) is envisaged, but the initial phase is strictly restricted to "the children"/Israel.[18] That, at least, was Jesus' working principle, which he pointedly breached on account of the faith of this feisty woman. Yet her acceptance of Jesus' stated priority of ministry for the "children" (= Israel) was the condition of his help to her, "dog" (= Gentile) though she was.

Matthew makes a critical addition to Mark's narrative where Jesus declares, "I was sent only to the lost sheep of the house of Israel" (Matt 15:24). Matthew's insertion of this logion from his special source strengthens further the exclusivity already present in Mark's narrative.

Nonetheless, once Mark's narrative brings Jesus to Jerusalem, we note a dramatic change of orientation. Jesus now declares that the message about him is to be proclaimed throughout "all the nations" of "the whole world."

And the gospel must first be preached to *all nations.* (Mark 13:10)

And truly, I say to you, wherever the gospel is preached in *the whole world,* what she has done will be told in memory of her. (Mark 14:9)

These texts are the more remarkable since they appear in a Gospel that lacks a specific "Great Commission" (cf. Matt 28:18-20; Luke 24:44-49).

---

16. The people of Israel are called God's "son" (Exod 4:22; Hos 11:1), "sons" (Deut 14:1; Isa 1:2), "first-born" (Jer 31:9); cf. *m. Avot* 3:15, "Blessed are Israel for they are called children of God. . . ."

17. Elsewhere (Matt 7:6 — "Do not give dogs what is holy") Jesus refers disparagingly to dogs as by implication "unholy" and bracketed with swine. The Mishnah is similarly derogatory about dogs (*m. Sotah* 9:15 — "the face of this generation is as the face of a dog"). Jews kept yard dogs provided they were chained (*m. Bava Qamma* 7:7). Dogs, like Gentiles, were deemed not susceptible to uncleanness since, by inference, they were already unclean (*m. Nedarim* 4:3; *m. Teharot* 8:6). Jews did not offer dogs as sacrifice (*m. Temurah* 5:5).

18. Contra R. H. Gundry, *Mark* (Grand Rapids: Eerdmans, 1993), 373, who argues that "children" = the Jewish disciples who are not yet "fully taught" and "[little] dogs" = Gentile children (like the woman's child). Gundry likely makes too much of the diminutive (*kynarios*/"little dog," as pointing to the child, not her adult mother); but Mark elsewhere uses a diminutive interchangeably with a full-length word (cf. "little boat"/"boat" — Mark 3:9; 4:1). According to Jeremias, "[q]uite apart from the fact that it is uncertain whether in contemporary Greek the diminutive had any mitigating force, it cannot be pressed since the Semitic has no corresponding form [i.e., for 'puppy']" (*Jesus' Promise,* 29 n. 2).

Nonetheless, the gospel "*must* be preached to all nations . . . in the whole world" before the end.[19]

These texts in Mark — 7:27, 13:10, 14:9 — imply that Jesus had a two-stage agenda that began in Israel and ended in the nations.

The Gospel of Matthew

Matthew's view is quite specific, stated in texts from his special source. Before the Twelve set out on their mission to Galilee, Jesus charged them: "Go nowhere among the Gentiles, and enter no town of the Samaritans, but go rather to the lost sheep of the house of Israel" (Matt 10:5-6). This logion demands recognition as authentic because of its descending rhetorical pattern (Gentiles, Samaritans, lost sheep of the house of Israel) and the "criterion of embarrassment" in its apparent contradiction of Jesus' Great Commission directing these same disciples to "go" to "all the nations" (28:19).

It is striking that Jesus placed himself under the same restriction as the Twelve. "I was sent only to the lost sheep of the house of Israel" (15:24). This logion, which arises from an Aramaic original,[20] likely belonged originally in Special Matthew in the context of Jesus' mission charge to the Twelve. It appears that Matthew has inserted it in Mark's narrative about the Syrophoenician woman[21] to underline the restrictive nature of Jesus' ministry. At the same time, we note Matthew's striking omission from Mark's narrative of Jesus' word "Let the children be fed *first*" (implying a *subsequent* feeding of the "dogs"/Gentiles). Matthew's insertion of one logion and his omission of another have the effect of emphasizing the restrictive character of Jesus' ministry to the people of Israel.

In short, when these texts (Matt 10:5-6; 15:24) are considered together, we have an unambiguous understanding that Jesus limited his ministry and the ministry of the Twelve to "the lost sheep of the house of Israel."

19. See M. Hengel, *The Four Gospels and the One Gospel of Jesus Christ* (London: SCM, 2000), 108, for the suggestion that these universals were written from the perspective of Roman world rule. Alternatively, it is difficult to avoid hearing echoes of the hopes of the prophets for the nations (e.g., Isa 43:8-13; 52:7-10).

20. So Jeremias, *Jesus' Promise*, 26 n. 3.

21. In Matthew's version she is "a Canaanite woman."

Matthew, however, incorporates a text from the Q source[22] that gives a radically different, indeed perplexing perspective. "When Jesus heard him [the Gentile centurion], he marveled, and said to those who followed him, 'Truly, I say to you, not even in Israel have I found such faith. I tell you, many will come from east and west and sit at table with Abraham, Isaac, and Jacob in the kingdom of heaven, while the sons of the kingdom will be thrown into the outer darkness; there men will weep and gnash their teeth'" (Matt 8:10-12).

Jesus is contrasting "many from east and west" (i.e., Gentiles like the centurion in Capernaum) with "sons of the kingdom" (i.e., people of Israel). He foresaw Gentiles seated with the patriarchs at the messianic banquet[23] while the "sons of the kingdom" were permanently excluded. Clearly Jesus is assuming a future ingathering of Gentiles, but he does not say how this will occur.

Matthew's Gospel, then, contains teachings of Jesus that appear contradictory. On one hand, his historic mission to Israel excludes the Gentiles, while in the eschatological future Gentiles will be members of the kingdom while the people of Israel are excluded. How are we to make sense of this exact reversal of Jew-Gentile circumstances?

Matthew's resolution, of course, is found in his Great Commission. Once more this text is found only in Special Matthew. "And Jesus came and said to them, 'All authority in heaven and on earth has been given to me. Go therefore and make disciples of all nations, baptizing them in the name of the Father and of the Son and of the Holy Spirit, teaching them to observe all that I have commanded you; and lo, I am with you always, to the close of the age'" (Matt 28:18-20).

Scholars debate whether "all nations" *(panta ta ethnē)* includes the "nation" Israel.[24] Matthew's usage of *ta ethnē* earlier in his Gospel seems to leave little doubt that he does not include the nation Israel.[25] How, then,

22. See Jeremias, *Jesus' Promise*, 56, for argument for the earliness and integrity of this text.

23. Jeremias, *Jesus' Promise*, 40-54, contrasts the merciful and inclusive attitude to the Gentiles with the harsh and censorious regard in which Gentiles were then held within the contemporary Jewish texts.

24. J. P. Meier, "Nations or Gentiles in Matthew 28:19?" *CBQ* 39 (1977): 94-102, argues that "all the nations" includes Israel, whereas D. R. A. Hare and D. J. Harrington, "Make Disciples of All Nations (Matthew 28:19)," *CBQ* 37 (1975): 359-69, take the opposite view.

25. In a number of references *ta ethnē* = Gentiles (6:32 — "the Gentiles seek all these

does it come to pass that "many from east and west"/Gentiles will be seated with the patriarchs eating at Messiah's banquet (Matt 8:10-12)? It is because the disciples of the Messiah will "go" to the nations of the Gentiles and make disciples from their people. On the last day these will sit with Abraham, Isaac, and Jacob in the kingdom of God.

Our conclusion, therefore, is that Matthew portrays Jesus as having a staged, Israel-to-nations worldview and that if he fulfilled the first stage (preresurrection), his disciples would fulfill the second (postresurrection).

Which "stage" finds the greater emphasis in Matthew, the former (to Israel) or the latter (to the nations)? It is not Israel but the nations to which Matthew's Gospel directs the attention of the reader. It is *in Galilee of the Gentiles* that the light of God falls on Jesus in his teaching and miracles (4:12-17), and it is *in Galilee* that Jesus instructs his disciples to "go" to the nations of the Gentiles.

Luke-Acts

Luke narrates Jesus' early life followed by his baptism and his ministry in Galilee. He then describes the journey to Jerusalem and the events that unfolded there. To achieve this intentional Galilee-to-Jerusalem story line, Luke omits altogether Mark's narratives of Jesus traveling to the north and the east in Gentile regions. This means that the critical pericope reporting Jesus' logion to the Syrophoenician woman (see above) finds no place in this Gospel.

Accordingly Luke's narrative of Jesus' movements and teaching gives us less sense of the two-stage Israel-to-nations approach that we found in Mark's and Matthew's accounts. Indeed, it appears that Luke can't wait to

---

things"; 10:5 — "go nowhere among the Gentiles"; 10:18 — "you will be dragged before . . . the Gentiles"; 12:18, 21 — "my servant . . . shall proclaim justice to the Gentiles . . . and in his name will the Gentiles hope"; 20:18-19 — "the chief priests and the scribes . . . [will] deliver [the Son of man] to the Gentiles"). Clear identification of *ta ethnē* = Gentiles in the above texts helps us understand that *ta ethnē* in the following references refers to the Gentile *nations* (21:43 — "the kingdom of God will be taken away from you [Israel] and given to a nation producing the fruits of it"; 24:7 — "nation will rise against nation, and kingdom against kingdom"; 24:9 — "you will be hated by all nations for my name's sake"; 24:14 — "this gospel of the kingdom will be preached throughout the whole world, as a testimony to all nations, and then the end will come"; 25:32 — "before him will be gathered all the nations").

move beyond Israel (in his Gospel) to direct our attention to the apostles' mission to the nations, in particular the mission of Paul to the nations (in the book of Acts).

Here three important qualifications must be made. First, Luke signals a mission-to-the-nations intent in his opening chapters. Simeon identifies the child Jesus as "a light for revelation to the Gentiles" (2:32); the advent of the Baptist signals the fulfillment of Isaiah 40:5 — "all flesh shall see the salvation of God" (3:6); Jesus' genealogy is traced back to Adam (3:38); at his rejection in Nazareth as the Spirit-anointed one, Jesus implies a future welcome instead by Gentiles (4:16-30).[26]

Second, Luke's "first book" is really an introduction to his "second book," whose missionary progress (Acts 1:8 — "Judea and Samaria and to the end of the earth") is immediately announced and whose trajectory quickly takes the reader to Philip's ministry to the Samaritans and the Ethiopian; to Peter's ministry to the Roman Cornelius; and to Paul's westward, Rome-ward missions. The mission-to-nations theme at the beginning of the first book (noted above) and articulated by the risen One at its end (24:44-49) becomes the driving story in the second book.

Third, the opening words of the second book state that it will narrate "all that Jesus *will continue* to do and to teach." That is to say, this volume is the record of works and words of the ascended Lord *through* the "servants of the word" (Luke 1:2). Since Paul, the gospel herald to the Gentiles, is the dominant "servant" in the book of Acts, it is *through him* that the Lord chiefly acts and teaches.

This is remarkably similar to Paul's own observation (noted above) that Christ had worked "through" him "to win obedience from the Gentiles" (Rom 15:18) and that Christ "came and preached peace [i.e., through Paul] to you [Gentiles]" (Eph 2:17).

We conclude, therefore, that for Luke Jesus' ministry to the people of Israel (in a restrictive sense) was relatively less prominent than it was for either Matthew or Mark. True, Jesus' works and words were of critical importance, for otherwise there could be no mission to the nations. But we sense that fundamental though those words and works were, they repre-

---

26. Luke's account of the healing of the centurion's slave (7:1-10) curiously does not include a reference to the messianic banquet where believing Gentiles are present and the sons of the kingdom are excluded (as in Matt 8:5-13). Did this item belong to Matthew's special source, or has Luke omitted it from Q?

sented a kind of prolegomenon to Luke's unfolding story of the risen Christ's mission to the "lost" ones in the nations, which he was to exercise mainly through Paul.

The Gospel of John

Few aspects in the Gospel of John illustrate its idiosyncratic character and difference from the Synoptics so clearly as the Israel-nations issue does. The verbal elements in common between Matthew, Mark, and Luke relating to Gentile mission are entirely missing in the Gospel of John.

True, the Fourth Gospel preserves a strong contrast between the pre- and postresurrection situations. In John's schema the risen Christ "sends" his disciples as Spirit-filled emissaries who are authorized to "retain sins" (20:21-23), to be "harvesters" (4:38), "fruit" bearers (15:8, 16), doers of "greater works" (14:12-13), and the means through whom others outside that immediate preresurrection circle "come to believe" (17:20).

But to whom are the original disciples "sent," and who are these "other sheep" (10:16) who come to believe through them? The Synoptics lead us to conclude that these postresurrection believers are Gentiles from the nations. This, however, would be a false inference here since this Gospel conspicuously lacks any reference to them.[27]

It is also true that John distinguishes between the land of Israel (which he refers to by its regions Judea, Samaria, and Galilee) and the Diaspora (7:35 — "the Diaspora among the Greeks [= Gentiles]").

Yet we should understand that these "added believers" are not Gentiles from the nations, but Hellenized Jews from the Diaspora among the nations, for two reasons. First, John intends us to understand that "the children of God[28] who are scattered abroad *(ta dieskorpismena),*" as distinct from "the nation [in Israel]," are Jews of the Diaspora (11:52). Second, those "Greeks" who approached Jesus in Jerusalem were most likely Greek-speaking Jews[29] who had come as pilgrims for the Passover (12:20). Since

---

27. True, the word *ethnos*/"nation" does appear in this Gospel, but it is always in the singular and refers to the nation Israel (John 11:48, 50, 51, 52; 18:35).

28. See n. 16 above, where "children of God" refers to God's historic people.

29. It is less likely that they were Jewish sympathizers/Godfearers since the interest of this Gospel is confined to those John calls Christ's "own people" (i.e., Jews — 1:11).

they did not speak Aramaic, they sought and found a bilingual translator in Philip from Hellenized Bethsaida.

In short, it appears that the Gospel of John displays little interest in the world of the Gentile nations. In my opinion this is due to the earliness of its (primary)[30] authorship and its identifiable Palestinian provenance.[31] John the author[32] had been one of the disciples closest to the historical Jesus, the second in the list of the Twelve after the resurrection (Acts 1:13), and a close associate with Peter in ministry to the circumcised in the early years in Palestine (Gal 2:9; Acts 3:1, 3, 4, 11; 4:13, 19; 8:14; cf. 12:2).

A key factor here is that Peter's apostolate in those early years was confined to the circumcised in the land of Israel,[33] a ministry that was likely in continuation of Jesus' restricted ministry to "the lost sheep of the house of Israel" (Matt 10:5-6; 15:24; see above). Since Peter had so close a colleague as John in the first decade or so, I conclude that both men believed they were called to bring the word of God only to the circumcised in the land of Israel, as their Master had done. Such an understanding would help explain a Gospel whose interests are limited to Jews in Eretz Israel with only a rather remote awareness of Jews who lived among the Greeks beyond the borders of the land.[34]

Conclusion

Our brief analysis of evidence from the Gospels yields two conclusions. First, the Synoptic Gospels (but not the Gospel of John) observe a distinc-

30. It may be allowed that the Gospel was "issued" in Ephesus, as Irenaeus notes (*Against the Heresies* 3.1.1). Yet this by no means precludes the likelihood that it reached its earlier, most definitive form in the land of Israel.

31. See P. W. Barnett, "Indications of Earliness in the Gospel of John," *RTR* 64 (2005): 61-75.

32. According to early authorities (Irenaeus, *Against the Heresies* 3.1.1; cf. Clement of Alexandria, quoted in Eusebius, *HE* 3.23.6; 5.20.4) and confirmed allusively internally (John 21:1-2). For a contra view see, e.g., M. Hengel, *The Johannine Question* (London: SCM, 1989), 80-83.

33. Only by special circumstances did Peter preach to the Samaritans and Cornelius (Acts 8:14-25; 10:1–11:18).

34. Contra Jeremias, *Jesus' Promise*, 37-38. For the view that the Gospel reflects a mission to Jews followed by a mission to Gentiles, see J. L. Martyn, "A Gentile Mission That Replaced an Earlier Jewish Mission," in *Exploring the Gospel of John*, ed. R. A. Culpepper and C. C. Black (Louisville: Westminster John Knox, 1989), 124-44.

tion between Jesus' preresurrection, limited ministry to Israel and his disciples' postresurrection ministry to the nations of the Gentiles.

Second, there is a soundly based argument that the Israel-to-nations schema in Mark, Matthew, and Luke-Acts reflects the teaching of Jesus as he applied it to himself and his disciples in their mission to Galilee. For Jesus' restriction of ministry to Israel we recall texts like Mark 7:27 ("Let the children *first* be fed, for it is not right to take the children's bread and throw it to the dogs"), Matthew 15:24 ("I was sent *only* to the lost sheep of the house of Israel"), and Matthew 10:5-6 ("Go *nowhere* among the Gentiles, and enter no town of the Samaritans, but go rather to the lost sheep of the house of Israel"). On the other hand, however, Jesus emphatically foresees the ingathering of the nations in Matthew 8:11-12 ("I tell you, *many will come from east and west* and sit at table with Abraham, Isaac, and Jacob in the kingdom of heaven, while the sons of the kingdom will be thrown into the outer darkness; there men will weep and gnash their teeth") and in Matthew 28:19 ("Go . . . and make disciples of all nations").

Let us now return to our consideration of Paul and his mission. Our presenting question is: Was Paul's mission to the Gentiles willful and idiosyncratic, making him a perverse "second founder" as claimed by many liberal Protestants, or was it according to the mind of Jesus and in valid extension of that ministry? In our view, there are good historical reasons supporting the latter answer to this important question.

This, however, raises a further question. How did Paul know that his mission was in genuine extension of the mission of the historical Jesus? Did this assurance come to him as part of the Damascus "revelation," or did he learn it from the disciples of Jesus?

Paul's Mission Was Jesus' Mission

Christ "Called" Paul

Paul's "call" to preach to the Gentiles came directly from Christ on the Damascus Road. True, Paul attributes that "call" to the Father who revealed his Son to/in him (Gal 1:15-16; cf. 2 Cor 3:6; 5:18-19; Gal 2:7; Eph 3:2-8). Yet within God's overarching interception of him Paul clearly identifies the Son himself as the immediate source of his commission to gather in the Gentiles. Paul declares that he was "seized" by Christ (Phil 3:12) and that

Christ "appeared" to him making him an apostle equal with others before him (1 Cor 15:8-9; cf. 9:1). Accordingly he identifies himself as an "apostle of Christ" and as an "ambassador for Christ" (2 Cor 5:20). Moreover, as noted earlier, Paul refers to himself extensively in 2 Corinthians as Christ's representative.[35] It was the ascended Lord who gave Paul the "authority" to "build up" the churches (2 Cor 10:8; 13:10).

The book of Acts confirms Paul's identification of Christ as the source of his mission to the Gentiles. Each of its three accounts of the Damascus event explicitly identifies Christ as the One who intercepted Paul and initiated the apostolic commission to Paul to take the message of Christ to the nations.[36]

It is possible that human instruments played some part in Paul's "call." As discussed earlier, Paul may have been affected by Stephen's rejection of the temple in Jerusalem as the center of God's purposes. As well, the influence of Ananias and the Hellenist fugitives in Damascus may have contributed to Paul's radical new direction. Such considerations, however, are inferential and conjectural. What is unavoidable and clear from Paul himself is that the risen and ascended Lord "seized" him and "sent" him to the Gentiles.

Jesus' Mission and Peter's and Paul's Missions: To the Jews First

Paul's declarations in Romans 1:16 and 2:9 that his preaching of the gospel was for the Jew "first" and "also for" for the Greek (= Gentile) coincide exactly with Jesus' statement in Mark 7:27 that his message of the kingdom was "first" for the "children" (= Israel) and only then for the "dogs" (= Gentiles).

This assertion by Paul of priority for the Jews is not tactical, nor merely historically descriptive, but *theological,* based on God's "irrevocable call" to Israel initially given to the patriarchs (Rom 11:29). Although Paul understood his own special role for the Gentiles in the second stage of Christ's two-stage mission (as set out in Rom 15:8, 18 and discussed above), this did not mean any lack of participation in his own

35. Chapter 5.
36. Chapter 5.

mission to "the Jews first." Likewise, it meant that even his ministry among Gentiles was with a view to the ultimate salvation of the descendants of the patriarchs.[37]

In Luke's presentation of speeches by Peter and Paul in the book of Acts, we find the same expression of priority for Israel. In Jerusalem Peter told the people: "You are the sons of the prophets and of the covenant which God gave to your fathers, saying to Abraham, 'And in your posterity shall all the families of the earth be blessed.' God, having raised up his servant, sent him to you *first*, to bless you in turning every one of you from your wickedness" (Acts 3:25-26).

God will bless all the families of the earth, but he will bless Israel "first" because its people are "sons of . . . the covenant which God gave to [their] fathers." By his easily missed reference to "the sons of the covenant . . . *first*," Peter is echoing Jesus' reference to "first" in the important logion to the Syrophoenician woman (Mark 7:27). God's "servant," Jesus, is now the risen and ascended Lord who is continuing to "teach" the people, *through* his "minister," Peter (cf. Acts 1:1; Luke 1:2).

Along similar lines we note Luke's quotation of Paul's sermon to the Jews in the synagogue at Antioch of Pisidia:

> And Paul and Barnabas spoke out boldly, saying, "It was necessary that the word of God should be spoken *first* to you. Since you thrust it from you, and judge yourselves unworthy of eternal life, behold, we turn to the Gentiles. For so the Lord has commanded us, saying,
>
> > 'I have set you to be a light for the Gentiles,
> > that you may bring salvation to the uttermost parts
> > of the earth.'" (Acts 13:46-47)

As Peter did, so too Paul insists on bringing the message of the Messiah "first" to God's covenant people (as in Rom 1:16; 2:9).[38] At the same time, Paul declared himself to be a "light to the Gentiles" to bring them salvation (which is similar in sentiment to Rom 15:18).

---

37. Rom 11:11-12, 25-27, 30-31. For discussion of the temporary "hardening" of Israel at the time of Paul's mission, see Köstenberger and O'Brien, *Salvation*, 185-91; see also chapter 10.

38. Luke by no means gives the impression that Paul was making a permanent break with the synagogue; Paul made preaching in the synagogue his priority wherever he went, including in the next city he visited, Iconium.

It is remarkable that Paul identified *himself* as the Lord's "light" to the Gentiles, as prophesied in Isaiah 49:6. This might suggest that Paul had an unduly high view of himself. This possible misunderstanding is corrected later in the book of Acts where Paul states that the risen *Christ* himself will proclaim "light" both to the people of Israel and to the Gentiles (Acts 26:23). In other words, the risen Christ was proclaiming the light to Israel and the Gentiles *through* Paul.[39]

We conclude, therefore, that Jesus' insistence that his message go *first* to the "children" (Israel) and only then to the "dogs" (Gentiles) was exactly followed in Peter's preaching (Acts 3:26) and in Paul's mission, as reflected in his own letters and where the book of Acts quotes from the mission sermons of both Peter and Paul.

Leading Apostles Confirmed Paul's "Call"

Our argument is that Paul was convinced within himself that Christ had "seized," "called," and "sent" him as his surrogate for his ministry to the Gentiles. Furthermore, Paul's letters reveal the same two-stage ethnological program as Jesus held, that is, the salvation of God belongs "first" to Israel and only subsequently to the nations. The sermons from both Peter and Paul that Luke quotes assert that the message must come "first" to the covenant people.

This, however, raises a question. Were these mission ideas the preoccupation of Paul himself, personal convictions that came to him (by whatever inward processes) that no one else agreed with? After all, this man was a Roman citizen from the Diaspora who had graduated from the leading Pharisaic academy in Jerusalem (not an uneducated fisherman from Galilee), one who had not followed the Lord during his ministry but who, on the contrary, had been a violent persecutor of the church of God in its earliest days. It would be difficult to imagine how different Paul was from the Galilean leaders of early Christianity, both in his mind and in theirs. Paul certainly felt the force of those differences, as reflected in his

39. See Wagner, "Heralds of Isaiah," 193-222, for argument against Paul's identification of himself as the Isaianic servant. Nonetheless, according to Wagner, "The Role of Isaianic Traditions in Paul's Missionary Theology: Romans," *SBL Abstracts* (Atlanta: Scholars, 1997), "Paul . . . carried on a sustained and careful reading of large sections of the book [Isaiah] through the lens of his own situation as an apostle and missionary" (72).

own (sometimes sarcastic) passing references (see, e.g., Gal 2:2, 6, 9; 1 Cor 9:2; 15:10).

Notwithstanding these (real) tensions, it is equally clear that the leading apostles in Jerusalem recognized that the Lord had "called" Paul and that his understanding of the Israel-to-nations trajectory was according to the mind of the historical Jesus. One obvious indication of this was their dispatch of Barnabas to Antioch in the 40s in the likely knowledge that he would recruit Paul from Tarsus to assist in this Gentile-orientated ministry in Syria (Acts 11:25).

Another more obvious indication was that the apostles directly recognized Paul's "call" and his grasp of Jesus' two-stage mission.

Paul's Meetings with Peter

Paul reports on two meetings where Peter was present. These occurred over a span of about a decade.

Circa 36 — the First Meeting (Galatians 1:18-19)

Within three years of his Damascus "call" Paul met Peter (who was at that time the leading apostle) and James, brother of the Lord. Paul's account of this meeting implies that Peter and James voiced no objections to Paul's account of the dramatic events that overtook him three years earlier near Damascus when God "called" Paul to preach his Son among the Gentiles (Gal 1:15-16).

Circa 47 — the Second Meeting (Galatians 2:1-11)

A decade or so later Paul met with James (the new leader in Jerusalem) and Peter and John. His account of this second meeting (now with Barnabas) is more expansive, with evidence of some tension due to the presence of their associate, the uncircumcised Titus.

Nonetheless, the "pillars" conceded that in his gospel message to the uncircumcised during the intervening years in Syria-Cilicia Paul had "not run in vain" (Gal 2:2). In confirmation of this the "pillars" did not compel Titus to be circumcised (despite pressure from those Paul calls "false brethren" — 2:3-5). In further confirmation of Paul by Jerusalem, Paul reports that James, Peter, and John fully agreed that Barnabas and Paul should "go" to the Gentiles in further mission (2:9).

These two meetings make it clear that whatever other misgivings they had about Paul, the leaders in Jerusalem endorsed the genuineness of the exalted Lord's "call" to Paul to "go" with the message of the gospel to the Gentiles in fulfillment of the second stage of the missionary program of Jesus of Nazareth.

We must regard Paul's accounts to be accurate since they appear in his apologia to the Galatian readers. Some Galatians who were critical of Paul already had acquired ammunition against him (5:11). Paul had to be very careful about his version of relationship with the Jerusalem leaders (as now stated to the Galatians), otherwise his entire relationship with these mission churches would be jeopardized.

Conclusion

Was Paul a true missionary of Jesus, genuinely extending the mission of Jesus of Nazareth from Israel to the nations? Our conclusion, based on historical inquiry, is that Jesus of Nazareth had a two-stage Israel-to-nations agenda and that Paul pursued that same order in his "Jews first, and *also* Greeks" policy.

How did Paul come to adopt and pursue Jesus' Israel-to-nations regime? Was it mere coincidence? Did it arise within his reflections or by the suggestions of others? The evidence from his letters (and the book of Acts) indicates that the risen Lord "seized," "called," and "sent" Paul to the Gentiles with the message of Christ crucified and risen.

True, the Lord had promised the ingathering of the nations through his servant Israel, as noted earlier. Yet, as Jeremias has shown, this great prospect was eclipsed in the Second Temple era by Jewish hostility toward Gentiles and a desire for divine vengeance upon them as corrupt military occupiers.[40] In the Damascus event, the Pharisee's likely hostile attitude to Gentiles underwent a profound moral conversion. He was now driven by "the love of Christ" for them (2 Cor 5:14).

Was Paul's radically new "calling" recognized and endorsed by the former disciples of Jesus who were now his apostles, based in Jerusalem?

40. Jeremias, *Jesus' Promise*, 40-41.

Despite the considerable differences between these uneducated Galilean men and the former elite Pharisee and persecutor, they did in fact recognize the remarkable fact of his conversion and calling. Paul records several meetings where Peter was present and where he confirmed Paul's apostolate to the Gentiles.

EIGHT

Light to the Nations and Minister to Israel

I have given you as a covenant to the people,
a light to the nations.

Isaiah 42:6

E. P. Sanders and T. Donaldson have issued serious challenges to long-standing interpretations of Paul's ministry, based on fresh assessments of the evidence. We will consider these views as we reflect on Paul's ministry to the Gentiles (in respect of Donaldson) and to Jews (in respect of Sanders).

Light to the Nations

Paul saw his own role more distinctively than any other leader we meet in the NT, apart from Christ himself. Based on the Damascus event and his subsequent career, Paul appears to have regarded himself and his life's work in *fulfillment* of a number of OT texts.

God . . . has shone in our hearts to give the *light* of the knowledge of the glory of God in the face of Christ. (2 Cor 4:6)	I will give you [my servant] as a *light* to the nations that my salvation may reach to the end of the earth. (Isa 49:6)

I have given you [my servant]
as a covenant to the people,
a *light* to the nations,
to open the eyes that are blind,
to bring out the prisoners from the
dungeon. (Isa 42:6-7; cf. Acts 13:37;
26:17)

But when he who had set me apart
before I was born,
and had called me through his grace,
was pleased to reveal his Son to me,
in order that I might preach him
among the Gentiles. . . . (Gal 1:15-16)

Before I formed you in the womb
I knew you, and *before you were born*
I consecrated you;
I appointed you a prophet to the
nations. (Jer 1:5)

A brief reading of these texts is enough to indicate that Paul had a specific identity, *a theology of himself,* or more precisely, a theology of himself as a consequence of the Damascus Christophany. In Paul's eyes he was a "servant" of the Lord to carry his light to the Gentiles (Isa 49:6; 42:6-7)[1] and was from "the womb . . . consecrated [by God] . . . a prophet to the nations" (Jer 1:5; cf. Isa 49:5, where the prophetic calling from the womb is also mentioned).[2]

We must note the origin of Paul's mission in contrast with the commissioning of "the twelve" and the other "apostles" who, like Paul, were proclaiming the gospel of the crucified and risen Christ (1 Cor 15:3-11). Whereas the missionary call of those other preachers was located in the "appearing" of the risen (historical) Christ to them, in Paul's special case it arose from the Damascus Christophany. While the resurrected Christ "appeared" to Cephas, the "twelve," the "five hundred," James, and "all the apostles," it was this heavenly "Lord," who was also *now glorified,* whom Paul "saw" near Damascus (cf. 1 Cor 9:1). Paul's was a special case since,

1. See further L. Cerfaux, *Christ in the Theology of St. Paul* (New York: Herder and Herder, 1959); G. K. Beale, "The OT Background of Reconciliation in 2 Corinthians 5–7 and Its Bearing on the Literary Problems of 2 Corinthians 6:14–7:1," *NTS* 35, no. 4 (1989): 550-81; S. Kim, *Paul and the New Perspective* (Grand Rapids: Eerdmans, 2002), 101-27.

2. For a persuasive argument that Paul saw himself as a prophet, see C. A. Evans, "Paul and the Prophets," in *Romans and the People of God,* ed. S. V. Soderlund and N. T. Wright (Grand Rapids: Eerdmans, 1999), 115-28.

unlike them, he was "untimely born" *(hōsperei tō ektrōmati)*.[3] It was through this Damascus event that Paul believed himself to be set aside and called to fulfill a role that marked him out uniquely as "servant" and "prophet."

Paul, Apostle to the Nations

There are numerous occasions where Paul asserts his apostleship to the Gentiles/the uncircumcised. These references are spread across the apostle's undisputed letters, as well as the so-called deutero-Pauline letters (Eph 3:1-8; Col 1:24-27) and the Pastoral Letters (1 Tim 2:7; 3:16; 2 Tim 4:17). We will concentrate on texts in Romans and Galatians.

Romans

In his magisterial letter to the Romans, in which Paul looks back on preaching to the uncircumcised for more than twenty years, he makes his most expansive claims about his apostleship to the Gentiles.

> But on some points I have written to you very boldly by way of reminder, because of the grace given me by God to be a minister of Christ Jesus to the **Gentiles** in the priestly service of the gospel of God, so that the offering of the **Gentiles** may be acceptable, sanctified by the Holy Spirit. In Christ Jesus, then, I have reason to be proud of my work for God. For I will not venture to speak of anything except what Christ has wrought through me to win obedience from the **Gentiles**, by word and deed, by the power of signs and wonders, by the power of the Holy Spirit, so that from Jerusalem and as far round as Illyricum I have fulfilled[4] the gospel of Christ. (Rom 15:15-19)

---

3. 1 Cor 15:8. For a review of the meaning of this opaque and widely disputed *hapax,* see A. T. Thiselton, *The First Epistle to the Corinthians,* NIGTC (Grand Rapids: Eerdmans, 2000), 1208-10. One possible interpretation (not widely canvassed) is that of a "premature" birth, suggesting that Paul's vision of the glorified *heavenly* Christ meant his "early" birth, a preview so to speak, into the new age ahead of those before him who had seen only the risen *earthly* Jesus.

4. Greek: *peplērōkenai to euangelion;* RSV has "fully preached the gospel."

Paul's statements in Romans, though measured, are emphatic.[5] He was "set apart for the gospel of God" (1:1), had "*received* grace and apostleship" (1:5), and "the grace . . . to be a minister of Christ Jesus to the Gentiles" had been "*given* [to Paul] by God" (15:15-16). The consistent use of verbs in the passive voice shows that Paul saw himself as the object of God's choice. In consequence of God's calling he was "under obligation *(opheiletēs)* both to Greeks and to barbarians" (1:14). Paul's sense of *indebtedness* to the Gentiles corresponds with his sense of "calling" by God and, indeed, "necessity" before God to preach the gospel (1 Cor 9:16; see below).

Galatians

In Galatians Paul was forced to make a spirited defense of the integrity of his apostleship to the Gentiles and the necessity of a circumcision-free message.[6] The drift of his argument suggests that various opponents are pointing to the supremacy of the Jerusalem apostles, to whom Paul is failing to defer. The implication is that Paul is self-appointed and willful and that, as a consequence, his doctrines are eccentric and wayward. Paul's reply to the Galatians has this context, or something like it.

The two major passages are Galatians 1:15-17 and 2:7-9.

> But when he who had set me apart before I was born, and had called me through his grace, was pleased to reveal *(apokalupsai)* his Son to (in) me, in order that I might preach him *(euangelizōmai auton)* among the **Gentiles,** I did not confer with flesh and blood, nor did I go up to Jerusalem to those who were apostles before me. (Gal 1:15-17)

> But on the contrary, when they saw that I had been entrusted with the gospel to the **uncircumcised,** just as Peter had been entrusted with the gospel to the circumcised (for he who worked through Peter for the mission *[apostolē]* to the circumcised worked through me also for the Gentiles), and when they perceived the grace that was given to me, James and Cephas and John, who were reputed to be pillars, gave to me and Barnabas the right hand of fellowship, that we should go to the **Gentiles** and they to the circumcised. (Gal 2:7-9)

5. See chapter 11.
6. See Barnett, *BC,* appendix B, for arguments for the early dating of Galatians.

Here we make the following observations:

i. God singled out the as-yet-unborn Paul for the unique moment of revelation at Damascus many years later.

ii. This moment of divine revelation coincided with the moment of divine calling to Paul. God's revelation of his Son was also his summons to Paul to proclaim this Son to the Gentiles. In Paul's mind God's christological "revelation" and God's vocational "call" were inseparable.

iii. The initiative for this intervention came solely "from God."[7] Paul did not stumble upon the Son of God; nor did others open his eyes to Jesus' hitherto hidden identity; nor was it Paul's idea, or the idea of others, that he must bring the message of the Son of God to the Gentiles.

iv. Pointedly, Paul asserts that he did not "confer with flesh and blood" about this "revelation" and "calling," including with those who were apostles before him, including Cephas and James. Paul was "an apostle — not from men nor through man, but through Jesus Christ and God the Father" (Gal 1:1).

v. Nonetheless, "after fourteen years," when the leading apostles in Jerusalem recognized that Paul had been entrusted (i.e., by God) with the mission *(apostolē)* to the uncircumcised, they confirmed this divine calling with the directive that Paul and Barnabas should "go" to the Gentiles.

vi. In short, Paul insists that he owed the "revelation" and "calling" to God alone, but that the leading Jerusalem apostles recognized and endorsed his *apostolē*/"mission" to the Gentiles.

In sum, then, Romans and Galatians teach conclusively that God gave Paul his commission to preach Christ to the Gentiles, so as to include them in the covenant of God.

Paul's assertion that God's mission "call" to preach to the Gentile nations began at Damascus calls into question the reconstructions of T. Donaldson, who claims that Paul's mission to the nations effectively predated Damascus.[8]

---

7. Cf. 2 Cor 2:17, where Paul declares that, in contrast with those who "peddle" the word of God, his "speaking" that word had its origin in God *(ek theou)*.

8. See T. L. Donaldson, *Paul and the Gentiles: Remapping the Apostle's Convictional World* (Minneapolis: Fortress, 1997), and his summary in "Israelite, Convert, Apostle to the Gentiles: The Origin of Paul's Gentile Mission," in *The Road from Damascus,* ed. R. N. Longenecker (Grand Rapids: Eerdmans, 1997), 62-84. The parenthetical page numbers in the text of the excursus refer to the article in Longenecker. In reply see S. Kim, *Paul and the New Perspective* (Grand Rapids: Eerdmans, 2002), 35-39.

Excursus: The Theory of Terence Donaldson

Donaldson rightly observes that Paul's "conversion" must not be taken to mean that he automatically embarked on a world mission to the Gentiles, as if that is what "converted" persons routinely did. By analogy he points to another "convert," James, and observes that he did not follow a course similar to Paul's.

Donaldson is concerned to discover a "subjective framework" for the complex of (1) Paul's "former life in Judaism" (Gal 1:13); (2) his "revelation of Jesus Christ" (1:12); and (3) his subsequent way of presenting and defending "the gospel that [he] proclaim[ed] among the Gentiles" (2:2) (Donaldson, 63-64).

This scholar, however, has problems with the key texts that relate to this Pauline complex. Acts was written long afterward, and Paul's letters contain "situationally conditioned arguments that are difficult to use." In any case, when Paul attributes to God actions that relate to himself, we should meet these "on the human side by an appropriate framework of understanding" (63). Accordingly, "answers to the question [about Paul's mission to the Gentiles] tend to be correlated with larger scholarly reconstructions of Paul's life and work" (64).

Donaldson rejects in turn various approaches to this question, whether that Paul developed his Gentile concern later (Francis Watson); or that this missionary concern was "part of his conversion experience" (Seyoon Kim); or that Paul was converted into a community that was already involved in a mission to the Gentiles (Heikki Räisänen).

After showing the deficiencies in these approaches, Donaldson points to the broad group in which his own explanation is located. That is to say, Paul's Gentile concern was "a pre-conversion disposition." His own stated position is that "Paul's mission to the Gentiles is to be accounted for in terms of his prior commitment to Jewish proselytism" (69).

As a basis for this Donaldson takes special notice of Galatians 5:11, where Paul is answering the charge of the inconsistency that in fact he "still preached circumcision." Donaldson comments: "In the context of Galatians, 'to preach circumcision' means 'to encourage Gentiles to be circumcised as a condition of entry into Abraham's family.' . . . [I]t suggests that there was a time when Paul had encouraged Gentiles to convert to Judaism . . . to a pre-Damascus stage in Paul's life" (81).

In short, he finds in this text a particular understanding that Paul had been a preacher of circumcision, which he finds to be substantial evidence for Paul's pre-Damascus proselytism of Gentiles that, post-Damascus, would be expressed as his apostleship to the Gentiles.

According to Donaldson, it wasn't that Paul was involved in a "full-scale" mission, but rather that he had a role akin to that of the Jew Eleazar who insisted that Izates, king of Adiabene, be circumcised (Josephus, *Ant* 20.34-48) (Donaldson, 82).

Donaldson contends that Paul's proselytism is to be located in the era of Second Temple Judaism, to which Paul belonged, a proselytism that implied a kind of universalistic outlook, an abandonment of Jewish particularism.

Where, then, does Donaldson locate Paul's specific apostolate to the Gentiles? Clearly "Damascus" was critical. "Paul's Damascus experience convinced him that God had raised Jesus and that Jesus was indeed Messiah and Savior. This experience necessitated a fundamental reconfiguration of his set of world-structuring convictions, with Christ replacing Torah as the means by which membership in the people of God was determined" (82).

Yet Paul's pre-Damascus proselytizing was also very important. "His encounter with the risen Christ released a whole new source of energy into the equation. Still, this energy flowed along channels of belief and activity that were already present" (82).

In sum, then, Donaldson argues that there must have been something different about the pre-Damascus Paul that accounts for his mission to the Gentiles, a unique and unparalleled activity. That "something" was his prior work in "preaching circumcision" to which the Damascus experience brought focus and the impetus of newly found energy.

How, then, do we evaluate this important proposal?[9]

To begin, Donaldson rightly asks what there was about Paul that made his mission different from others like James (and, we would add, every other leader in the NT).

In our view, however, he is too dependent on just one text (Gal 5:11), and on a specific interpretation of that text. Donaldson cautions against using "situationally conditioned arguments" in Paul, yet his whole reconstruction inconsistently rests on a text that is truly "situational."

The problem is not that of using "situational" texts, since most of Paul's writings are "situational," but rather of Donaldson's exclusive de-

9. See Kim, *Paul,* 35-39.

pendence on a single text, one that is capable of other meanings. In fact, the "situational" character of Galatians, that is, Paul's need to defend his apostleship, is an argument in favor of his accuracy. Paul's Jewish opponents in Galatia belonged to a worldwide network whose center was Jerusalem, so that any overstatement or deceit on his part would be used against him to devastating effect.

Furthermore, Donaldson's example of Eleazar's proselytism in the circumcision of Izates must be questioned. Eleazar insisted on circumcision to *hinder* Izates from becoming a proselyte on the Jew Ananias's terms of admission to Judaism that were *too easy,* that is, circumcision-free. In fact, Eleazar's insistence on circumcising the king of Adiabene was, if anything, antiproselytism. Eleazar was a circumciser, but he was no proselytizer. Donaldson's prime example of a supposed parallel to the pre-Damascus Paul actually works against him.[10]

When we turn to Donaldson's key text, Galatians 5:11,[11] we find there are other explanations of its meaning, for example, the circumcision of Timothy (Acts 16:1-3). Paul, however, did not circumcise Timothy to make him a proselyte, but because of his unusual situation as the uncircumcised son of a Jewish woman and a Gentile man. An early dating of Galatians, which I think likely, would prevent any text from Galatians applying to the circumcision of Timothy. Nonetheless, it does illustrate an act of circumcision that was unrelated to proselytism.

Likewise, we should consider Paul's likely attitude to Jewish believers and their attitudes toward circumcising their sons. Is it likely that Paul would instruct them against circumcising their sons? On the contrary, it is inconceivable that Paul would give such advice.[12] Paul's critics could certainly seize upon this as an example of inconsistency on his part.

Our response, then, to Donaldson's use of Galatians 5:11 is that this one text is required to bear too much weight and that it is, in any case, open to alternative interpretations.

---

10. See earlier, chapter 3.

11. See earlier, chapter 3.

12. When Paul visited Jerusalem circa 57, he was confronted with the charge that the Jewish believers in Jerusalem had been told (by Jews of the Diaspora?) that Paul was teaching "all the Jews who are among the Gentiles to forsake Moses, telling them not to circumcise their children or observe the customs" (Acts 21:21). This complaint, however, rests on misunderstanding (or mischief), since Paul insisted that he gave "no offense to Jews" (1 Cor 10:32) and that to Jews he "became as a Jew" (1 Cor 9:20).

Of greater importance, however, is Donaldson's neglect of Paul's own testimony in Galatians 1:15-16 and 2:7-9, as discussed above. In these texts Paul insists that God's "revelation" to him of "his Son" and the "call" to "evangelize him among the Gentiles" occurred together in the single Damascus encounter.

Minister to Israel

Although Paul is famous as the apostle to the Gentiles (Rom 1:13), it is clear that he also preached to Jews. This rather surprising aspect of Paul's ministry emerges both from Romans and from 2 Corinthians, and it is confirmed by passing references elsewhere in his letters (1 Cor 9:20; 10:32; 2 Cor 11:24) as well as in the book of Acts (9:15; 13:5-14; 14:1; 17:1-4, 10, 17; 18:4, 19; 19:8; see chapter 7 above).

Significantly, Paul saw himself as a minister to Israel under the long-promised new covenant. In 2 Corinthians 3 Paul contrasts two covenants (old and new) and two ministers (Moses and himself). Moses and the old covenant are implied types that are now fulfilled by Paul and the new covenant. Paul hints that he regarded himself as a symbolic counterpart to Moses who superseded Moses. Paul was "sufficient" for his role (v. 6), whereas Moses was "not sufficient" for his (*ouk hikanos eimi* — "I am not sufficient" — Exod 4:10 LXX).[13] In short, Paul's new covenant ministry was, like Moses' old covenant ministry, a ministry to *Israel*.

Romans

Pointedly he told the Romans that he had fulfilled the gospel in an arc *(en kuklō)* "from *Jerusalem* and as far round as Illyricum" (Rom 15:19), and he reminds the Thessalonians that the Jews "drove [him] out" of Judea (1 Thess 2:15). These references from his own pen about his ministry to Jews — including Palestinian Jews — confirm the claim he made in the presence of King Herod Agrippa II that he declared the message "to those . . . at Jerusalem and *throughout all* the country of Judea" (Acts 26:20). Paul's rhetorical question about the Jews ("Have they not heard? Indeed

13. See earlier, 63-64.

they have" — Rom 10:18) most likely includes his own preaching to Jews in Judea as well as in the Diaspora.

As we shall argue, Romans is Paul's comprehensive response to the Jewish-Christian, Jerusalem-based countermission.[14] Indeed, the greater part of Romans is devoted apologetically to *Jewish* concerns. We note for example that the critical word "law" *(nomos)* occurs more than seventy times in the letter. The notional hostile interlocutor Paul answers throughout Romans is a Jew (2:1, 17-24; 3:7; 9:19). The extent of Paul's apologetic to Jewish readers in Romans implies that Paul engaged in significant ministry among the Jews and that Jewish issues were dominant in that letter.

2 Corinthians

Jewish issues also dominate 2 Corinthians (2:14–4:6; 11:1–12:13). Much of the letter is devoted to Paul's apologetic response to recently arrived preachers from the Jerusalem-based Jewish-Christian countermission. Like him, they are "ministers *(diakonoi)* of Christ" (11:23), Hebrews, Israelites, and descendants of Abraham (11:22). They are, however, "false apostles" (11:13) and "ministers *(diakonoi)* of Satan" (11:15) who preach "another Jesus" (11:4) and contend against Paul for an alternative "righteousness" (11:15).

These preachers of "a different gospel" (11:4) are to be identified with "those who peddle the word of God" who appear earlier (2:17; cf. 4:2).[15] Paul's sequence in 2:14–3:11 is important. He locates the "peddlers" *after* the antitriumphalist passage (2:14-16) and *before* his declaration that the old covenant is now "abolished" (3:1-11). The "peddlers" reference ties together the antitriumph passage with the old covenant passage.

Paul's mention of these triumphalist peddlers is deliberate, and implies that they were attempting to reimpose the "righteousness" of the now-abolished *Mosaic* covenant (3:9) upon the members of the church in Corinth, possibly in particular upon Jews in the congregation.[16]

---

14. See chapter 11.

15. This view rests upon the conviction of the unity of 2 Corinthians. True, the letter appears disjointed and uneven. This may be explained by (i) Paul's emotional turmoil at the time of writing, and (ii) the likelihood that he wrote the letter over a period of time. See further, P. Barnett, *The Message of 2 Corinthians: Power in Weakness* (Leicester, England, and Downers Grove, Ill.: InterVarsity, 1988), 15-25.

16. P. Barnett, "Opposition in Corinth," *JSNT* 22 (1984): 3-17.

Double Darkness under the Old Covenant (2 Corinthians 3)

Paul was convinced that the old covenant (as he called it — v. 14) had run the course God had predetermined for it. God had appointed its *telos* ("end" or "goal") from its inception so that, from that time, it had been "abolished" in principle.[17] The advent of the "ministry" *(diakonia)* of the new covenant (3:6) has outglorified and therefore de-glorified the "ministry" of the old covenant that these peddlers seek to perpetuate.

That "covenant" was given at Mount Sinai, written on "tablets of stone" (v. 3), which Paul calls "letter" *(gramma* — v. 6). This *gramma* is not, as is popularly believed, the "letter of the law" (Pharisaic legalism), that is, a corruption of the law given at Mount Sinai. Rather, *gramma* is the law *itself,* as given in its pristine, undistorted form. This is clear enough from verses 3 and 6, but indisputably so in Romans 7:6: "But now *(nuni de)* we are discharged *(katērgēthēmen)* from the law, having died to that in which we were held, so that we serve in the newness of Spirit and not in the oldness of letter" (author's translation).

It is clear from the parallelism in this text that "law" and "letter" are identical in meaning and refer to an "old" dispensation of "captivity" from which those under the law are now "discharged," set free to "serve" in the "new" dispensation of the Spirit. "Law" and "letter" are synonymous and point back to a now superseded old covenant. The observation that "law" *(nomos)* does not appear in 2 Corinthians, while technically correct, is irrelevant since *gramma* has the same meaning.

According to Paul, the "letter," "tablets of stone," and "letters carved in stone" are one and the same thing (vv. 6, 3, 7), that is, the law given through Moses as the basis of the old covenant. This "letter" "kills" (v. 6) because it is a "ministry" of "condemnation" and of "death" (vv. 9, 7).

Most likely, those who "peddle the word of God" (2:17) seek to legitimate their ministry by "letters of recommendation" (v. 1). Paul makes a connection between the "ink" on these letters and the "letters carved in stone" by Moses (vv. 3, 7). This connection points to the peddlers as preaching a version of the "word of God" that focused on "the letter" (v. 6), that is, the law-based old covenant. They are "ministers of Moses."

---

17. A. T. Hanson, *Jesus Christ in the Old Testament* (London: SPCK, 1965), 23-25, is correct in translating *tēn katargoumenēn* (v. 7), *to katargoumenon* (v. 11), *tou katargoumenou* (v. 13), *katargeitai* (v. 14) as "abolished" rather than "fading" (as in RSV).

Their "ministry," however, is now futile since that covenant is now "abolished" by its *telos*/end, Christ (v. 13; cf. Rom 10:4). Furthermore, as we have noted, that ministry only mediated "death" and "condemnation."

In the second part of chapter 3 Paul speaks of the plight of those who live under the old covenant. Israelites "to this day" hear "Moses"/the old covenant read with a veil over their minds (vv. 14, 15). Centuries earlier at Mount Sinai Moses used a veil to cover the glory on his face, the glory that was yet to come, whose *telos*/end was Christ. Despite the advent of the new covenant, Israelites sit in their synagogues hearing the old covenant read, but their veiled blindness prevents them from seeing the now-fulfilled glory of the old covenant in the "face" (not of Moses but) of Christ (cf. 4:6). Theirs is a "double darkness," due to Moses' veil covering the glory and the veil lying over their own minds. Accordingly, both Moses and the Israelites are without "hope" and in bondage (3:12, 17).

How different it is for a Jew like Paul who has "turned to the Lord (Jesus)" so that the veil is now "lifted" from his "face" (vv. 17, 18). God has taken the veil from the minds of Paul and other Jews who have believed in Jesus as Messiah. They now understand that the glory in Moses/the law anticipated and pointed onward to Christ. Furthermore, God has blessed them with "righteousness" in place of "condemnation" (v. 9), and the transforming presence of the eschatological Spirit in place of stagnation and death (vv. 7, 17-18).

Paul, a Minister under the New Covenant (2 Corinthians 4:1)

Paul's words "*this* ministry" contrast powerfully with his grim description of the ministry of the old covenant, which the "peddlers" are seeking to revive (among Jews?) in Achaia.

> Therefore, having this ministry, even as we have been shown mercy, we do not lose heart. (2 Cor 4:1)

a. The initial "therefore" *(dia touto)* springs from blessings flowing from the ministry of the new covenant, namely, the God-given comprehension that the OT promises pointed on to Christ (1:18-20) and the presence of the eschatological Spirit who is transforming the people toward the *imago Christi* of the coming age (3:6, 9, 12, 16, 18; cf. 4:16–5:1).

b. Because the new covenant will never be superseded (as the old covenant ministry has been), Paul accordingly says he "*has* this ministry" so that he does not "lose heart" or "give up." He will not refer to new covenant ministry in a past tense.

Paul's "ministry" under the long-awaited "new covenant" was a ministry he exercised toward his fellow Jews, to Israel, whether in Palestine or the Diaspora.

Paul's assertion of his new covenant ministry *to Israel* raises issues for E. P. Sanders's theory of covenantal nomism that asserts the *continuing* character of the covenant, which Israel is "in" due to God's mercy and her practical observation of the law *(nomos)*.

Excursus: E. P. Sanders's Theory of Covenantal Nomism

The observation that Paul's "new covenant ministry" was directed to his fellow "Israelites" who were "condemned" and in "double darkness" in a now obsolescent covenant is of considerable importance. It is a commonplace that at Damascus God commissioned Paul to be apostle to the Gentiles. But in 2 Corinthians 3:6 Paul indicates that he was a "minister" in the new covenant, which was ministry that God promised to *Israel*, and not to the Gentiles.

Of course, everyone assumes that Paul had *some* ministry to Israel. But few have noticed that the "new covenant" was promised to the "house of Israel and the house of Judah," that is, *to the Jews* (Jer 31:31). The force of 2 Corinthians 4:1 is that God gave to Paul the "ministry" in the newly fulfilled new covenant to Israel, the elect people who have hitherto lived under the old covenant. Paul implies that just as Moses "had been" the "minister" under that "old" dispensation, he, Paul, was "now" the "minister" to Israel under the "new covenant" (2 Cor 3:6).

This infrequently noted observation has significant implications for the reconstructions of E. P. Sanders's "new perspective" on Paul.[18] In Sanders's view the covenant of Israel had always been a covenant of grace, which Israel had upheld and which was still current. He refers to "covenantal nomism" (the covenant based on *nomos*/law), which he de-

---

18. The origin of this phrase is attributed to J. D. G. Dunn in 1982. See J. D. G. Dunn, "The New Perspective on Paul," in *Jesus, Paul, and the Law: Studies in Mark and Galatians* (Louisville: Westminster John Knox, 1990), 183-206.

fines as "[t]he view that one's place in God's plan is established on the basis of the covenant and that the covenant requires as the proper response of man his obedience to its commandments, while providing means of atonement for transgression."[19]

Sanders has a positive attitude to that covenant and the ability of its people to observe its *nomos*/law, which they did willingly and effectively. Its only deficiency was that it was not something else: "This is what Paul finds wrong in Judaism: it is not Christianity."[20]

Sanders further argues that Paul allows the notion of "covenantal nomism" for Israel also to be applied to that "ministry" to which he had been called in the Damascus event. "Thus one can see already in Paul how it is that Christianity is going to become *a new form of covenantal nomism,* a covenant religion which one enters by baptism, membership in which provided salvation, which has a specific set of commandments, obedience to which (or repentance for the transgression of which) keeps on in the covenantal relationship, while repeated or heinous transgression removes one from membership."[21] Here Sanders is arguing that God's covenant with Israel based on covenantal nomism was successful and that Paul was attaching Christianity to Judaism as an adapted version of covenantal nomism.

There are several (connected) objections to this reconstruction, based mainly on 2 Corinthians 3.

The first is that Paul indeed found *something else* wrong with Judaism, something so fatally wrong that it had to be abolished. That is to say, God has actually finished with that covenant, de-glorified it and abolished it. Why? It was written on tablets of stone and (due to their sin) brought the people only (spiritual) "death" and "condemnation" (2 Cor 3:7, 9). It was now obsolete because it had proved to be ineffective.

Furthermore, due to their "hardened" minds, the people who hear Moses read (in the synagogues) cannot discern the promises in "Moses" that are fulfilled in the One who was to come (2 Cor 3:14-15). The Messiah

---

19. E. P. Sanders, *Paul and Palestinian Judaism* (Philadelphia: Fortress, 1987), 75. Whether or not Sanders is accurately describing Second Temple Judaism is open to question, which I will leave to others to discuss. See generally D. A. Carson, P. T. O'Brien, and M. Seifrid, *Justification and Variegated Nomism: A Fresh Appraisal of Paul and Second Temple Judaism,* WUNT 140 (Tübingen: Mohr Siebeck, 2001).

20. Sanders, *Paul and Palestinian Judaism,* 552.

21. Sanders, *Paul and Palestinian Judaism,* 513.

has come, but the people are blind to recognize him, even though the law prophesied him.

Accordingly, God has "abolished" that covenant (and Judaism with it). It is not, as Sanders proposes, a benign entity to which Paul could merely attach Christianity, a Christianity that was likewise based on the principle of "covenantal nomism."

In short, 2 Corinthians 3 rejects both Sanders's sunny verdict on Judaism/the old covenant and his proposal that Paul merely annexed Christianity to it along similar lines.

For Paul the former covenant that had been based on "letter" *(gramma)* was now "ended" by the advent of Christ and the "righteousness" that now belongs to those who are "in Christ" (2 Cor 3:13; 5:21).

Paul makes it clear in Romans that the advent of the law under Moses merely revealed the existing fallenness of the covenant people, Israel (Rom 5:13). Both Gentiles and Jews are "under sin" (*huph' hamartian* — 3:9). Accordingly, both Jews and Gentiles are the children of Adam whose "righteousness from God" can be found only in the "Adam" who "was to come" (5:14). In 2 Corinthians Paul teaches that those who are alienated from God find their "righteousness from God" in the sinless One, whom God made "to be sin" for them (2 Cor 5:21). Any implication that "righteousness" or "justification" is relevant only to Gentiles is mistaken; Jews stand in the same desperate need.[22]

Conclusion

The Damascus Christophany as an objective and historical event is crucial for the understanding of Paul, since it opened the way for him to become the "apostle of Christ to the Gentiles," on one hand, and a "minister of the new covenant" to Israel, on the other.

---

22. See also Gal 2:15-16 ("We ourselves, who are Jews by birth and not Gentile sinners, yet who know that a man is not justified by works of the law but through faith in Jesus Christ, even we have believed in Christ Jesus, in order to be justified by faith in Christ, and not by works of the law, because by works of the law shall no one be justified") and Acts 13:38-39 ("Let it be known to you therefore, brethren, that through this man forgiveness of sins is proclaimed to you, and by him every one that believes is freed from [justified from — *dikaiōthēnai*] everything from which you could not be freed by [justified by — *dikaioutai*] the law of Moses").

Accordingly, we must doubt those reconstructions that argue that he had practiced circumcision beforehand as a form of universal proselytism (Donaldson) or that his ministry to Gentiles post-Damascus was a kind of ongoing "covenantal nomism" (Sanders). On the contrary, the Damascus event spelled an end, radically, to Paul's previous life and work as a Pharisee (and circumciser) and to any sense that the old covenant remained current. Damascus was both a radical end to the old and a radical beginning to the new. Other reconstructions do not do justice to the evidence about Paul.

NINE

Mission and Countermission (ca. 47-57)

What I do I will continue to do, in order to undermine the claim of those who would like to claim that in their boasted mission they work on the same terms as we do. For such men are false apostles. . . .

2 Corinthians 11:12-13

On frequent journeys, in danger from rivers, danger from robbers, danger from my own people, danger from Gentiles, . . . danger from false brethren. . . .

2 Corinthians 11:26

About A.D. 57 Paul offered a brief review of the twenty-five years he had been a believer and an apostle: "From Jerusalem and as far round as Illyricum I have fulfilled[1] the gospel of Christ" (Rom 15:19).

As we have seen, however, for the first decade and a half Paul confined his ministry to locations within the Levant, to Damascus, "Arabia," Judea, and Syria-Cilicia. Circa 47, however, all that changed, and Paul began a series of westward missions that would take him to the Roman provinces of Galatia, Macedonia, Achaia, and Asia.

Writing circa 57, Paul saw the Levantine ministry and the westward missions seamlessly as one apostolate. Luke, however, had a differ-

---

1. Greek: *peplerōkēnai;* there is no verb "preached" here.

ent perspective, passing over Paul's initial fifteen years in relative silence and directing detailed narrative attention instead to the decade of westward missions. There is no real conflict here; it is a matter of differing perspectives.

Luke's viewpoint is worth noting since Paul's ministry in that decade was materially different from all that had gone before. Paul's achievements during that "glorious" decade were so remarkable as to change the course of history. How different world history would be had Paul remained in Syria-Cilicia.

Paul's mission immediately provoked the rise of a Jerusalem-based countermission in churches that insisted Gentile believers be circumcised. This countermission was active throughout the decade of Paul's mission in the provinces, and it was the major problem Paul faced during those years. This in turn provoked Paul to write major letters (Galatians, 2 Corinthians, Romans, and, later, Philippians) contending for a law-free gospel against the circumcision demands of the countermissionaries.[2]

In fact, most of Paul's letters were written during this missionary decade (which was effectively ended by years of imprisonment in Palestine and Italy).[3] True, not all of Paul's letters addressed the demands of the countermissionaries upon Gentiles. In the two letters to the Thessalonians and in 1 Corinthians (and in the two lost letters to the Corinthians), Paul is mainly addressing the theological, moral, and spiritual challenges that former idolaters now faced as believers.

How different, then, our Bible would be without the letters Paul wrote during his mission decade, in particular those answering the countermissionaries in which he made his great defense of the grace of God in the message of the cross.

---

2. Note, however, that while 2 Corinthians makes no mention of circumcision, its (implied) insistence on Moses/old covenant/"letter" (= law) establishes a continuity with those other letters that connect "law" and "circumcision."

3. Paul wrote (a) Philippians from prison in Rome circa 60, (b) 1 Timothy and Titus circa 63/64 during a subsequent period of freedom, and (c) 2 Timothy from prison in Rome circa 64.

Movements and Letters

I will not trace in any detail Paul's movements in Anatolia and Greece,[4] nor will I discuss at any length the specific connections between Paul's travels and the writing of the letters that occurred during this decade.[5]

The chronology for this decade is based on the view that (i) Barnabas and Paul's private meeting in Jerusalem (Gal 2:1-10) circa 47 preceded (ii) the mission to Cyprus, Pisidia, and Lycaonia that was followed (iii) by the "incident in Antioch" in about 49, and (iv) (later that year) the so-called Jerusalem Council.[6]

ca.

47	Barnabas and Paul meet with "pillars" in Jerusalem
48	Paul and Barnabas go to Cyprus, Pisidia, and Lycaonia
49	"Incident in Antioch" and the Jerusalem meeting
50-52	Paul, Silvanus, and Timothy in Galatia, Macedonia, and Achaia
52-56	Paul in Asia
56-57	Paul in Macedonia and Achaia

Paul's burst of letter writing occurred during this decade, beginning with Galatians[7] and ending with Romans. We know of no letter by Paul written beforehand,[8] and his only writings after 57 are his letter to the Philippians and his "pastoral" treatises to Timothy and Titus. Paul's letters from the decade 47-57 are "occasional" (except for Ephesians, which is a circular), written to address a current "situation" in a church. It seems that Paul wrote as many as eleven letters during these years.

---

4. See, e.g., E. J. Schnabel, *Early Christian Mission* (Downers Grove, Ill.: InterVarsity, 2004), 1073-1231.

5. See, e.g., J. B. Polhill, *Paul and His Letters* (Nashville: Broadman and Holman, 1999), 82-378; U. Schnelle, *Apostle Paul: His Life and Theology*, trans. M. Eugene Boring (Grand Rapids: Baker Academic, 2005), 138-386.

6. Agreeing with Polhill, *Paul and His Letters*, 80. The dating by R. Riesner, *Paul's Early Period: Chronology, Mission Strategy, Theology* (Grand Rapids: Eerdmans, 1998), 322, of the events of Paul's "mission decade" approximates the chronology above.

7. For the earliness of Galatians, see Barnett, *BC*, appendix B.

8. See Barnett, *BC*, 42-54.

ca.		
48	Galatians	written from Antioch
50	1 and 2 Thessalonians	written from Corinth
53	(Lost) "Previous" letter	
	to the Corinthians	written from Ephesus
54	1 Corinthians	written from Ephesus
55	Philemon, Colossians,	
	Ephesians	written from Ephesus[9]
56	(Lost) "Severe" letter	
	to the Corinthians	written from Ephesus
	2 Corinthians	written from Philippi (?)
57	Romans	written from Corinth

Why Paul Went to the Gentiles: 1. Apocalyptic Ferment

We have already noted the uneven length of various phases of Paul's ministry. His years of relative obscurity in the Levant (Damascus, "Arabia," Judea, Syria-Cilicia — Gal 1:17-22) occupied "fourteen years" (ca. 34-47), whereas his very public westward missions in the provinces of Anatolia and Greece (Acts 13–20) were of a mere ten-year duration (ca. 47-57).

During the Levantine years Paul remained in places familiar to him (apart from "Arabia"?) and most likely limited his ministry to Gentiles who were already Godfearers. By contrast, the succeeding period of westward missions involved extensive travel with a more intentional outreach to Gentile idolaters outside the synagogues.

Historians have not often noted the uneven amounts of time Paul spent in these successive mission phases or sought an explanation for his (apparent) dramatic change in modus operandi. In this regard we note, first, the importance of Paul's ministry in Antioch, which Barnabas shared with him, though as his junior associate. Upon arriving in Antioch in the early to mid-40s, Paul discovered that numerous "Greeks" had already "turned to the Lord" (Acts 11:21).

When Barnabas arrived in Antioch from Jerusalem and Paul from Tarsus, they came upon a vibrant and entirely new phenomenon. Here for

---

9. Most scholars believe Paul wrote Philemon during his Roman imprisonment (ca. 60-62), and many classify Ephesians and Colossians as deutero-Pauline. See appendix D.

the first time was a mixed congregation of the circumcised and the uncircumcised acknowledging but also likely proclaiming Jesus as "the Christ," having the epithet *Christianoi* attached to them by the people of Antioch (Acts 11:26). It is likely that Paul was influenced by what he saw in Antioch.

A second factor that likely contributed to Paul's decision to seek the approval of the "pillar" apostles in Jerusalem for a more intentional "going" to the Gentiles was the stability of Claudius's era. The chaos and near civil war between Greeks and Jews in Alexandria and the cities of the eastern Mediterranean including Antioch that arose during the years of Gaius's principate (37-41)[10] had been replaced by the greater stability of Claudius's rule. This may have encouraged Barnabas and Paul to travel to the west to bring the message of Christ to the Gentiles.

A third observation is that Judea at that time was in the grip of apocalyptic fervor. While Claudius's principate brought greater political stability to the empire at large, the same cannot be said for Judea during the 40s, where circumstances led to a burst of apocalyptic preaching and activity.

In 44 the untimely death of King Herod Agrippa I brought his brief rule over a united Israel to an end, to the disappointment of the Jews. Worse still, Claudius reannexed Judea and Galilee for the first time, extending considerably the limits of Roman rule. Compounding this problem, Claudius appointed as governors "procurators,"[11] administrators with a more explicitly tax-gathering function than their predecessors, the military "prefects" appointed under Augustus and Tiberius.[12] It might be expected that the first such procurator would have been both sensitive and judicious. Cuspius Fadus (44-46), however, proved to be neither wise nor competent. He attempted to seize the vestments used by the high priest, unsuccessfully as it turned out,[13] and he put down a regional uprising with unnecessary force.[14]

During Fadus's tenure a significant apocalyptic event took place. A self-styled prophet named Theudas, accompanied by a great multitude,

10. M. Hengel and A. M. Schwemer, *Paul between Damascus and Antioch: The Unknown Years* (London: SCM, 1977), 180-91.

11. See P. A. Brunt, "Procuratorial Jurisdiction," *Latomus* 25 (1966): 461-87.

12. For a general account of the instability of Judea during this period, see M. Goodman, *The Ruling Class of Judea* (Cambridge: Cambridge University Press, 1987), 5-14.

13. Josephus, *Ant* 20.13.

14. Josephus, *Ant* 20.2-4.

marched from Jerusalem to the Jordan, where he attempted to part the waters of the Jordan in the manner of Joshua (or Moses at the Red Sea).[15] The governor's violent suppression of Theudas's "enacted prophecy" is a measure of the seriousness with which he viewed it. Nonetheless, Theudas's attempted miracle-sign signaled the hope of a Joshua-like reconquest of the land and the expulsion of the Roman occupying forces.

The sense of apocalyptic urgency was likely heightened by the severe famine (and the accompanying civil unrest) that gripped the entire eastern Mediterranean from the mid-40s. This, too, might have been viewed as a supernatural portent.

Why Paul Went to the Gentiles: 2. Israel "Hardened"

The final and most important "apocalyptic" element to have influenced Paul's explosion of missionary activity among the Gentiles was his conviction that Israel had entered a period of divine "hardening." It appears that Paul had come to understand that the people of Israel (both in Palestine and in the Diaspora) had comprehensively rejected the claims of the Messiah, Jesus.

Paul and others had been "sent" to "preach" to the people of Israel (Rom 10:14-15). There had been little response:

> But they have not all obeyed the gospel; for Isaiah says, "Lord, who has believed what he has heard from us?" . . . But I ask, have they not heard? Indeed they have; for "Their voice has gone out to all the earth, and their words to the ends of the world." Again I ask, did Israel not understand? First Moses says, "I will make you jealous of those who are not a nation; with a foolish nation I will make you angry." Then Isaiah is so bold as to say, "I have been found by those who did not seek me; I have shown myself to those who did not ask for me." But of Israel he says, "All day long I have held out my hands to a disobedient and contrary people." (Rom 10:16-21)

Paul refers to this rejection as the "mystery" of "a hardening [that] has come upon part of Israel, until the full number of the Gentiles come in" (Rom 11:25; cf. 11:7 — "the rest [of Israel, apart from the elect] were

15. Josephus, *Ant* 20.97-99.

hardened"). This is no passing observation, but a direct appeal to scriptural fulfillment. God had sent Isaiah to "make the heart of this people fat, / and their ears heavy, / and [to] shut their eyes" until they are reduced to a tiny "stump" (Isa 6:9-13). Paul cites that very oracle (which he combines with Deut 29:4 LXX — "God gave them a spirit of stupor") to establish that God is now fulfilling the promise of his "hardening" upon Israel.[16]

This in turn gave Paul the signal that the moment had arrived for the "coming in" of the Gentiles (Rom 11:25), an idea that picks up Jesus' own references to people "coming into" the kingdom of God or "coming into" life (see, e.g., Mark 9:43, 45, 47; 10:15, 23-25; Matt 5:20; 7:13-14, 21; 18:3; 19:17; John 3:5). Paul doubtless also saw the fulfillment of many prophetic oracles promising the nations' "coming" to Jerusalem, for example: "For I know their works and their thoughts, and I am coming to gather all nations and tongues; and they shall *come* and shall see my glory" (Isa 66:18; see also 60:3-7, 14), and "Many peoples and strong nations shall *come* to seek the LORD of hosts in Jerusalem, and to entreat the favor of the LORD" (Zech 8:22; see also 8:20).

In short, it was against this political, apocalyptic, and prophetic background and under the conviction that God had "hardened" Israel that Paul decided to leave Syria-Cilicia and strike out toward Rome,[17] bringing the message of Jesus the Messiah and his impending return in salvation and judgment (1 Thess 1:10; 4:13–5:11; 2 Thess 1:9; 2:1-12; 1 Cor 7:29; 15:23).

Gathering in the Gentiles

When we reflect on Paul's "glorious" decade of ministry in Anatolia and Greece, we are struck by how different were the patterns of his activity as compared to the prior decade and a half in the Levant. These include his more intentional creation of churches as a means of spreading the gospel

---

16. Other references to the "hardening" of Israel include Mark 6:52 ("For they did not understand about the loaves, but their hearts were hardened"; cf. 8:17); John 12:40 ("[God] has blinded their eyes and hardened their heart"); 2 Cor 3:14 ("But their minds were hardened; for to this day, when they read the old covenant, that same veil remains unlifted"); see K. L. Schmidt and M. A. Schmidt, *TDNT* 5:1025-28.

17. See Riesner, *Paul's Early Period*, 241-56, for argument that Paul followed a travel itinerary foreshadowed in Isa 66:19, and Barnett *BC*, 267-69, for a contrary view.

locally, his use of various traveling coworkers, his employment of envoys between himself and the churches, and his identification of key figures in the churches as exemplars of faith and practice.[18] In short, Paul created a mission, a movement of considerable size and influence. So far as we can tell from the available evidence, Paul did not follow these strategies in his earlier Levantine years.

The greatest and most significant element of this missionary decade, however, was Paul's intentional evangelization of Gentile idolaters.

In the Levantine years Paul appears to have limited his Gentile ministry to Godfearers in the circle of the synagogue.[19] During the mission decade, however, he began gathering Gentile idolaters into the membership of his messianic assemblies *(ekklēsiai)*.

This is evident in his letters to the churches in Anatolia and Greece. Prominent references from Galatians, 1 Thessalonians, and 1 and 2 Corinthians clearly establish that significant numbers of former idol-worshiping, temple-attending Gentiles had come to belong to the Pauline mission churches.

> Formerly, when you did not know God, you were in bondage to *beings that by nature are no gods (theoi);* but now that you have come to know God, or rather to be known by God, how can you turn back again to *the weak and beggarly elemental spirits (stoicheia),* whose slaves you want to be once more? You observe days, and months, and seasons, and years! I am afraid I have labored over you in vain. (Gal 4:8-11; cf. 5:20 — "idolatry"/*eidōlolatria*)

> For not only has the word of the Lord sounded forth from you in Macedonia and Achaia, but your faith in God has gone forth everywhere, so that we need not say anything. For they themselves report concerning us what a welcome we had among you, and how you turned to God from *idols (eidōla),* to serve a living and true God, and to wait for his Son from heaven, whom he raised from the dead, Jesus who delivers us from the wrath to come. (1 Thess 1:8-10)

---

18. See, respectively, classical studies by E. E. Ellis, "Paul and His Co-Workers," in Ellis, *Prophecy and Hermeneutic in Early Christianity,* WUNT 1/18 (Tübingen: Mohr, 1978), 3-22; M. M. Mitchell, "New Testament Envoys in the Context of Greco-Roman Diplomatic and Epistolary Conventions: The Example of Timothy and Titus," *JBL* 111 (1992): 641-62.

19. See earlier, chapter 6.

Therefore, my beloved, shun the *worship of idols (eidōlolatria).* (1 Cor 10:1; cf. 1 Cor 8–10 passim)

What agreement has the temple of God with *idols (eidōla)?* . . . Therefore come out from them, and be separate. (2 Cor 6:16, 17)

In short, the documents of Paul from the missionary decade reveal that he gathered into his churches significant numbers of idol worshipers as well as those Godfearers who had already left the temples to join the synagogues.

The decade from 47 to 57 represented a "paradigm shift" for Paul's approach to the Gentiles. Whereas during the Levantine years Paul appears to have preached mainly in the synagogues with ancillary ministry to Godfearers, the next decade saw Paul shifting his emphasis from the synagogues to new "synagogues" (called "churches") whose members were now predominantly *Gentiles.*

This new emphasis, in turn, provoked a new reaction from the Jewish Christian mission based in Jerusalem.

The Jewish Mission in Jerusalem

Both Galatians and the book of Acts reveal three main viewpoints within the Jewish mission in Jerusalem regarding Paul's ingathering of Gentiles.[20]

First, Peter's baptism of Godfearers in Caesarea (based on the revelation in Joppa and the Spirit-inspired tongues speaking in Caesarea) indicated his openness in the late 30s to the incorporation of Gentiles on a *circumcision-free* basis (Acts 10:9-16, 45; 11:4-18; 15:7-11; Gal 2:14).

Secondly, at the other extremity were "those of the circumcision" (*hoi ek peritomēs* — Acts 10:45; 11:2), who insisted on the circumcision of Gentile believers. The context shows that these were not merely Jews, but *believing* Jews who belonged to the church in Jerusalem. Most likely those

---

20. The identity and mission(s) of the opponents of Paul have generated considerable interest and difference of opinion. For critical reviews see E. E. Ellis, "Paul and His Opponents," in *Christianity, Judaism, and Other Greco-Roman Cults,* ed. J. Neusner, Festschrift for Morton Smith (Leiden: Brill, 1975), 264-98; or, more briefly, S. J. Hafemann, "Paul and His Interpreters," in *Dictionary of Paul and His Letters,* ed. G. F. Hawthorne et al. (Downers Grove, Ill.: InterVarsity, 1993), 666-71, who concluded that the issue was "deadlocked." The position taken in the pages following is broadly in line with Ellis's viewpoint.

who came later to Antioch circa 49 were from the same group. They said, "Unless you are circumcised according to the custom of Moses, you cannot be saved" (15:2).

Luke further reveals them to be "believers who belonged *to the party of the Pharisees*" (Acts 15:5). They likely sustained some kind of overlapping membership in the Jerusalem church and the Pharisaic enclaves. So far from being a splinter group, however, "those of the circumcision" were the majority within the Jewish church in Jerusalem. The deepening crisis of the Roman occupation in the 40s and 50s likely drove many Jews to a more conservative expression of Judaism, including *believing* Jews. By the late 50s the elders of the Jerusalem church were able to point Paul to "many thousands . . . among the Jews . . . who have believed; they are all *zealous for the law*" (21:20).

Our sources do not reveal the names of the leaders of this potent faction; they remain nameless and faceless. They did, however, bring considerable pressure to bear on the known leaders of the Jewish mission in Jerusalem. They were unsuccessful in overturning the baptism of the Godfearers in Caesarea in the late 30s (Acts 11:16-18) and in their demands for the circumcision of Titus circa 47 (Gal 2:3-5). In Antioch circa 49, however, they did force Peter, Barnabas, and the Jewish believers to separate from Paul and the Gentile believers (Gal 2:11-15).

Thirdly, James, leader of the Jerusalem church from the time of Peter's flight from King Herod Agrippa I in the early 40s (Acts 12:17), was more conservative than Peter but less extreme than "those of the circumcision." After Peter and John and other apostles left Jerusalem during the 50s, James appears to have been surrounded by conservative forces within the Jewish mission.

James's relative moderation on the circumcision issue was reflected in his disavowal of his envoys' circumcision demands in Antioch (Acts 15:24; cf. 15:1; Gal 2:11-12) and his pronouncement not to require circumcision from Gentiles "who turn to God" (Acts 15:19, 28). James's concern, rather, was that Gentile believers should not offend Jews (including those outside the churches) by eating food sacrificed to idols, by unchastity, and by eating nonkosher meat (15:20, 29). Paul delivered these decisions to the churches of Syria and Cilicia and of Lycaonia and Pisidia (15:30, 40; 16:5). Pointedly, however, Paul did not impose James's decisions (on food sacrificed to idols) on later mission churches (see 1 Cor 10:27-28).

The Countermission

The countermissionaries attacked Paul's circumcision-free policy toward Gentile believers in two ways: firstly, by direct visits to Pauline churches (to Galatia, Antioch, Corinth, and Philippi), and secondly, through local agitators influenced by the worldwide network connections from Jerusalem (in Colossae [?] and Rome).

Traveling Countermissionaries

In Galatia

The churches in Galatia were being "troubled" circa 48 by a group of Jews led by an unidentified individual (Gal 5:10, 12; 3:1; 1:6) who told the churches that unless Gentile members were circumcised, they were not "children of Abraham," not members of the "Israel of God" (3:6-14; 6:16). These "agitators" were putting pressure on their fellow Jews within the churches to compel Gentile believers to submit to circumcision (6:12).

Who were these Jews who penetrated the churches of Galatia and where did they come from? It is almost certain that they came from Jerusalem and were "those of the circumcision" (cf. 2:12; 4:25). Paul was responding to a skewed portrayal of himself that could not have been known in Galatia and that most likely came from Jerusalem. Their line on Paul appears to have been that he had no authority in his own right but was entirely subject to the authority of the Jerusalem apostles (1:1, 11-12, 18-19; 2:1, 7-9, 11). Moreover, he was a mere man-pleaser, practicing circumcision when convenient, failing to do so at other times (1:10; 5:11). This information must have been close enough to the raw facts that Paul felt compelled to correct it. These unidentified "agitators" appear to have come to Galatia from Jerusalem.

In Antioch

Both Paul and Luke explicitly state that those who insisted that Gentile believers must be circumcised circa 49 came from Jerusalem (Gal 2:12; Acts 15:1, 5).

Around 49, after Paul's return from his missionary tour to Pisidia and Lycaonia (southern Galatia), a very serious incident occurred in Antioch.[21] Some men from Jerusalem representing James[22] demanded that Jews withdraw from table fellowship with Gentile believers.[23]

> But when Cephas came to Antioch I opposed him to his face, because he stood condemned. For before certain men came from James, he ate with the Gentiles; but when they came he drew back and separated himself, fearing the circumcision party. And with him the rest of the Jews acted insincerely, so that even Barnabas was carried away by their insincerity. But when I saw that they were not straightforward about the truth of the gospel, I said to Cephas before them all, "If you, though a Jew, live like a Gentile and not like a Jew, how can you compel the Gentiles to live like Jews?" (Gal 2:11-14)

This was the most serious crisis in the history of early Christianity to date, since it potentially spelled the end of Paul's mission to the Gentiles on a circumcision-free basis. James's demand, in effect, was that Gentile believers must become Jews (by means of circumcision) to be acceptable to God as true members of the covenant.

Paul accused Peter of hypocrisy (because he had earlier entered the house of the Gentile Cornelius and eaten there?) and of failure to understand that even Jews like himself were "justified by Christ" and not by "works of the law" (like circumcision — Gal 2:15-17). Paul insisted that both Jews and Gentiles find common table fellowship only on the single

21. I follow the chronology that locates the "incident in Antioch" as prior to and the reason for the Jerusalem Council that was held soon afterward.

22. For discussion of James's role and influence beyond Jerusalem, see M. Bockmuehl, "Antioch and James the Just," in *James the Just and Christian Origins*, ed. B. Chilton and C. A. Evans (Leiden: Brill, 1999), 155-98.

23. We know from other sources that Jews would not eat with Gentiles. The much-traveled Philostratus, the biographer of the wonderworker Apollonius of Tyana, commented on the distinctiveness of the Jews. "For the Jews have long been in revolt not only against the Romans but against humanity; and a race that has made its own a life apart and irreconcilable, that cannot share with the rest of mankind the pleasures of the table nor join in their libations or sacrifices" (*Life of Apollonius* 5.33). The historian Tacitus, a former senator and consul in Rome who became proconsul of Asia early in the second century, had extensive opportunities to observe their behavior in a province where there were large concentrations of Jews. "[T]he Jews . . . sit apart at meals, and they sleep apart. . . . They adopted circumcision to distinguish themselves from other people by this difference. Those who are converted to their ways follow the same practice" (*Histories* 5.5).

basis of a common participation in "righteousness of God" in the Messiah crucified and raised up.[24]

Peter and Barnabas and the whole group of Jewish believers in Antioch effectively opposed Paul's circumcision-free gospel message to Gentiles (which he calls "the truth of the gospel" — Gal 2:3, 14), which he had been proclaiming throughout the sixteen or so years since the Damascus event, and threatened to overthrow the grace-based character of his preaching to the uncircumcised.

The "incident at Antioch" calls for an explanation. What had happened between the meeting in Jerusalem in about 47 (Gal 2:1-10) and the meeting in Antioch (Gal 2:11-14) not more than two years later that brought about such a dramatic change of attitude (by James, Peter, and Barnabas) over the circumcision issue? Two comments may be offered.

We note, first, that in the intervening period Paul had engaged in an intentional mission *journey* (to Cyprus, Pisidia, and Lycaonia) in which he had assumed leadership by reversal of roles with Barnabas (who came to Antioch representing the church of Jerusalem). Furthermore, during that mission journey Paul was not content merely to secure the support of synagogue-based Godfearers, but actually went to idolaters, rank outsiders among the Gentiles.

Second, it is significant that the impetus for the crisis in Antioch came from Jerusalem, initiated by James.[25] Here we must take account of

---

24. Most likely Luke also refers to this incident, though in different terms: "Some men came down from Judea and were teaching the brethren, 'Unless you are circumcised according to the custom of Moses, you cannot be saved.' And . . . Paul and Barnabas had no small dissension and debate with them" (Acts 15:1-2). In common with Paul's own account, Luke identifies the circumcision of Gentiles as the heart of the dispute. Luke, however, portrays Barnabas as siding with Paul, whereas Paul himself states that Barnabas was "carried along" by the "hypocrisy" of "those of the circumcision [party]." Furthermore, the book of Acts makes no reference to Peter's "insincerity" that led the Jews to follow his example to "withdraw" and "separate" themselves from table fellowship with Gentiles. Clearly, there are differences between these two versions, as well as similarities. Did Paul overdramatize a crisis that was perhaps only temporary in duration or sectional in its effects? Alternatively, did Luke place so much emphasis on the resulting meeting in Jerusalem that the situation in Antioch was effectively diminished in the flow of the narrative? While from this historical distance any explanation must be tentative, it does appear that greater weight should be given to Paul's version since it was written closer to the events and, moreover, subject to scrutiny and criticism by Paul's opponents.

25. See, however, Acts 15:24, where James distances himself from those who went to Antioch.

the escalating problems in Judea after the death of Herod Agrippa I in 44 and the Roman reoccupation of the province.[26] These external circumstances likely intensified religious nationalism in Judea that in turn provoked the conservative wing of the Jerusalem church to bring pressure upon James. This likely explains the dramatic change of attitude from two years earlier.

26. Under Claudius (41-54) governors were no longer "prefects" (with a primary military role) but "procurators" (with a primary fiscal role). This implied a new tax-raising priority for these governors, a major source of tension since its controversial institution in A.D. 6 (cf. Mark 12:13-17 par.), which in any case provided further opportunity for rampant extortion and corruption by the tax gatherers. (Tiberius likened his provincial governors to bloodsucking flies — Josephus, *Ant* 18.17-178.)

The procurators whose administration coincided with the Jerusalem leaders' increasingly hard line on circumcision around 49 were Tiberius Alexander (46-48) and Ventidius Cumanus (48-52), each of whom provoked major problems.

Tiberius Julius Alexander (Josephus, *JW* 2.220, 223; *Ant* 20.100, 102-103) was from a prominent Jewish family in Alexandria (and a nephew of Philo); however, he had abandoned his faith. Josephus sends mixed messages about Tiberius Alexander. On one hand, he comments that "by abstaining from all interference with the customs of the country he kept the nation at peace" (*JW* 2.220), while on the other he reports that the procurator hunted down and crucified the sons of Judas the Galilean, the patriot who led the uprising over the imposition of the Roman tax in A.D. 6-7 (*Ant* 20.102). Perhaps Josephus praises him because he was a highborn Jew who advanced to further greatness after leaving Judea, when he became in turn prefect of Egypt and, later, Titus's chief of staff in the siege of Jerusalem. Josephus, himself a highborn Jew who also enjoyed imperial patronage, is likely to have portrayed Tiberius Alexander in a favorable light.

It is possible that the rule of Tiberius Alexander, an apostate Jew, raised doubts that Paul's opposition to Gentile circumcision meant that he too was an apostate, if the truth were known.

The dire famine that afflicted the entire eastern Mediterranean struck during the rule of Tiberius Alexander, bringing an increase of banditry and general lawlessness.

Ventidius Cumanus, by contrast with his illustrious predecessor, was typical of the undistinguished and mediocre administrators the Romans sent to this troublesome province. Cumanus emerges from the sources as one of the worst of an appalling series of governors in the "Second Procuratorial Period" (44-66). Eventually the inept and corrupt Cumanus was recalled in disgrace, but not before Jewish scruples were repeatedly violated and many Jewish lives were lost. Cumanus appears to have brought trouble to Jerusalem from the time of his arrival. His tenure is known to have provoked resurgent religious nationalism.

Was it in this worrying time in Judea under Tiberius Alexander and Ventidius Cumanus that Paul's anticircumcision policies in the Diaspora began to be called into question by conservative, nationalistically minded members of the Jerusalem church? Believers in Judea were not insulated from the events in the wider world.

In Corinth

A measure of the earnestness of the countermission of these members of the Jerusalem church is that they were prepared to travel circa 55 as far as Corinth. It is, of course, an inference that they had come from Jerusalem, though a reasonable one.[27]

Several details are clear enough. First, they were Jews who had "come" to Corinth, trespassed into Paul's "field" there, and bore letters of recommendation from outside authorities (2 Cor 11:22; 11:4; 10:13-15; 3:1-2). Secondly, they were missionaries who "preach [another] Jesus," declaring themselves to be "apostles" and "ministers" of Christ (11:4, 12-13). Thirdly, they were contending that the old covenant (of Moses) based on "letter"[28] (i.e., law — cf. Rom 7:6) was still current and applicable. Fourthly, Paul's dispute with them was based on his assertion that the now-abrogated Mosaic covenant issued in condemnation, whereas Christ, who fulfilled the "promises of God" (2 Cor 1:20), was the only means to the "righteousness of God" (3:9; 5:21; cf. 11:15).

In short, these countermissionaries from the extreme wing of the Jewish mission in Jerusalem were so opposed to Paul's law-free (circumcision-free?) message to Gentiles that they were prepared to travel as far as he did to modify or even overturn his teachings.

Like Paul, they were Pharisaic in theological orientation (cf. Acts 15:5; Gal 1:13-14). This helps explain why key argumentative passages in Galatians and 2 Corinthians are so densely scriptural. It appears that the opponents have their scriptural texts, which Paul rebuts with his own interpretation of those texts. In Galatians 3:6-14 the countermissionaries are likely appealing to Genesis 17:10-13 ("Every male among you shall be circumcised. . . . So shall my covenant be . . . an everlasting covenant"), whereas Paul is replying with Genesis 15:6 ("[Abraham] believed the LORD; and he reckoned it to him as righteousness"). In 2 Corinthians 3:7-18 both countermissionaries and Paul appear to be contending for their respective interpretations of Exodus 34:29-35. Clearly, such reconstructions, though plausible, even likely, are conjectural; we hear only Paul speaking.[29] None-

27. See chapter 10.

28. 2 Cor 3:6.

29. For a critique of the various reconstructions of a supposed textual battle between Paul and his opponents in 2 Cor 3, see E. Richard, "Polemics, Old Testament and Theology," *RB* 3 (1981): 340-67.

theless, it is evident that Paul and his opponents are engaged in a theological battle based on their respective use of proof texts, consistent with their common background in Pharisaism.

In Philippi

A majority of scholars agree that Paul wrote Philippians from Rome, most likely circa 60 during his two-year imprisonment.[30] Paul was writing from a situation of conflict in Rome (see below) to one of conflict in Philippi. From whom does this conflict in Philippi arise? Apart from the "opponents" of the persecuted believers in Philippi (Phil 1:27-28), who appear to be Gentile unbelievers, the other references to conflict in Philippi (3:2-3; 3:17-19) point to members of the Jewish Christian countermission who have come to the city.[31]

> Look out for the dogs, look out for the evil-workers, look out for those who mutilate the flesh. For we are the true circumcision, who worship God in spirit, and glory in Christ Jesus, and put no confidence in the flesh. (3:2-3)

> Brethren, join in imitating me, and mark those who so live as you have an example in us. For many, of whom I have often told you and now tell you even with tears, live as enemies of the cross of Christ. Their end is destruction, their god is the belly, and they glory in their shame, with minds set on earthly things. (3:17-19)

Most likely both passages refer to the same people.[32] The intervening verses 4-16 clearly flow from verses 2-3 and spell out the example of Paul that is to be "imitated" in verses 17-19. The entire passage (vv. 2-19) is a coherent entity.

In this, Paul's most trenchant attack on the Jewish Christian countermission, he portrays their members as "dogs" (a Jewish slur on Gentiles) and as "workers of evil" (because they are "enemies of the cross of Christ").

---

30. Schnelle, *Apostle Paul*, 367-69.

31. See P. T. O'Brien, *Commentary on Philippians*, NIGTC (Grand Rapids: Eerdmans, 1991), 26-35, for a review of opinion about the identity of these persons, and for argument that they were "Judaizers" (i.e., members of the Jewish Christian countermission).

32. So also O'Brien, *Commentary on Philippians*, 34.

Why is Paul so passionate? It is because these people are circumcisers[33] who are requiring circumcision of Gentile believers as a necessary basis of "righteousness" (3:9). But this would be a "righteousness . . . based on law" *(dikaiosunēn tēn ek nomou)*, which Paul had been eminently qualified to have (having been "circumcised on the eighth day" — 3:5) and which he now regarded "not as profit but as loss" (3:7).

The "righteousness of God," however, cannot be acquired by "the flesh"/by "circumcision"/"from law" but only "in [the] Spirit"/"in Christ"/ by "means of faith"/by "the cross of Christ." Accordingly, these "mutilators" who require circumcision have made themselves "enemies" of that "cross," since they effectively argue against the adequacy *in itself* of the message of Christ crucified for "righteousness."

Underlying Paul's uncompromising attitude is his own "Damascus" experience when, as he said, "Christ Jesus . . . made me his own" (3:12 — *katelēmphthēn hypo Christou Iēsou*).[34] It was not the mere impact of the Christophany, however, but the revelation to Paul the persecutor of the stark meaning of the cross as a message of love. As a man "in Christ," Paul came to discover a depth of his subservience to sin that he only dimly felt beforehand and, with that, an understanding of the cosmic adequacy of the cross of Christ to meet and more than meet the grim realities of the power of sin and of the evil powers.

In this passage once again we see the demand for circumcision as the central plank of the Jewish Christian countermission against Paul. This demand by the countermissionaries is evident at the beginning of Paul's westward mission circa 47-48 (in the Galatian churches and in Antioch) and at its close circa 60 (in Philippi).

Paul's extreme language in presenting circumcision or the "cross" as stark and absolute alternatives demonstrates that circumcision was as critical in their theology as the cross was in his. For Paul circumcision was no mere detail within a broader raft of halacha that Gentile believers should accept at their discretion for the sake of fellowship with Jews. That perhaps is how we should view James's decree from Jerusalem circa 49 in regards various dietary items. Circumcision, however, was for Paul's opponents *the* salient and nonnegotiable requirement (symbolizing law keeping in the

33. Metaphorically they are "mutilators" where *katatomē* = "mutilation" is a wordplay on *peritomē* = "circumcision."

34. See chapter 5.

broad) that Gentile believers had to fulfill to find righteousness from God and, consequently, to stand alongside Jewish believers in the covenant of Messiah Jesus.

Were these "enemies of the cross" local Jewish believers or, as in the Galatian churches and at Antioch and Corinth, had they traveled to Philippi from elsewhere? On balance, the vigor of Paul's language suggests they were outsiders. They may have traveled all the way from Jerusalem or perhaps from centers closer to Macedonia. We know, for example, that those who came with "letters of recommendation" to Corinth also sought letters of recommendation *from* Corinth (2 Cor 3:1), to perform similar countermissionary work elsewhere. Either way, these circumcisers belonged to a network whose center was located in the conservatives in the church of Jerusalem.

Local Jewish Christian Opposition to Paul

Colossae

Paul had not visited the church in Colossae established by Epaphras, a local evangelist and a "fellow minister" in the Pauline mission.[35] In recent times the church had been exposed to "philosophy and empty deceit" that was "Jewish" in character, as in references to "circumcision," fasting, new moons, "sabbaths," and "angels" (Col 2:8, 11, 13, 16, 18). This Judaism, however, appears to be syncretistic with Gnostic overtones.[36]

The letter does not resolve the question whether the Colossian "heresy" was introduced by itinerant countermissionaries or by means of local influence. It appears that the (likely) syncretized Jewish gnosticism evident in the letter was a local belief that some church members held prior to their baptism and that had seeped back into the church's religious culture. There are no hints within the letter that the Jewish influence evident in Colossae was connected with the Jerusalem-based countermission.

---

35. Col 1:7-8; 4:12; Philem 23. For arguments supporting Pauline authenticity of Colossians, see Appendix D.

36. E.g., implied by "fullness"/*plērōma* — 1:19; 2:9; cf. 1:25; 2:10. For a review of opinion on the nature of the Colossian "philosophy," see P. T. O'Brien, *Colossians, Philemon*, WBC 44 (Waco: Word, 1987), xxxii-xxxviii.

Rome

Evidence in Romans   Paul's letter to the Romans, universally regarded as his most comprehensive statement, was written from Corinth circa 57 at the end of his "glorious" decade. It is almost universally held that Paul understood the circumstances of Roman Christianity and that his letter was directed to that pastoral situation.[37]

Paul is aware of those who accuse him of justifying (even encouraging?) Jewish opposition to his message because of the benefit it brings to Gentiles (Rom 3:8). These critics also claim that he encourages continuance in sin (i.e., a law-free life = a circumcision-free life?), that grace might be "multiplied" (6:1; cf. 6:15). Further, he must answer the inference that he is a renegade Jew holding a kind of "supersessionist" belief that God has now entirely finished with Israel and is concerned only for Paul's mission to Gentiles with an exclusively Gentile church as his end-time intention (9:1-29).

While these critics and objectors are in the shadows of the audience in Rome, they are nonetheless within the fringes of the Christian meetings. Most likely they are the same persons who "cause divisions and put obstacles in your way that are contrary to the teachings you have learned," who "deceive the minds of naïve people" and are to be avoided (16:17-18).

Paul is writing to his known friends in Rome (16:3-16) to "strengthen" them against his opponents in the Jewish-Christian circumcision-based mission who are seeking to capture them. He is not offering his apologia to Jews who are outside the circle of faith, but to those Jewish believers in Rome who may be open to the views of the conservative members of the Jerusalem church.

Evidence in Philippians   As noted above, Philippians reflects situations of conflict both for Paul in Rome and for his readers in Philippi. Whereas it is reasonably straightforward to identify the opposition in Philippi, it is less so in Rome.

Who is opposing Paul in Rome? He refers to those who "preach Christ from envy and rivalry . . . out of partisanship, not sincerely but thinking to afflict me in my imprisonment" (1:15-17) and less trenchantly

---

37. Contra J. Drane, "Why Did Paul Write Romans?" in *Pauline Studies,* ed. D. Hagner and M. Harris, Festschrift for F. F. Bruce (Exeter, Devon: Paternoster, 1980), 209-27.

to those who "look after their own interests, not those of Jesus Christ" (2:21). The "partisanship" (1:17) of the one and the self-interest (2:21) of the other suggest that both texts refer to the same group.

Clearly they are "Christian," since they "preach Christ," but are they Jews or Gentiles? It is possible they are Jewish believers who belong to the same stream of opposition that Paul addresses throughout Romans (in particular in 16:17 — "I appeal to you, brethren, to take note of those who create dissensions and difficulties, in opposition to the doctrine which you have been taught"). In this case they were local Jewish believers who were influenced (from a distance) by conservative members of the Jewish mission in Jerusalem.[38] Paul, their longtime opponent, had finally reached Rome — under house arrest, but facing a trial — and he was vulnerable to their schemes. Perhaps by preaching Christ (in the synagogues?) they envisaged an uproar that would come to the attention of the authorities, to the disadvantage of Paul.

Summary

The combined evidence from Paul's letters written throughout the decade from 47 to 57 and the retrospectively written Acts of the Apostles point to a determined countermission against Paul's westward mission to win Gentiles for Christ *on a circumcision-free basis.* For Paul, to demand circumcision was one and the same thing as to demand Gentiles to submit to the entire burden of the law. This was entirely inimical to Paul, who insisted that access to the "righteousness of God" was through Christ alone (2 Cor 5:21).

The Collection

It is striking that the agreement that Paul should raise a "collection for the saints" (*logeia tēs eis tous hagious* — 1 Cor 16:1) in Judea was made when his westward mission began in about 47 (Gal 2:10) and that he brought the collection to Jerusalem in about 57 when he had completed his Jerusalem-

---

38. Contra O'Brien, *Commentary on Philippians,* 102-5, who reviews various opinions and concludes that Paul is being opposed in Rome out of personal rivalry.

to-Illyricum circuit (Rom 15:25-33). Having "fulfilled the gospel" in the eastern provinces, Paul could have gone directly to Spain, with or without an extensive visit to Rome. He embarked on his intervening journey back to Jerusalem, time-consuming and dangerous as it was, for one reason only — to take the collection and the accompanying Gentile delegates to the Holy City.

Once Paul had decided upon ending his Aegean ministry circa 54, he made arrangements with the churches in the four provinces for the money to be brought to Corinth prior to being taken to Judea (Acts 19:21; cf. 1 Cor 16:5; 2 Cor 1:16; Rom 15:25).

Accordingly he sent Titus to Corinth (2 Cor 8:6, 10; cf. 1 Cor 16:1-4) and, we presume, an envoy to southern Galatia (cf. 1 Cor 16:1), to make arrangements. The Asian churches also participated (Acts 20:4), along with the Macedonians, though on account of their poverty they were not initially invited to do so (2 Cor 8:1-5). After many difficulties, including the sheer magnitude of the task and the Corinthians' discontinuance of their contributions culminating in the revelation in Corinth of a Jewish conspiracy for a shipboard interception of the money, the collection with its impressive body of delegates from the Gentile churches arrived in Jerusalem.

Why was the collection arranged? We must note, first, that it was requested by the "pillars" in Jerusalem in reciprocity for their agreement that Paul should "go" to the Gentiles (Gal 2:9-10). No reason is recorded, only that Paul readily agreed. He and Barnabas had already brought money from Antioch for famine relief in Jerusalem. The request of the "pillars" may have been motivated by merely practical concerns for such further assistance that may have been available arising from Paul's hoped-for harvest of Gentiles through his projected mission.

Initially Paul's agreement may have been along similar lines. It is possible, however, that his thinking evolved during the course of his mission in Anatolia and Greece, especially in the face of the Jerusalem-based countermission that was directed at capturing the churches of his mission. Did Paul reason that the collection would establish bonds between his Gentile churches and the (Jewish) mother church in Jerusalem, to create unity within the new covenant people of God? If Paul was immovable over the countermissionaries' demands for the circumcision of Gentile believers, he was equally unyielding and tenacious in completing the collection, despite the problems.

It may not have been diplomatic to articulate this line of thought. Paul's explanation was rather broader. Paul declared it to be the "debt" the Gentiles owed to the saints of Jerusalem for the "spiritual blessings" that had flowed out from them to the Gentiles (Rom 15:27). As reported in Acts, Paul called these gifts "alms and offerings" that he had brought after some years "to my nation" (Acts 24:17). This resembles Queen Helena's "desire to go to the city of Jerusalem and to worship at the Temple of God . . . and to make thank offerings there."[39] Implied, perhaps, is the underlying motive that the Gentiles sent such gifts to secure a place in the covenant in lieu of circumcision.

Paul was very careful to raise the collection on the basis of "grace." Paul referred to it as a "contribution for the saints" (1 Cor 16:1); a "gift" (2 Cor 9:5); "grace" (2 Cor 8:6, 7, 9; 9:14; cf. 1 Cor 16:3); a "service" (2 Cor 9:12; cf. Rom 15:27); and a fellowship (2 Cor 8:4; 9:13; Rom 15:26). It is likely significant that as Peter expressed his "fellowship" in the gospel for Paul's "going" to the Gentiles (Gal 2:9), so Paul reciprocally created this "fellowship" between the Gentile and Jewish churches by means of the collection.

The rationale stated here is more cogent than some other theories. One such theory is that his strategy embodied his teaching in Romans 9–11, namely, that Jews would be provoked to become believers on account of the ingathering of the Gentiles (Rom 11:14), a view associated with J. Munck. According to this hypothesis, the Gentiles' delivery of the collection to Jerusalem would provoke the conversion of Israel and would be quickly followed by the parousia.[40] Paul, however, would hardly have planned to go to Spain if he had expected the parousia to occur as a result of the coming of these Gentile converts to Jerusalem. Paul makes no explicit connection between the collection for the saints and the bringing of the Gentiles to Jerusalem as an offering to the Lord, whether in 2 Corinthians 8–9 or in Romans 15:15-33.

So far as we can tell, the collection was not successful in fulfilling Paul's hopes. His cool reception from the elders of the Jerusalem church suggests that, initially at least, his hopes for strengthening the fellowship between Jews and Gentiles with consequent recognition of the Gentile churches were not realized (Acts 21:17-26). James and the Jerusalem elders

---

39. Josephus, *Ant* 20.49.

40. Cf. Isa 2:2-3; 60:5-6; Mic 4:1-2. See R. Aus, "Paul's Travel Plans to Spain and the 'Full Number of the Gentiles' of Rom 11:25," *NovT* 21 (1979): 232-62.

made it clear that they didn't need any help from Paul or his Gentiles for the conversion of Israel! Moreover, there was an implied criticism of Paul for encouraging the collapse of religious culture among Jews in the Diaspora (Acts 21:20-24). To be sure, the elders confirmed the Jerusalem decree of a decade earlier setting out requirements for the inclusion of the Gentiles that, however, Paul must continue to uphold. They appear to be implying that Paul has failed also in this. In short, they are unimpressed with Paul's Gentile companions and their money! In their eyes Paul has succeeded only in alienating the Jewish community from himself and therefore from them! Let him demonstrate his genuineness as a Jew in a public act in the temple, the payment for purifying four men who had taken a Nazirite vow. Paul's submission to their request was to have disastrous consequences for him; he would be imprisoned for the next five years, first in Caesarea Maritima and then in Rome.

Conclusion

At the time Paul wrote Romans he looked back on about twenty-five years during which he had "fulfilled the Gospel from Jerusalem and as far round as Illyricum" (Rom 15:19). Paul counted his decade and a half as a nonitinerant in the Levant as part of that grand sweep. Luke, however, gave Paul's earlier phase only passing scattered reference in Acts, whereas he devoted full and exclusive attention to the decade from about 47 to 57 in Acts 13–20.

While Paul's and Luke's perspectives are each valid, the latter's must be given greater priority. During that "glorious" decade Paul, in a burst of energy, established churches over a vast area and wrote as many as nine (extant) letters, including his longest and most important letters. It is no overstatement to claim that Paul changed the course of world history during those few years.

As to what prompted Paul to break free from his relative obscurity in Syria-Cilicia, we may only speculate. There were likely several interlocking factors, including a heightened apocalypticism in Judea, the new stability in the empire under Claudius, and Paul's sense that the coinciding realities of the "hardening" of Israel and the beginnings of Gentile inclusion (in Antioch) were the divine signal for him to begin his westward, Rome-ward missions.

From the beginnings of his new missionary thrust Paul adopted new approaches. He established churches in rapid succession as a means of spreading the gospel locally; he drew others into partnership with him as traveling coworkers and as envoys; he pioneered letter writing as a means of instructing his churches in absentia. By far the most significant difference, however, was his deliberate outreach to rank pagans, idol-worshiping, temple-attending Gentiles. Soon his churches were mainly composed of such Gentiles as well, no doubt, as synagogue-connected Godfearers (his primary interest in the Levantine years).

While Paul received a mandate from the "pillars" of the Jerusalem church for this thrust into the Gentile world, there were many (a majority?) of the Jerusalem church who opposed Paul's insistence that Gentile believers not be required to submit to (male) circumcision. It appears, then, that from the beginning of Paul's new mission, a countermission arose that was dedicated to circumcising (male) Gentile believers. So convinced were these Jerusalem-based Christian Jewish countermissionaries that they were prepared to travel to southern Galatia, Antioch, Corinth, and Philippi to preach their message and to secure the circumcision of Gentiles. Even in distant Rome the influence of this doctrine was being felt even though the countermissionaries had not actually come to the city.

While the conversion of idolaters brought with it large theological and moral concerns (see, e.g., 1 Corinthians), we may say with confidence that the circumcision mission of Jerusalem-based Jewish believers (whom Paul calls "false brothers") was the greatest challenge he faced during that decade. In response, however, he wrote such major texts as Galatians, 2 Corinthians, [Ephesians], Romans, and Philippians in which he contended for a grace-based, law-free, Christ-centered, Spirit-empowered theology and praxis.

If during this "glorious" decade Paul's travels brought Christianity to Europe, and consequently to the world, his letters responding to the circumcision mission articulated the doctrines of grace that inspired the Protestant Reformation centuries later.

Broadly coinciding with this westward Gentile-directed mission was Paul's agreement with the Jerusalem "pillars" to raise money among the Gentiles for the "poor" in Judea.

This may have been proposed (by the "pillars") and agreed to initially circa 47 (by Barnabas and Paul) to relieve Jews affected by the famine. By the time Paul came to implement the collection in the mid-50s, he may have embraced a rather different rationale. It is plausible to suggest that Paul saw a comprehensive gift from all the churches of his Gentile mission as an instrument of unity between the disparate Jewish and Gentile missions. By that reasoning, the collection (based on the arguments of grace) was to secure unity within the new covenant people of the Messiah. The collection for the Jewish mission from the Gentile mission may have been Paul's attempt to answer and neutralize the campaigns of the circumcision faction in the Jerusalem church.

TEN

Conflict in Corinth (ca. 54-56):
Paul, a Christ-Shaped Emissary

Have you been thinking all along that we have been defending ourselves before you?

2 Corinthians 12:19

It is evident from his letters that Paul was sometimes under criticism from within the churches he founded[1] and that his reason for writing to them (in part, at least) was to defend himself from those criticisms.[2] Nowhere is this more evident than in Paul's relationship with the troublesome Corinthian church that he visited twice after its initial foundation and to which he wrote no fewer than four letters (two of them lost to us).

This apologetic element is present in 1 Corinthians, but it is dominant in Paul's Second Letter to the Corinthians, much of which is devoted to his self-defense. The apologetic element in 2 Corinthians is without par-

---

1. We note (implied) apologetic elements also (a) in Galatians, where Paul was accused of preaching "man's gospel" (1:11-13), of not telling the truth (4:16; cf. 5:7-10), and of inconsistently "still" preaching circumcision (5:11); (b) in 1 Corinthians, where Paul answers criticism that as an apostle he should have accepted payment (9:3-18); (c) in Romans, where Paul responds to the Jewish-Christian (2:3; 16:17-19) opponents' accusations of antinomianism (6:15) and of teaching that God opportunistically does the evil of rejecting Israel for the good outcome of saving Gentiles (3:8; cf. 9:6; 11:1). Clearly Paul faced many questions and considerable opposition in his churches, most of it originating from fellow Jewish believers.

2. See P. W. Barnett, "Paul, Apologist to the Corinthians," in *Paul and the Corinthians,* ed. T. J. Burke and J. K. Elliott, Festschrift for Margaret Thrall (Leiden: Brill, 2003), 313-26.

allel in the Pauline corpus and appears to have been necessitated by an extremity of criticism and opposition. In this chapter our chief focus will be on the second letter, though we must also give prior consideration to the first letter.

Paul and the Corinthians

Paul wrote 2 Corinthians (ca. 56) about six years after he established the church. In the meantime he had written three letters,[3] dispatched his envoys Timothy and Titus to sort out problems,[4] and come himself on an emergency visit (2 Cor 2:1-3; 13:1-2). Clearly these relationships were turbulent, to say the least!

2 Corinthians is a complex letter whose edgy tones and uneven structure likely correspond with a passionate mutual lack of trust between author and readers. It comes as no surprise that many believe it to have been a later compilation of various earlier fragmentary epistles, though this writer contends for the unity of the letter.[5]

Sources of Their Criticism

It is not easy from Paul's text to identify precisely the Corinthians' criticisms of him, not least since they were themselves divided by factional loyalties (1 Cor 1:10-12; 3:3-4, 21; 4:6) and the Jew-Gentile (1 Cor 1:24; 12:13) cultural and religious chasm within the church. Various criticisms issued from differing sections of the congregation. Furthermore, we must attempt to distinguish between the criticisms of well-established "insiders" and the outright opposition of newly arrived "outsiders" (addressed indirectly in Paul's "Fool's Speech" — 2 Cor 11:1–12:13).

Broadly speaking, however, the criticisms of Paul arose from three

3. Paul wrote four letters to the Corinthians: the "previous letter" (1 Cor 5:9); 1 Corinthians; the "severe letter" (2 Cor 2:1-4; 7:8-13); 2 Corinthians.

4. Timothy (1 Cor 4:17; 16:10), Titus (2 Cor 2:13; 7:6, 13; 8:6, 16-17, 23; 12:18).

5. Present discussion of 2 Corinthians is based on the unity of the extant letter, a view not universally held. See, e.g., P. Barnett, *The Second Epistle to the Corinthians* (Grand Rapids: Eerdmans, 1997), 15-25; contra M. E. Thrall, *II Corinthians,* ICC (Edinburgh: T. & T. Clark, 1994), 3-49.

sources: (i) those influenced by the Greco-Roman religious environment in Corinth, (ii) Paul's own practices, and (iii) influential Jewish-Christian visitors to the city during Paul's absences (including the countermissionaries referred to in 2 Corinthians as "false apostles").

Corinth's Greco-Roman Religious Environment

Gentile idolaters baptized as believers brought vestiges of their powerful religious culture into the messianic assembly in Corinth. At several points in 1 Corinthians Paul addresses ideas and practices from the Greco-Roman world that were inimical to the apostolic faith.

Prominent among these was a disbelief in a cosmic resurrection of the dead. For Jewish believers the anticipation of a general resurrection and the accompanying end-time judgment presented few difficulties since this was part of their eschatological universe. For Gentile converts, however, a world resurrection was nonsense, as reflected in Paul's question to the Corinthians, "How can some of you say that there is no resurrection of the dead?" (1 Cor 15:12).

N. T. Wright has conducted an exhaustive survey of beliefs about the resurrection among the Greeks of that era. His conclusion is as follows: "In so far as the ancient non-Jewish world had a Bible, its Old Testament was Homer. And in so far as Homer had anything to say about resurrection, he was quite blunt: it doesn't happen."[6] Such skepticism likely inspired the Corinthian disbelief, and also the Athenians' mockery of Paul's preaching of the resurrection as narrated in the book of Acts (Acts 17:32).

No less important than disbelief in the resurrection were the two Greco-Roman practices from which Paul exhorts his readers to "flee" — *porneia* (extramarital sexual practices; 1 Cor 6:18) and *eidolatria*[7] (worshiping in pagan temples). 1 Corinthians 8:1–11:1 is devoted to the problem of the believers' interface with Greco-Roman "temple" culture, the vocabulary of which abounds throughout those chapters (idol/*eidōlon* [8:4, 7; 10:19]; meat sacrificed to an idol/*eidōlothutos* [8:1, 4, 7, 10; 10:19]; slain sac-

---

6. N. T. Wright, *The Resurrection of the Son of God* (London: SPCK, 2003), 32. In Aeschylus's *Eumenides* Apollo observes, "Once a man has died and the dust has soaked up his blood, there is no resurrection" (*outis est' anastasis* — *Eumenides* 647).

7. 1 Cor 10:14. B. Rosner, "The Structure and Argument of 1 Corinthians: A Biblical/Jewish Approach," *NTS* 52, no. 2 (2006): 205-18, argues that the text of 1 Corinthians was arranged structurally around Paul's twofold injunction to "flee" from these practices.

rifice/*hierothutos* [10:28]; temple containing an idol/*eidōleion* [8:10]; worship of an idol/*eidōlolatria* [10:14]). It is widely and no doubt correctly believed that *porneia* occurred within the temple precincts and as an accompaniment of the practice of *eidōlatria*.[8]

These twin evils were deeply embedded within Greco-Roman culture. Not long after Paul first left Corinth, it was necessary for him (in the now-lost "previous letter") to enjoin the Corinthians not to associate with fellow believers who were *pornoi*/sexually immoral (1 Cor 5:9, 11). Those concerns also dominate 1 Corinthians (5:1–11:1 passim). Paul's second, emergency ("painful") visit to the city and his follow-up "severe letter" were likely necessitated by related matters (2 Cor 2:1-11; 7:8-12; 10:1-11; 12:20–13:4). Likewise, in 2 Corinthians his powerful call to separation from pagan shrines indicates the tenacious power of the temple culture in the lives of the new believers (6:14–7:1).

While there is some evidence of local criticism against Paul in 1 Corinthians (e.g., 4:8-21), this seems to have increased dramatically after Timothy's follow-up visit. Paul's "second" visit was "painful" (2 Cor 2:1-2; 12:20–13:2), and his next letter was written "with many tears" and brought grief to the Corinthians (2:4).

Paul's Own Practices

Paul's practices and behavior rankled the Corinthians at a number of points and necessitated his self-defense. One sore point was his refusal to accept payment for his teaching. While he endorsed the dominical mandate that other traveling apostles had the "right" to be given food and drink, Paul himself steadfastly refused to receive payment from the church in Corinth (1 Cor 9:3-18; 2 Cor 11:7-12). In status-conscious Corinth, wealthy patrons expected to provide generous gifts to traveling rhetoricians, which they expected to be gladly received.[9] Paul's stubborn resistance against this convention must have struck the Corinthians as eccentric at best and proudly superior at worst.

The other matter related to money concerned the collection Paul es-

8. See B. S. Rosner, "Temple Prostitution in 1 Corinthians 6:12-20," *NovT* 60 (1998): 336-51.

9. See J. K. Chow, *Patronage and Power*, JSNTSS 75 (Sheffield: Sheffield Academic, 1992), 107-12 and 130-41; T. Savage, *Power through Weakness: Paul's Understanding of the Ministry in 2 Corinthians*, SNTSMS 86 (Cambridge: Cambridge University Press, 1996).

tablished in the churches of his mission for the benefit of the saints in Judea (Rom 15:25-33; 1 Cor 16:1-4; 2 Cor 8:1–9:15; Gal 2:10; 6:7-10; Acts 24:17; see chapter 9 above). Prior to the writing of 1 Corinthians, Paul's envoy Titus had initiated the Corinthians' "contribution *(logeia)* for the saints" in Jerusalem (1 Cor 16:1; 2 Cor 8:6, 10). Their letter to Paul sought clarification, which he provided *(peri de* — 1 Cor 16:1; cf. 7:1). The disciplinary problems demanding his "painful visit" and its corollary, the "severe letter," had, so it appears, halted the Corinthians' weekly "contributions," necessitating Paul's pastoral sermon in 2 Corinthians 8–9.

A second area of disagreement (or, more likely, misunderstanding) was Paul's policy and practice of church discipline. As a Roman city, Corinth was subject to the coercive justice of the local praetors and other officials. Magistrates in Roman cities had a free hand in the exercise of *coercitio* (summary correction or chastisement). Paul himself knew the force of Roman punishment ("Three times I have been beaten with rods" — 2 Cor 11:25). Jews were also used to severe physical punishment that was administered in the synagogue, as Paul knew to his personal cost ("Five times I have received at the hands of the Jews the forty lashes less one" — 2 Cor 11:24). Paul's discipline of the morally wayward, however, differed markedly from both Roman and Jewish practice. To be sure, it involved "due process" with some kind of a trial procedure (1 Cor 5:3-5; 2 Cor 13:1-2). The punishment of the guilty, however, meant no more than admonition, the expression of profound sorrow, and ultimately, in the absence of genuine repentance, exclusion.

When Paul came in his second visit to discipline the offender where the outcome was inconclusive, the Corinthians regarded him as irresolute and weak. His "severe letter," written later from Ephesus, which did provoke repentance, served only to confirm their worst opinion about him, that "his letters are weighty and strong, but his bodily presence is weak, and his speech [is] of no account" (2 Cor 10:10; cf. 10:2-9; 13:1-4). The Corinthians judged Paul by the disciplinary standards of Romans, on one hand, and of Jews on the other, and found only disappointment in him based on those comparisons.

A third area of criticism was their perception of his duplicity. Paul had to defend himself from two charges in 2 Corinthians. The first was that he broke his promise of an immediate return visit following the "painful visit," and compounded his sin by sending the "severe letter" instead (2 Cor 1:15-17; 1:23–2:4; 10:10). Accordingly they accused him of acting out of "fleshly wisdom" *(en sophia sarkikē* — 1:12; cf. "making his plans *kata sarka*" — 1:17) so that he did not even know his own mind (saying yes and no at the same time — 1:18).

Their second charge was that he acted "craftily" (*peripatountes en panourgia* — 4:2; *hyparchōn panourgos dolō* — 12:16). Most likely they had come to believe that his refusal to be paid ("be a burden" — 12:16) was a ruse, to gain some kind of moral leverage. His question ("Did I take advantage of you *through* any of those whom I sent to you?" — 12:17) suggests that they believed their payment to Titus ended up in Paul's pocket anyway.

How does Paul respond to these Corinthian criticisms relating to his policies and actions? We might conclude that he will answer his critics with some kind of straightforward defense, correcting misunderstandings and perhaps apologizing for mistakes. The closest he comes to offering an apology is his expression of "regret" upon sending the "severe letter" (2 Cor 7:8).

Paul, however, does not engage with his churches on the basis of ordinary human relationships. Rather, he views everyone and everything through eschatological and christological eyes, as a man "in Christ."

Thus, to their complaint that he acts out of duplicity, Paul says he does not, but that his good motives will be revealed and vindicated eschatologically, on "the day of the Lord Jesus" (2 Cor 1:12, 14, 23) and "in the sight of God" (1:23; 2:17; 4:2; 12:19; cf. 5:10).

Regarding their complaint about his refusal of payment and his insistence on working, he declares this to be his settled policy, which he will not alter despite pressure to do so from newly arrived opponents who claim apostolic status and who did receive payment (11:7-11). Paul's determination to "abase" himself (by working) that they might be "exalted" (11:7) is overtly christological, echoing his earlier statement that the incarnate Christ impoverished himself to make them rich (8:9). Paul characterizes the whole of his sufferings christologically as one who was "poor" to make "many rich" (6:10).

In a similar vein he defends his practice of church discipline by the example of Christ, that is, "by the meekness and gentleness of Christ" (*prautētos kai epieikeias tou Christou* — 10:1), adding that he is "humble" *(tapeinos)* when present with them. Two of these three words are calculatedly christological, indicating that Paul exercised moral discipline according to the tradition that carried Jesus' words and known character.[10]

---

10. See, e.g., "Blessed are the meek" (*praus* — Matt 5:5); "I am meek and lowly of heart" (*praus eimi kai tapeinos* — 11:29); "your king is coming to you humble" (*praus* — 21:5).

It appears, then, that even in his response to criticisms in mundane matters involving petty grievances and misunderstandings, Paul discloses an inner universe that elsewhere he calls "the mind of Christ" (1 Cor 2:16). We cannot escape the conclusion that Paul saw himself to be in the closest relationship with Christ. This was indeed no remote or distant thing for Paul, who understood that he was "in Christ" and that Christ was "in" him. Paul was "loved" by him, "justified by his blood" but also crucified and risen "in him," and indwelt by him (Gal 2:20; Rom 5:9; 6:4-9). Paul's greatest "gain" was that he "knew" Christ Jesus his Lord, and his deepest passion was to "know" him on the last day (Phil 3:9-10).

Furthermore, Paul did not separate his persona from his ministry. For Paul life and work coalesced "in Christ." His entire ministry, characterized as it was by hardship and suffering, was driven by the "love of Christ" (2 Cor 5:14), that is, by his sense of Christ's love for him expressed in his sacrificial death.

As we shall soon see, Paul the apostle of Christ sought to conform his thinking and behavior according to the example of Christ. Indeed, this will become his major defense to those who dismiss his ministry as inferior and weak.

Jewish-Christian Visitors

Various Jewish-Christian visitors came to Corinth, which by accident or design occurred while Paul was absent from the city. Between Paul's initial foundation of the church (ca. 50-52) and his second visit (ca. 55) the city was visited by Apollos (Acts 18:27; 1 Cor 1–4 passim), "other apostles and the brothers of the Lord and Cephas" (1 Cor 9:5), and perhaps Barnabas (9:6).

We know nothing else about the visits of other apostles and brothers of the Lord (and Barnabas?). Their arrival does not appear to have created problems for Paul's relationship with the church in the Achaian capital. It was otherwise, however, with Apollos and Cephas, who are mentioned as points of loyalty to church factions in Corinth (1:12; 3:5, 21-22; 4:6).

In 1 Corinthians Paul does not say outright that the visitors intentionally created the factions in the church or that the factions were unintended consequences of their ministries. The letter leaves open both possibilities. N. A. Dahl is likely correct, however, in observing that the slogans

"I belong to Apollos" and "I belong to Cephas" (1:12) are to be understood as "declarations of independence from Paul."[11] Paul's appeal in that context is not so much for unity between these parties (and his own) as for unity under his apostolic leadership. It does appear, though, that Paul is rather cool about Cephas's visit (9:5) and less than enthusiastic about the Corinthians' request[12] for a return visit by Apollos (16:12).

Apollos The assertion that Paul was uneasy about Apollos's return to Corinth depends on an accumulation of references in 1 Corinthians.[13] To begin, Paul's reminder that he preached "Christ crucified" (1:23) but not in the "wisdom of speech" (*sophia logou* — 1:17; cf. *peithois sophias logois* — 2:4) is most likely a corrective of the Corinthians' appreciation of Apollos's recent ministry among them.[14] It scarcely needs arguing that rhetoric was highly prized in the cities of the Greco-Roman east.

The precise nature of the Alexandrian Jew's expertise is not known, though the fact of its impact (noted in the book of Acts) is not in doubt (Acts 18:24, 28, *anēr logios . . . dunatos . . . en tais graphais*). From 1 Corinthians 1–4 it may be inferred that Apollos's ministry had the effect of elevating rhetorical preaching among local Corinthian preachers,[15] perhaps in the direction of "Alexandrian" exegesis, as in Philo's allegorical style.[16] Lack of further information, however, leaves us unsure of Apollos's ap-

11. N. A. Dahl, "Paul and the Church in Corinth according to 1 Corinthians 1–4," in *Christian History and Interpretation: Studies Presented to John Knox,* ed. W. R. Farmer et al. (Cambridge: Cambridge University Press, 1967), 322.

12. Most likely *peri de* in 1 Cor 16:12 signals Paul's answer to the Corinthians' request for a return visit from Apollos (contra M. M. Mitchell, "Concerning PERI DE in 1 Corinthians," *NovT* 31 [1989]: 229-56).

13. See D. P. Ker, "Paul and Apollos — Colleagues or Rivals?" *JSNT* 77 (2000): 75-97.

14. According to D. Litfin, *St. Paul's Theology of Proclamation: 1 Corinthians 1–4 and Greco-Roman Rhetoric,* SNTSMS 79 (Cambridge: Cambridge University Press, 1994), the practice of rhetoric was associated with *sophia,* which in the first century was largely "decorative," drawing attention to the speaker (11.109-134).

15. Most likely in 3:10 Paul is referring to local Corinthian preacher(s) rather than Apollos (so D. R. Hall, "A Disguise for the Wise," *NTS* 40 [1994]: 143-49, contra Ker, "Paul and Apollos," 88-89, 92, following M. D. Hooker, "'Beyond the Things That Are Written'? An Examination of 1 Corinthians 4:6," *NTS* 10 [1963]: 127-32).

16. Ker, "Paul and Apollos," 81, warns against overconfidence in identifying too precisely the character of *sophia* rhetoric or of overconfidence about Apollos's background (83). For a list of texts devoted to wisdom, rhetoric, preaching, and the cross, see A. Thiselton, *The First Epistle to the Corinthians,* NIGTC (Grand Rapids: Eerdmans, 2003), 134-35.

proach. At the least, it must be pointed out that there were many Jews in Alexandria besides Philo!

From 1 Corinthians 1–4 it seems that in Paul's mind in recent times the "substance" of the kerygma of the crucified Messiah had been diminished by the "style" of its presentation. The "faith" of the Corinthians was now "rest[ing] . . . in the wisdom of men" (2:5 — *en sophia anthrōpōn*). Equally, it meant that a different "building" was being erected upon Paul's "foundation," which was Christ crucified and risen (3:10-11). An immediate consequence was the devaluing in their eyes of the less fluent Paul.[17]

Furthermore, in 1 Corinthians 3–4 Paul quietly but firmly asserts his primacy over Apollos. True, Apollos is with Paul both "a *sunergos* of God" (3:9) and a *diakonos*[18] "through whom" the Corinthians believed (3:5). Yet, in the agricultural image Paul planted and Apollos fulfilled the subsidiary role of watering (3:6), and in the architectural image Paul is the foundation-layer, with no role attributed to Apollos. More to the point, though the Corinthians may have "countless guides" (including Apollos, presumably), Paul is their sole "father" (4:14-15). In short, Paul is "the planter," "the foundation-layer," and "the father." With great diplomacy Paul manages to relegate Apollos to a subsidiary role while not disaffirming his ministry and thereby bringing continuing division in Corinth.

Nonetheless, Paul's last words about Apollos provide a cautious endorsement of his ministry. Paul calls Apollos "our brother" and mentions him alongside "the other (approved) brothers" (Timothy, Stephanas, Fortunatus, and Achaicus), and indicates that Apollos will indeed come to Corinth, as requested by the Corinthians, but later, at a more convenient time (16:12).

It does not appear that Apollos set out to undermine or compete with Paul. Rather, the problem lies with (some of) the Corinthians who have elevated Apollos above Paul while prompted to move off in unhelpful directions in the prizing of *sophia* rhetoric.

---

17. This was a continuing problem in Corinth, as reflected several years later by Paul in the second canonical letter when he is forced to defend his "knowledge" against his "speech" (11:6 — *ei de kai idiōtēs tō logō, all' ou tē gnōsei*). True, the context of that remark was his perceived lack of effectiveness in disciplining his opponent during the second visit. Nonetheless, it boiled down to the same thing in their eyes, that is, his unimpressive personal presence and his lack of rhetorical power (2 Cor 10:10).

18. According to E. E. Ellis, "Paul and His Co-Workers," *NTS* 17 (1971), "the diakonoi appear to be a special class of co-workers, those who are active in preaching and teaching" (442).

The two men were different, both as to their names and their education. Saul of Tarsus was named after the first king of Israel, and Apollos after a Greek god! Saul was educated in the strict Pharisaic academies in Jerusalem, whereas Apollos of Alexandria, who was an *anēr logios* (Acts 18:24), would have been nurtured in an educational culture that we sense was different without knowing exactly how.[19]

Critical to the problem between them, however, was that Apollos had never been subject to Paul's tutelage. Apollos arrived in Ephesus sometime after Paul's brief visit en route from Corinth to Jerusalem (Acts 18:19-20). By the time Paul arrived back in Ephesus, Apollos had been instructed by Priscilla and Aquila and had moved on to Corinth with the written commendation of the Ephesians (Acts 19:24, 26-28). Paul called Apollos a "brother," yet he was not part of Paul's mission. Most likely he had withdrawn from Corinth sometime earlier and had by now returned to Ephesus. We sense a continuing ministry for Apollos in Ephesus, but parallel with Paul's and not integrated within it (1 Cor 16:12).

Notwithstanding Paul's caution about Apollos, we sense no hostility, or any need by Paul to engage in sustained self-defense. It was otherwise, however, with the other prominent Jewish visitor to Corinth, the apostle Cephas.

Cephas   1 Corinthians 8:1–11:1 is devoted to the problem of the Christian interface with Greco-Roman "temple" culture whose vocabulary abounds throughout these chapters (see earlier in this chapter).

Yet, unexpectedly, in the midst of his instruction Paul digresses, or appears to digress, in 9:1-18 about his "right" *(exousia) not* to exercise his "right" (as an apostle) to be supported financially. To be sure, his exposition about "rights" springs from the use of the word in the previous chapter (8:9) and provides the basis for his implied exhortation to the readers not to stand on their supposed cultural "rights." Yet this tangential discussion beginning in 9:3 is curious.[20]

---

19. Ker, "Paul and Apollos," 78, follows Litfin in making a connection between "eloquence" and (rhetorical) "education." True as this was for Greeks and Romans, it was not true for Jews. Apollos was an educated *Jew*. The assumptions regarding educated/eloquent Gentiles do not likely apply for Jews. The education of Apollos the Jew and his "eloquence" could not have been more distinct from the educated and eloquent Gentile.

20. See P. D. Gardner, *The Gifts of God and the Authentication as a Christian* (Lanham, Md.: University Press of America, 1994), 67-110.

Significantly Paul calls his exposition "my defense *(apologia)* to those who would examine *(anakrinousin)* me" (9:3). Both *apologia* and *anakrinein* have forensic associations. Who are these "examiners" of Paul? Not the Corinthian readers, since for them his apostleship is not in dispute (9:2) — at least, not yet! Most likely they are outsiders who have come to Corinth.

Given Paul's insistence that he has "seen Jesus our Lord" (9:1) and his specific bracketing of himself with apostolic witnesses to the resurrected Christ (15:5-8), it would make sense if these "examiners" were connected with the "apostles" whose names Paul supplies. In saying, "I am no less an apostle than these," he implies that they are questioning his status as an apostle.

Since Cephas had visited Corinth circa 52-54 (1:12; 3:22; 9:5), it is likely that Paul is alluding to Cephas as his "examiner" on the basis that he had raised doubts about Paul's equal status with other apostles, or qualified his apostolicity in some way.

In this regard, Paul's problems were threefold. He had not been a follower of Jesus of Nazareth; he had attempted to destroy the church of God; and his manner of seeing the risen Lord was different from that of the original disciples of Jesus.[21]

Since traveling apostles (like Cephas — 9:5) were paid for their ministry, Paul's refusal to act on his "right" and his stubborn insistence on working were in effect tantamount to removing the badge of apostleship. Paul had his own good reasons for his policies (see, e.g., 9:12b, 15-18; 2 Thess 3:7-10). Yet those who regarded Paul's preaching as idiosyncratic for other reasons easily placed him outside the circle of true apostles and witnesses on account of his policy and practice of working to support himself, independent of gifts from church members. In a sense Paul invited his own marginalization. Yet notwithstanding the evident difficulty for him reflected by his "defense" in 1 Corinthians 9:3-18, he insisted on

---

21. Whereas Cephas was the first to "see" the Lord, Paul was "last of all" (15:5, 8). Worse still, Cephas, the Twelve, the five hundred, James, and "all the apostles" saw the risen One "on earth" within a limited number of days (Acts 1:3). Paul, however, saw and heard the Lord "from heaven" many months after the ascension. Theirs was a seeing of "bodily" manifestations of the risen Lord, Paul's a heavenly Christophany. To be sure, he stoutly insists that he and they proclaim the same kerygma of the crucified and risen Christ (15:11). But he concedes that his manner of "seeing" the Lord was as one "untimely born" (15:8 — *tō ektrōmati*), which may be a reference to seeing the glorified Lord *ahead* of others at the parousia, "prematurely," as it were.

continuing this policy, as he also declared in 2 Corinthians 11:12, "what I do [work] I will continue to do."

Our argument, then, is that during his visit in Corinth Cephas raised questions (directly or by inference) about the nature of Paul's apostleship and authority. Perhaps Cephas suggested that Paul was a subsidiary apostle dependent for his authority upon Jerusalem leaders like Cephas himself. Whatever the case, Cephas's presence in the city (especially with the Jewish believers?) may have created doubts in the minds of the people about Paul's leadership. For his part, however, Paul in no way diminishes the fundamental primacy of Cephas and the Twelve as the first witnesses of the risen Christ (1 Cor 15:5), conceding that he, Paul, is the "least of the apostles" (15:9). We infer that Cephas prompted questions about Paul's apostleship but that Paul did not reciprocate regarding Cephas.

In short, from 1 Corinthians we sense that the visits to the church in Corinth by Apollos and Cephas raised real though different concerns for Paul the founding apostle. These, however, were of a different order than the issues associated with the arrival of those Jewish-Christian countermissionaries Paul calls "false apostles."

The Mission of the False Apostles *(pseudapostoloi)*   These preachers also arrived in Corinth while Paul was absent from the city, between his second and third/final visits (ca. 54-56). Possibly these countermissionaries[22] **came to Corinth precisely because Peter had visited the city and, as it were, (unintentionally?) planted a flag there for (their extreme version of) the Jewish mission.**

It will be helpful to note Paul's references to them in his second letter,[23] as:

triumphalist "peddlers" who preach the word of God	2:14-17; cf. 4:2
letter-bearing "Moses" revisionists	3:1-18
boastful of external (ecstatic) qualities	5:12
trespassers into Paul's "field" of ministry	10:13-18
"superlative apostles" who preach "another Jesus" who are "superior" speakers	11:1-6

22. See chapter 9.
23. This is based on the view that 2 Corinthians is a unity.

"false apostles," "ministers of Satan" masquerading as "ministers of righteousness"	11:7-15
those who "make slaves" of the Corinthians	11:16-21
Hebrews, Israelites, descendants of Abraham, "ministers of Christ"	11:22-23
"superlative apostles" who have "visions and revelations" (?)	12:1
"superlative apostles" who work miracles (?)	12:11-13

From these references it is evident that Paul's concern about these "false apostles" was his major reason for writing this second letter to the church in Corinth.

Who were these men and what was their mission and message? C. K. Barrett's famous verdict that these "intruders" were "Jews, Jerusalem Jews and Judaising Jews" who "constituted a rival apostolate to Paul's"[24] is broadly correct.

Their Origin and Identity That they were Jews is incontrovertible (11:22), and that they came from Jerusalem (where else?) is almost as certain. Apart from these elements, however, Barrett's tersely stated judgment needs amplification and qualification. They were, as Barrett observed, "a rival apostolate," that is, a countermission.

By way of amplification, we suggest that Jerusalem Jews who came to Greek-speaking Corinth and whose speech impressed the people (11:5-6) must have been accomplished Greek speakers. Furthermore, since they were attempting to reimpose the Moses covenant (3:1-18), we reasonably assume them to have been Pharisaic in their sympathies (cf. Acts 15:5).[25] In short, like Paul himself in his "former life in Judaism" (cf. Gal 1:13), these men were Jews, Jerusalem Jews, *Greek-speaking Pharisaic* Jews.

Significantly they were Jews who were *Christian believers.* They claim to be ministers of Christ (11:23) and "apostles of Christ" (11:13) who preach "another Jesus," "a (different) gospel," a corrupted "word of God" (11:4; 2:17; cf. 5:12).

---

24. See C. K. Barrett, "Paul's Opponents in II Corinthians," *NTS* 17 (1971): 251.
25. See chapter 9.

Their Mission and Message What, then, of Barrett's description of them as "judaizing Jews"? In my view[26] we should cease using this word (also "Judaizers"), for two reasons. First, the NT does use the word "judaize" to describe those who seek to impose Judaism on Gentiles.[27] Second, the term implies that they are Jews who straightforwardly seek to demand Jewish practices from Gentiles, obscuring the fact that these are Jewish *Christians* who are seeking to impose their version of *Jewish Christianity* on the churches of Paul's mission.

What did these preachers preach that stirred Paul to condemn them in such strong terms as "false apostles, deceitful workmen . . . ministers of Satan" (2 Cor 11:13-14)? That the word "circumcision" does not appear in the letter might mean that they did not seek the rite in Corinth, though the absence of the word does not necessarily demand that conclusion.

What, then, about the other striking omission from the letter, Paul's failure to use the word "law"? The *idea* of law, however, is present even if the word is absent; for Paul the word "letter" *(gramma)* is synonymous with "law."[28] Paul's great issue with these rival apostles relates to the "righteousness [of God]" *(dikaiosynē)* and its antonym, "condemnation" *(katakrisis)*.

The countermissionaries preached that the dispensation of "letter"/ "Moses" (= law) remained in place, current and applicable, notwithstanding the death of the Messiah and the coming of the Spirit. Paul, however, insisted that the advent of the new covenant of the Spirit and of "righteousness" had displaced the old covenant dispensation of "condemnation" and "death" (3:9). Paul locates that "righteousness of God" in the sin-bearing death of Christ (5:21) and reciprocally locates "condemnation" arising from "letter" (= law).[29]

Paul's assertion that the new covenant of the Spirit and righteousness has "abolished"[30] the covenant of Moses and "the letter" provides the clue that identifies the alternative theology of the countermissionaries.

---

26. As argued earlier, 142-43.

27. In Gal 2:14 *Ioudaizein* means "to live as a Jew."

28. See 128-29.

29. See chapter 8.

30. Paul's use of the verb *katargeō* (in the passive voice) in 2 Cor 3:7, 11, 13, 14 carries the meaning "abolished" or "abrogated," as it also does in Rom 7:6. Paul is asserting that Moses/the old covenant was "abolished" in principle from its inception, awaiting its *telos* (= goal/end) in Christ (2 Cor 3:13; Rom 10:4).

Clearly they contended that "Moses"/"the letter" was undisplaced, unabolished, and unabrogated — in a word, still applicable.

In other words, the dispute between them was over the source of divine righteousness. It was essentially *eschatological, christological, soteriological,* and *pneumatological* in character. They argued that the covenant of Moses *continued* and that Jesus was part of that unabrogated dispensation. Paul, however, insisted that God's "day of salvation" had come in the death and resurrection of Christ and the proclamation of a grace-based, law-free, Christ-centered, Spirit-empowered gospel (5:14–6:2) and that, in consequence, God had now "abolished" the old covenant.

Their Credentials Paul's repeated apologetic acknowledgment "we are not commending ourselves" (3:1; 5:12) was forced on him by the perception that he did in fact commend himself. Such a perception was likely sharpened by the earlier visit of Cephas, disciple of the historical Jesus, first witness to his resurrection, and initial leader in the apostolic band dispatched by Jesus. Paul is driven to claim a merely *indirect* commendation from the Lord that he contended was evident in the quality and fruits of his missionary labors (6:3; 10:17).

More immediately, however, the intruders sought to legitimate themselves by paranormal phenomena, characterizing themselves as ecstatics (5:13) who experienced revelatory "visions" (12:1, 7) and who, perhaps, performed miracle signs (12:12). Barrett attributed these phenomena to the "readiness of the intruding apostles . . . to adopt a measure of hellenization . . . of Corinthianization."[31]

Barrett is right in inferring that by these means they sought to legitimate themselves as "superior" to Paul. Yet it is more likely that such paranormal phenomena were inherently Jewish (rather than Hellenistic), and well documented within the Palestinian Judaism of that era. Josephus reports that during the mid-50s "Deceivers and imposters under the pretence of divine inspiration . . . led the multitude into the desert under the belief that God would give them signs of redemption *(sēmeia eleutherias)*."[32]

In addition to (attempted) miracles, mystical experience was a well-known aspect of the apocalyptic thought and practice of Second Temple

---

31. Barrett, "Paul's Opponents," 251.
32. Josephus, *JW* 2.258-259.

Judaism. According to one seer, "I went . . . and sat in the valley of Cedron. . . . I sanctified my soul there, and ate no bread . . . and I drank no water, and I was there till the seventh day . . . it came to pass that my soul took much thought, and I began to speak in the presence of the Mighty One" (2 *Bar* 21:1-3). Other apocalyptic writings speak in a similar vein: "[T]hose men . . . led me up to the third heaven . . . in that place where the Lord rests, when he goes up into paradise of Eden" (2 *En* 8).

Our conclusion is that the superior Greek speech and the paranormal behavior of these Jewish newcomers to Corinth are consistent with a Jerusalem origin.

These elements, however, were not merely ordinary matters that Paul may have mentioned in passing. Rather, these men intentionally emphasized these aspects of their ministry to demonstrate their "superiority" over Paul. Paul sarcastically called them *hyperlian apostoloi* (11:5; 12:11), ironically declared himself to be "superior" *(hyper)* in missionary *weaknesses* (11:23–12:10), and pointedly characterized them by words compounded with the prefix *hyper* to illustrate their self-styled "superiority" (10:12, 14 — they *over*extended themselves into lands *beyond;* 12:7 — they boasted of an *abundance* of revelations with resultant *super*elation).

By contrast, much of the letter is devoted to Paul's catalogues of his own *sufferings* and *failures*.[33]

Christ parades him as his prisoner in a victory parade	2:14-17
He is a fragile earthen vessel, handed over to death	4:7, 11
He "endures" in ministry under suffering and calumny	6:3-10
He is a "fool" experiencing greater sufferings	11:1–12:13

It is evident from these texts that Paul devotes much of 2 Corinthians to details of his missionary sufferings. Furthermore, he is echoing in his own words the opponents' assertions of his inadequacy in ministry. But why does he do this? Why does Paul so readily acknowledge these elements of suffering and weakness that his opponents point to as evidence of his "inferiority" to them?

Here we must understand that a war of words is being fought for the

---

33. See generally J. T. Fitzgerald, *Cracks in an Earthen Vessel: An Examination of the Catalogues of Hardships in the Corinthian Correspondence*, SBLDS 99 (Atlanta: Scholars, 1988), 148-207.

loyalty of the Corinthians; the contenders are Paul and the Jewish-Christian countermissionaries. They have come to Corinth to subvert Paul's authority and to capture his converts for their own Jewish-Christian mission, and Paul is fighting the fight of his life to retain the Corinthians' loyalty for his law-free gospel.

How does Paul defend himself so as to secure the commitment of the Corinthians to his apostleship?

Paul's Legitimacy in 2 Corinthians

2 Corinthians is Paul's great apologia in which he both defends himself against criticism and advances argument for his legitimacy as an apostle of Christ and a minister of the new covenant. C. K. Barrett rightly notes that "II Corinthians poses the question how the legitimacy of an apostle, and therefore the legitimacy of the gospel, may be recognised."[34]

Paul wrote the letter from Macedonia (Philippi?) in response to Titus's report on the reaction of the Corinthians to the "severe letter." Titus brought back the good news that the crisis necessitating Paul's "painful visit" had been resolved and the offender disciplined (2:5-11; 7:8-12). Apart from that, however, Titus's report was negative. The Corinthians had stopped setting aside money weekly for Paul's collection for Judea (8:10), resenting the severity of the recent letter (10:10) and his failure to return in spite of promising to do so (1:15-23); and there was a rising suspicion that his refusal to receive payment was "crafty" (4:2; 12:16; cf. 1:12; 2:17), a "sin" (11:7), and a "wrong" done to them (12:13).

Worse still, their comprehensive repudiation of Paul is matched by their fulsome welcome of recently arrived preachers (11:4), despite the problematic nature of their doctrines (11:14-15).

Paul expresses his apologia in deeply emotional terms, making it the most personally revealing of his letters. Arguably it stands alone in antiquity for its emotional self-disclosures until the publication of Augustine's autobiography, the *Confessions* (ca. 397-400).

The emotional passion of the letter and its considerable length are measures of the depth of Paul's feelings and indicative of the breakdown of

---

34. Barrett, "Paul's Opponents," 231, following E. Käsemann, "Die Legitimtät des Apostels," *ZNW* 41 (1942): 33-77.

relations between him and the Corinthians. This letter represents Paul's desperate effort to rebuild mutual trust prior to his upcoming third and final visit (2:1; 10:2; 13:1).

Paul speaks to them as their heartbroken "father." Even today we feel Paul's sense of rejection in his cry to these petulant children: "Our mouth is open to you, Corinthians; our heart is wide" (6:11). He pleads with them to reciprocate the breadth of his love for them. As their "father" he had betrothed them to their husband-to-be, Christ, but they are being seduced by "another Jesus" (11:4). They warmly welcome this adulterous interloper while wearily "tolerating" Paul (11:1, 4, 19-21). He asks, Is it "wrong" that he, their father, provides for them, his children, by working to support himself (12:13-15)? Let them "examine" themselves and conclude that they are "in the faith," thereby authenticating his apostleship (13:5; cf. 3:2; 10:18). That "faith," however, is what really matters, not that Paul will have been "approved" by them (13:6). In short, throughout this letter, alongside his theological arguments, Paul is appealing to them in human and deeply emotional terms.

At the same time, however, Paul makes his argument for authority on the grounds of his apostolicity. This is evident in his opening address, "Paul, an apostle of Christ Jesus by the will of God" (1:1), and is restated by his claims that "the signs of a true apostle were performed among you" (12:12). He amplifies this apostolicity by portraying himself as an "ambassador of Christ" (*Christou . . . presbeuomen* — 5:20), an idea that was well understood in a world familiar with various "embassies" whose members represented their nation abroad.[35] The ambassador came in the name of his nation and bore its authority; thus to meet the one "sent" was, in effect, to meet the sender.[36] Paul had come to Corinth in precisely that role, "in Christ's place" (*hyper . . . Christou* — 5:20).

When did Paul's apostolicity begin? Although he makes no direct reference to the Damascus revelation, we are in no doubt that his apostolic ministry began at that critical moment.[37] Paul intentionally uses aorist tense verbs to point to the single occasion when God made him "sufficient" for the ministry of the new covenant (3:6); when God "shone" in his "heart" to give that light to others (4:6); when he "received mercy" and be-

---

35. See, e.g., Thucydides, *The Peloponnesian War* 8.45.4; 1 Macc 14:21-22; cf. M. M. Mitchell, "New Testament Envoys in the Context of Greco-Roman Diplomatic and Epistolary Conventions," *JBL* 3, no. 4 (1992): 641-42.

36. In Jewish understanding "a man's agent is as himself" (*m. Berakhot* 5:5).

37. See chapter 5.

gan to exercise his "ministry" (4:1); when he began to "live for [Christ]" (5:15); when God "gave" him "the ministry of reconciliation" (5:18); when the Lord "gave" him "authority . . . for building up the church" (10:8; 13:10). Clearly, Paul's entire ministry as an apostle of Christ and as Christ's ambassador flowed from that single moment twenty-five years earlier.

It was one thing for Paul to claim to be Christ's "sent one" and his "representative," but how does he *validate* that claim? Did he attempt to match his opponents' "triumphalist" (2:13) assertions of "superiority" by means of paranormal works? On the contrary, he mocked and derided such claims by his scathing tag *hyperlian apostoloi* (11:5; 12:11), by the heavy irony of the "fool's speech" with its catalogue of *sufferings* (11:1–12:13) and its climax that he was "lowered *down*" the wall and (almost comically?) "caught *up*" to paradise (11:33; 12:2), concluded by his calculatedly offhand, twice-repeated "in the body or out of the body I do not know" (12:2, 3).

Rather, Paul sought to identify himself in the closest way with Christ as Christ's "representative." At the end of his catalogue of missionary sufferings he asserted, "For the sake of Christ *(hyper Christou)*, then, I am content with weaknesses, insults, hardships, persecutions, and calamities" (12:10). In other words, Christ's sufferings *continue* in Paul, who "abundantly" shares those sufferings (1:5). He is "always being given up to death for Jesus' sake" (*dia Iēsoun* — 4:11). His life is a "sacrificial offering" so that wherever he goes (and is rejected) he is the "aroma of Christ" (2:15) so that (metaphorically) as the bystander "smells" Paul as sacrifice (in ministry), he also "smells" Christ (the Levitical sacrifice acceptable to God).

Furthermore, such is the closeness of his identification with Christ that, as Christ suffered "for" *(hyper)* others (as in 5:21), so too did Paul. Paul has been "afflicted for *(hyper)*" the Corinthians' "comfort and salvation" (1:6); he has been "spent for *(hyper)* [their] souls" (12:15). Paul does not use the specific language of "imitating" Christ in this letter, as he does elsewhere,[38] but the idea is present nonetheless. By this identification of himself as a vicarious sufferer, Paul legitimates himself as a true apostle and representative of Christ, as opposed to the opponents who portray themselves as men of power and who say that Paul is a man of weakness (cf. 11:21, 29; 12:9-10).

So close is this identification with Christ that Paul actually describes his ministry in terms almost identical with those he applies to Christ.

---

38. Cf. 1 Cor 11:1 — "Be imitators of me, as I am of Christ."

Paul	Christ
As poor	by his poverty
yet making many	you . . . have become
rich	rich
2 Cor 6:10	2 Cor 8:9

Not so explicit yet nonetheless striking are these words:

Paul	Christ
I humbled myself	he humbled himself . . .
that you might be exalted	God has highly exalted him
2 Cor 11:7	Phil 2:8-9

Paul closely modeled his own life and ministry on the life and ministry of Christ, and he pointed to that identification to legitimate his ministry, in particular in the face of those self-styled apostles who sought legitimacy on the basis of religious power and "superiority."

It is not true that Paul avoided all references to "power" in his own life. Paul referred to power in two ways (at least) that differed from the newcomers. On one hand, Paul was the *recipient* of God's power, whereas the newcomers were (professed) executors of power; and on the other, God's power rested upon Paul *in weakness*, whereas the newcomers believed that God multiplied his power out of their power.

> We felt that we had received the sentence of death; but that was to make us rely not on ourselves but on God who raises the dead; he delivered us from so deadly a peril, and he will deliver us. (2 Cor 1:9-10)

> Always carrying in the body the death of Jesus, so that the life of Jesus may also be manifested in our bodies. For while we live we are always being given up to death for Jesus' sake, so that the life of Jesus may be manifested in our mortal flesh. (2 Cor 4:10-11)

> As dying, and behold we live; as punished, and yet not killed. (2 Cor 6:9)

> But he said to me, "My grace is sufficient for you, for my power is made perfect in weakness." I will all the more gladly boast of my weaknesses, that the power of Christ may rest upon me. For the sake of

Christ, then, I am content with weaknesses, insults, hardships, persecutions, and calamities; for when I am weak, then I am strong. (2 Cor 12:9-10)

These passages, which are scattered throughout the letter, point to God's repeated deliverances of Paul from missionary sufferings and calamities. Paul has taken the facts of Christ's death and resurrection and made them a metaphor or notional template for his own sufferings ("death") and deliverance ("resurrection"). He wants his readers to consider his own life and ministry as "Christ-shaped" or "Christoform" and to acknowledge their legitimacy *on that basis.*[39]

This means that Paul as a concrete embodiment of Christ's death and resurrection incarnates his apostolic word, focused as it is in Christ's death and resurrection. Paul preached Christ crucified and risen, and he embodied Christ crucified and risen. By this he validates both his apostleship and his gospel.

Conclusion

Paul's relationships with the church in this major Greco-Roman city extended throughout most (i.e., ca. 50-57) of his "glorious" missionary decade (ca. 47-57) and are documented in his extant letters and the book of Acts. Beginning less than two decades after the historical Jesus, they represent a fascinating window into the sustained relationships between the first world missionary and his converts, the more so since he was a Jew and they (for the most part) were Gentiles.

As we trace Paul's dealings with the Corinthian believers, we sense a trend toward increasing difficulties between them. These reach a climax with Timothy's return to Ephesus and Paul's subsequent "painful visit" and "severe letter," and finally with the writing of (canonical) 2 Corinthians.

Nonetheless, the church (presumably) received that powerful letter,

39. M. J. Gorman, *Cruciformity* (Grand Rapids: Eerdmans, 2001), follows Hans Küng in locating Paul's essential spirituality in the idea of "cruciformity." Paul, however, connects Christ's *resurrection* with his death throughout 2 Corinthians and takes Christ's *incarnation* and death as his moral and ethical inspiration in Phil 2:4-9. See also S. Kraftchick, "Death in Us, Life in You: The Apostolic Medium," in *SBLSP,* ed. E. H. Lovering (Atlanta: Scholars, 1991).

otherwise it would not have survived in the Pauline corpus. Perhaps Paul's three-month sojourn there in the house of Gaius helped heal the wounds and bring reconciliation (Acts 20:2-3; Rom 16:23).

By any reckoning 2 Corinthians is a remarkable text. It is a unique window into Paul's mind revealing his intense identification with Christ his Lord and his passionate concern to replicate Christ's ministry ("the meekness and gentleness of Christ"), Christ's death (in missionary "afflictions"), and Christ's resurrection (in "deliverance" from afflictions).

Paul argued his case for legitimacy with the Corinthians on the grounds that he was identifiable with Christ himself, and with the core elements of the gospel of the crucified and risen Lord. Paul's legitimacy was not based in the materialistic power plays of the newcomer triumphalists but in his evident replication of Christ himself in Paul's life and ministry. Unlike them, Paul was a true missionary of Jesus. Thereby, from this unique letter, Paul establishes from that time a pattern for pastoral ministry that is truly "Christian."

ELEVEN

Romans:
Paul's Final Answer (ca. 57)

Do you not see that Paul put to flight the whole world, that he was more powerful than Plato and all the rest?

Chrysostom, *Homily on Titus* 2

Paul wrote his letter to the Romans during a three-month period in about 57 from the house of Gaius in Corinth, by means of the amanuensis Tertius (Rom 16:22-23; Acts 20:2-3). He was writing for the sake of the twenty-six named persons of whom he speaks in warm tones, and those many more unnamed ones connected with them who gathered in the various house churches in the imperial capital (Rom 16:3-16). Paul dispatched the letter with the trusted sister Phoebe, whom he expected the readers generously to welcome (16:1-2).

Phoebe the envoy and the letter she carried were (so to speak) Paul's "advance party," since he planned personally to go to Rome after delivering the collection[1] to Jerusalem, to "pass through" on his way to Spain (15:22-29). Paul was not to know that his writing of this letter would be the climax of his apostolate and, in effect, its end. The book of Acts draws the curtain on Paul under house arrest in Rome circa 62, after which we hear no more about him from his friend Luke. His literary output after Romans is slight, consisting only of Philippians and his pastoral tracts to Timothy and Ti-

---

1. See chapter 9.

tus.[2] From scattered references in these texts it appears that Paul enjoyed a brief period of freedom traveling in the Aegean region before his final imprisonment and execution (in the mid-60s).

The Situation in Rome

Two groups of people are in Paul's mind as he writes this letter: (1) the readers who belong to his mission and their associates in the house churches (Rom 16:3-16; cf. 6:1-4, 17), and (2) the hostile interlocutors (2:1, 17-19; 3:7; 9:19) who likely are also those Paul accuses of creating dissension and obstacles for the faith in which the first group has been instructed and baptized (16:17-19; cf. 6:3, 17).

Paul's major purpose in writing is to "strengthen" the faith of group 1 against the destructive influence of group 2. Accordingly, the letter is implicitly polemical against group 2, while also being necessarily apologetic for Paul and his credentials in view of the influence he seeks to bring for the benefit of his mission supporters.

Paul's Mission Friends and Their Associates in Rome

Paul addresses this group warmly, acknowledging with approval their worldwide reputation for the "faith" (1:8) into which they had been instructed and baptized (6:3, 17; cf. 16:17), their "goodness" (15:14), and their "obedience" to the gospel, which is "known to all" (16:19; cf. 1:5 — "the obedience of faith").

At the same time, he diplomatically writes this letter for their "strengthening" (1:11; 16:25) and their "wise" discernment of what is "good" (16:19), which likely is against the negative influence of group 2.

As well, hints of external "secular" pressure are likely implied by the sequential admonitions "Bless those who persecute you," "never avenge yourselves," and "let every person be subject to the governing authorities" (12:14, 19; 13:1). Possibly Suetonius, *Nero* 16.2 ("Punishment was inflicted on the Christians, a sect devoted to a new and mischievous superstition")

---

2. See appendix D for argument that Ephesians, Colossians, and Philemon were written from Asia (Ephesus).

refers to a situation of persecution even before the great fire in A.D. 64, possibly as early as the writing of Romans.[3]

Paul's most critical exhortations are directed to real-life Jew-Gentile tensions between believers in the house churches in Rome. These include the admonition to the Gentiles not to be "proud," but to be in awe of God lest they be cut out of the olive tree (11:20; cf. 12:3), for them (the "strong," i.e., Gentiles — cf. 15:1) to welcome those who are "weak in faith" (i.e., Jews — 14:1), and for each to "welcome" the other (15:6), that "together you may with one voice glorify the God and Father of our Lord Jesus Christ" (15:6).

The Countermission Network in Rome

Paul's major concern, however, which is identifiable throughout the length and breadth of the letter, is his polemic against the Jewish Christians, who have been influenced by the Jerusalem-based countermission that seeks to impose circumcision on the male members of the Pauline churches.[4] As argued earlier,[5] this countermission arose at the beginning of Paul's westward missionary journeys (from ca. 47) and continued throughout Paul's ministry to Gentiles in Anatolia and Greece.

While these critics and objectors are in the shadows of the audience in Rome, they likely had overlapping associations with the Jews of the synagogues, with whom they would have had strong sympathies (against Paul). At many points the objections of the Jewish Christians were probably indistinguishable from those of the Jews of the synagogues.

Once more we note the decadelong importance of the circumcision issue[6] that dominates Romans 2:25–3:12 and culminates in the case study of Abraham, forefather of the Jews, who "*believed* God, and it was reckoned to him as *righteousness*" (4:3) apart from and prior to his own circumcision (4:10).

---

3. So U. Schnelle, *Apostle Paul: His Life and Theology*, trans. M. Eugene Boring (Grand Rapids: Baker Academic, 2005), 306.

4. See chapter 10. This argument depends, to a degree, on P. Stuhlmacher, *Paul's Letter to the Romans* (Louisville: Westminster John Knox, 1994), 5-6, who in turn acknowledges the influence of F. C. Baur and C. Weizsäcker.

5. See chapter 9.

6. See chapter 9.

Purpose of the Letter

Paul's primary reason for writing[7] is to expound his "gospel" ("my gospel" — 2:15; 16:25) for his Roman supporters in the knowledge that he was about to come to them (by a roundabout route) for a temporary visit, and in the understanding that his declared enemies in the Jewish-Christian countermission were wielding their influence in the Eternal City. In Romans, then, Paul sets out his comprehensive statement of the "gospel" (as he calls it; see below) to buttress his sympathizers and to answer his enemies.

Closely connected is Paul's own apologetic for himself as apostle and bearer of the word of God to the nations, which he argues in two ways. First, he immediately sets out a major statement of the gospel of God:

> The gospel of God
> which he promised beforehand through his prophets in the holy scriptures,
> the gospel concerning his Son,
>> who was descended from David
>>> according to the flesh, and
>> designated Son of God in power
>>> according to the Spirit of holiness
>>> by his resurrection from the dead,
> Jesus Christ our Lord. (1:1-3)

Various elements suggest that Paul is adapting a preformed confession,[8] one that may have predated Paul's own conversion and that the Roman believers may have known. This short passage has many elements in common with the earliest "teaching of the apostles" (Acts 2:42; cf. 5:28) in Jerusalem, into which some Roman Jews present had been baptized.[9] As

---

7. See K. P. Donfried, ed., *The Romans Debate* (Peabody, Mass.: Hendrickson, 1991); R. Miller, "The Romans Debate, 1991-2001," *CurBS* 9 (2001): 306-49; Schnelle, *Apostle Paul*, 307-9.

8. Those elements include: (i) the gospel as fulfillment of the prophets; (ii) reference to Jesus as "his Son"; (iii) balancing participial phrases with contrastive elements ("flesh"/ "Spirit"); the archaic-sounding "Spirit of holiness." For references for this view see E. E. Ellis, *The Making of the New Testament Documents* (Leiden: Brill, 1999), 94 n. 203.

9. The teaching included (i) Jesus' descent from David (Acts 2:25, 29, 34; 4:25); (ii) his present status as "Lord and Christ" through resurrection (2:31, 36, 38; 4:10, 26, 33); (iii) the

well, there are other passages in Romans that were likely preformed and pre-Pauline in origin (e.g., Rom 4:25; 11:33-36)[10] that Paul likely cites (among other reasons) to validate his credentials and authority.

Secondly, Paul makes significant claims about his apostolic authority over them in Rome, notably at the head of the letter.

> Paul, a servant of Jesus Christ, called to be *an apostle*, set apart for the gospel of God. (1:1)

> Jesus Christ our Lord, through whom we have received grace and apostleship to bring about the obedience of faith for the sake of his name among all the nations, *including yourselves* who are called to belong to Jesus Christ. (1:5-6)

> For God is my witness . . . that without ceasing I mention you always in my prayers, asking that somehow by God's will I may now at last succeed in coming to *you*. For I long to see *you*, that I may impart to you some spiritual gift to strengthen *you*. (1:9-11)

> I have often intended to come to *you* . . . in order that I may reap some harvest among *you* as well as among the rest of the Gentiles. (1:13)

> So I am eager to preach the gospel to *you* also who are in Rome. (1:15)

We note with interest Paul's "I . . . you" statements at the beginning of the letter that clearly assert his apostolic authority in respect *of them*.

Likewise assertive is his doxology at the end of the letter, which completes a kind of *inclusio*, picking up references to "gospel," "preaching," "strengthening," "prophetic writings," "nations" (= "Gentiles"), and "obedience" that appear in the opening passage (1:1-15).

> Now to him who is able to *strengthen* you according to my *gospel* and the *preaching* of Jesus Christ, according to the revelation of the mystery which was kept secret for long ages but is now disclosed and through the *prophetic writings* is made known to all *nations*, according

---

outpouring of the Holy Spirit (2:38; 3:19; 4:31). See further Barnett, *BC*, 90-93; P. W. Barnett, "Romans and the Origin of Paul's Christology," in *History and Exegesis*, ed. San-Won Son, Festschrift for E. E. Ellis (Edinburgh: T. & T. Clark, 2006), 90-103.

10. Ellis, *New Testament Documents*, 94 n. 203.

> to the command of the eternal God, to bring about the *obedience* of faith — to the only wise God be glory for evermore through Jesus Christ! Amen. (16:25-27)

Paul's apostolic assertiveness in relationship to those in Rome is seen in his words "strengthen *you* according to *my* gospel," where his "my . . . you" reference corresponds with his "I . . . you" relationship noted above.

In fact, the tone of Romans throughout is authoritative; Paul expects his apostolicity to be acknowledged and his various admonitions heeded (11:13). This is true, even though he will not come to Rome for direct ministry (apart from a brief period in transit to Rome) because he follows the settled policy of limiting his sustained ministry to virgin territory (15:20-24). The apostolic letter, however, bears the same authority as the apostolic presence.

Yet, as noted above, Paul seeks to identify with the theological understanding of his Roman readers. He refers to their "obedience" to the "standard of teaching" *(typos didachēs)* to which they were "committed" *(paredothēte* — 6:17), which must be read alongside the later reference to "the doctrine which you have been taught" *(tēn didachēn . . . humeis emathēte* — 16:17). This "rabbinic" language ("standard of teaching," "handed over," "learned," "obeyed") points to the instruction at the time of baptism that was as likely true for Paul as it had been for his readers (*"all of us* who have been baptized" — 6:3).

Paul's close identification with the twenty-six named persons he urges his readers to "greet" (that is, who are approved by Paul as part of or sympathetic to his mission — 16:3-16) also serves to isolate those whom he said the "brothers" should "take note of" (16:17). These unnamed ones raise obstacles against the very doctrines that Paul and his readers share. In all likelihood these are the same people (or represent the same viewpoint) that Paul is answering throughout the letter, as noted above (2:1, 17-19; 3:7; 9:19).

In short, Paul's purposes in writing to the Romans are threefold and overlapping. The letter is *pastoral* to "strengthen" his mission supporters in the true gospel, *apologetic* for Paul's defense of his apostolic authority, and *polemical* against those "fringe" insiders who oppose the doctrines that Paul and his supporters share.

Paul's Gospel

Our contention, then, is that Romans is an "occasional" letter. True, it is his most systematic and closely argued text, but Paul did not plan it as his "last will and testament" (so Bornkamm) but as a comprehensive response to the particular crisis facing the believers in Rome created by the countermission against Paul. Ironically, though, Romans proved to be Paul's unintended "last will and testament," since the writing of it coincided with the practical end of his missionary and letter-writing apostolate. After Romans Paul wrote only shorter works.

The argument of the letter is well known, but nonetheless worth stating in brief.

Chapters

1–4	The "one" God has justified both Gentiles and Jews the same way, by faith in Christ, who was made a propitiation for sins in his death.
5	Adam, who plunged humanity into sin and death, was the "type" of the one who is to come, Christ.
6–8	God delivers Gentiles and Jews by faith in Christ from the power of sin, and he empowers them by the Holy Spirit to fulfill the just requirement of the law.
9–11	Although a "hardening" has come to Israel, God will ultimately save (the elect of) Israel in keeping with the promise to the patriarchs.
12–14	How believers in Rome are to conduct themselves in their life together and with the governing authorities.
15	How the Romans are to pray for Christ's apostle Paul in Jerusalem, and how upon his arrival in Rome they are to "send" him on to Spain.
16	The Roman readers are to greet twenty-six named persons but are warned about those who intend to divide the community of faith.

Other analyses of the letter are possible, yet the above gives the reader a reasonable overview.

Some have said that chapters 1–8 are Paul's "purest gospel" (Luther), since here we find the great doctrines of grace, that sinners are justified only by faith in Christ and not by works of the law. Here the tendency is to regard the remainder of the letter as a kind of appendage. Others have argued for the prior significance of chapters 9–15, where God's plan to gather in Gentiles and graft them to "olive tree" Israel is dominant. Here the tendency is to regard the earlier chapters as "introductory" (Munck).

There are disadvantages in regarding one half, or the other, as the "real" message of Romans. If our exclusive focus is on chapters 1–8, we have the impression that the gospel is only about what happened *back then* in God's justifying work for sinners in the death and resurrection of his Son. We would not understand from those chapters that God's task through his servants is *continuing* (through his "workers" like Prisca and Aquila [16:3] and "apostles" like Andronicus and Junia [16:7]). Alternatively, if our interest centers on chapters 9–15, we would not understand that in the death and resurrection of his Son God has superseded the dispensation of law (symbolized by the call for the circumcision of Gentiles) and inaugurated the dispensation of the Spirit. Both parts, that is, all of Romans, must be read to discover Paul's gospel.

The Universal Character of Romans

In asserting that Romans is a "responsive" letter, it may be readily acknowledged that it is not narrowly occasional. We can understand why Melanchthon declared Romans to be a "compendium of Christian doctrine."[11] The global and comprehensive character of the letter justifies that conclusion even if he did not recognize that the letter was one side of a fierce debate.

Six elements give the letter its universal and cosmic appearance.

Its Teaching about God

Here some statistics must be noted.[12] Apart from everyday words (like "and"), the word most frequently appearing in Romans is "God," which appears more times in Romans than in any other book in the New Testa-

---

11. Quoted in Stuhlmacher, *Paul's Letter*, 2.

12. See L. Morris, "The Theme of Romans," in *Apostolic History and the Gospel*, ed. W. Gasque and R. P. Martin (Exeter: Paternoster, 1970), 249-63.

ment. God is "eternal" (16:26) and "wise" (16:27), the "God of hope" (15:13), the "God of peace" (16:20), but the God who judges justly and without partiality. But Romans is not so much about who God is as about what God *does,* about God in action, justifying the unjust from Israel and the Gentile nations, in Christ (cf. 3:26).

God is not God of Jews only, but equally of Gentiles. He has one and the same way of saving both, that is, "through their faith" (3:30) in the Son God "sent" and "did not spare" (8:3, 32). Paul declares that "God is one," echoing the great confession of Israel (the Shema), and he is God to *all* people, Jews and Gentiles (3:30).

Paul Makes Many References to "All"

We are struck by the numerous references to "all," whether in regard to sin and death, or to the universal Lordship of Christ, or to the universal judgment of God. Fundamental to the idea of "all" is that it covers the two great peoples who compose humanity, Jews and Gentiles, who however stem from the one fountainhead, Adam.

3:9	*all* (both Jews and Greeks) are under sin
3:23	*all* have sinned and fall short of the glory of God
5:12	death spread to *all* men because *all* sinned
5:18	one man's trespass led to condemnation for *all* men
10:12	the same Lord is Lord of *all*
14:10	we *all* shall stand before the judgment seat of God

Paul Teaches the Universal "Day of Wrath"

At several points we encounter the "day of wrath," the absolute terminus of this age, when God judges all.

2:5	"You are storing up wrath for yourself on the day of wrath when God's righteous judgment will be revealed."
11:15	"If [the Jews'] rejection [of Christ] means the reconciliation of the world, what will their acceptance [of Christ] mean but life from the dead?"

13:11   "Salvation is nearer to us now than when we first be-
         lieved; the night is far gone, the day is at hand."
14:10   "We shall all stand before the judgment seat of God."

Paul Teaches about Jesus as the
Unique and Universal Lord

Throughout Romans Paul argues for the highest view of Christ.

1:3   The gospel concerning [God's] *Son,*
             who *came* of the seed of David
             who is *marked out* as Son of God in power
                 according to the Spirit of holiness
                 by his resurrection from the dead.
5:11   We were reconciled to God by the death of *his Son.*
8:3   God sent *his own Son* (cf. 4:19) in the likeness of sinful
        flesh.
8:32   He did not spare *his own Son* but gave him up for us all.
9:5   Christ, who is *God* over all. . . .
10:6   "Do not say in your heart, 'Who will ascend into heaven?'
        (that is, to bring Christ down)."
10:12   "There is no distinction between Jew and Greek; the same
        Lord is Lord of all and bestows his riches upon all who
        call upon him."
14:8   Whether we live or whether we die, we live and die to *the
        Lord.*

Paul Insists on the Universality of Justification
Only through the Gospel

God has judged his Son now (3:24-25), so that those who take refuge in
him now will be spared the wrath of the last day. This God declares
through his word, the gospel.

1:16   The gospel is the power of God for salvation for all who
        believe.

3:22   The righteousness of God through faith for all who be-
        lieve.

5:18   One man's act of righteousness leads to acquittal and life
        for all men.

In Consequence, Paul Exhorts the Body of Believers Composed of Jews and Gentiles to Be "One"

The ethical section of the letter is dominated by Paul's appeal (12:1) to believers — Jew and Gentile — as in "one body" (12:3) to serve one another
(12:3-8), "love one another" (12:10 — unhypocritically), and "welcome one
another" (15:7).

These six observations point to the global character of the letter and might
well justify the verdict "compendium." This is Paul's considered view look-
ing back on an apostleship extending over a quarter of a century throughout a vast geographic arc from Jerusalem to Illyricum, preaching in Syria,
Arabia, Judea, Syria-Cilicia, Galatia, Macedonia, Achaia, and Asia.

   Paul's preaching of Christ had attracted strong opposition from both
Gentiles and Jews, as witnessed by the lists of suffering (called *peristaseis*)
set out in 1 Corinthians (4:8-13) and 2 Corinthians (1:3-11; 4:7-12; 6:3-10;
11:21b-12:13), and also in Romans (8:35-39), so that his gospel was tempered
in the fires of affliction.

   A significant source of Paul's missionary sufferings was the
countermission of the Jerusalem-based Jewish Christians who sought to
impose circumcision on Gentile believers. As a measure of the danger
these countermissionaries posed, Paul calls them "false apostles"
(*pseudapostoloi* — 2 Cor 11:13) and "false brothers" (*pseudadelphoi* — Gal
2:4; 2 Cor 11:26), even though they are "ministers of Christ" (*diakonoi
Christou* — 2 Cor 11:23).

   This also explains why Paul on occasion speaks in such muted tones
even about the apostles Peter (cf. 1 Cor 9:1-14) and James, despite their un-
doubted status as apostles and leaders in the Jewish mission and their
proclamation of the crucified and risen Christ (1 Cor 15:11). The problem
was that the unnamed countermissionaries on occasion seemed able to
impose such pressure on Peter and James that they appeared to vacillate
over the circumcision issue (Gal 2:1-21). It may be recalled that from the

mid-40s Judea was sliding toward war with the occupying Romans. In that emotion-charged situation it would not have been easy to defend Paul's mission to Gentiles that offered such easy, pain-free (i.e., circumcision-free) access to the messianic covenant.

In short, then, we recognize the universal and comprehensive nature of Romans. Yet this is not due to a situation in Rome that was either unknown or unproblematic; Romans is not merely Paul's inspired essay setting out his version of the gospel theoretically, as it were. In minor part, the comprehensive character of Romans is due to the stage Paul had reached as he completed his gospel work in the eastern provinces as he prepared to go to the western extremity (Spain) through the world capital. More to the point is the recognition that Paul had been struggling with the countermissionaries' skewed gospel for a decade, and he had reason to believe that its influence in Rome was significant.

"Righteousness" in Romans

Our argument is that Romans is Paul's comprehensive response to the Jewish Christian countertheology that required Gentiles to submit to the Mosaic law, in particular for (males) to be circumcised. Paul countered this by his appeal to the "righteousness of God" that both Gentiles and Jews lacked (through Adam's sin) but that was theirs through the propitiatory death of Christ (see Rom 3:21-26). There are six Greek words belonging to the "righteousness" group, and these appear more than one hundred times in Paul's letters and more than fifty times in Romans. It appears that the "righteousness of God" was the theological battleground contested by Paul and the countermission.

"Righteousness of God" for Paul meant being acquitted by God of wrongdoing (negatively) but being declared to be "in the right" with God (positively).[13] This "righteousness" is God's gift to the unworthy made

---

13. Several of Paul's "incidental" uses of the "righteousness" vocabulary help us understand its meaning in the more intensely argued passages: Rom 2:13 — "For it is not the hearers of the law who are righteous before God *(dikaios tō theō)*, but the doers of the law who will be justified *(dikaiōthēsontai),*" where the parallelism shows that to be "justified" means to be "righteous before God"; 1 Cor 4:4 — "I am not aware of anything against myself, but I am not thereby acquitted *(dedikaiōmai)*. It is the Lord who judges me." Here, to be *"righteoused"* means to be "acquitted."

possible by Christ's death and "revealed" in the message of the gospel (1:16-17). Critical to Paul's argument was the case of Abraham, the forefather of Israel (4:1-3), whose "faith" was "reckoned to [him] as righteousness . . . *before* he was circumcised" (4:9-10). "Righteousness of God," then, is possessed only by those who "believe" God's promises, not by those who attempt to fulfill the law (including by circumcision). To be "*righteoused*[14] by faith" is possible only through faith in Christ the faithful One, who is the God-given means of "access" to a "right" standing with God and to "peace with God" (5:1-2).

It is our understanding that Paul's viewpoint on "righteousness" is historically evident ten years earlier than expressed in Romans (i.e., ca. 47), as revealed in Paul's opposition to the circumcision of Gentile believers in Jerusalem, Antioch, and Galatia (Gal 2:1-21; 5:2-12). Paul the Jew believed that he was "*righteoused* by faith" at the time of the Damascus event (Gal 3:24).[15] In short, from the beginning of his life "in Christ," Paul believed that the "righteousness of God" was his possession and that he fought for that "truth of the gospel" for Gentiles throughout the entire period of his mission, from Damascus to Corinth (where he wrote Romans).

"Righteousness of God" and the "Kingdom of God"

This, however, raises a major question: Was this doctrine so passionately held by Paul the "sent one" *also* the doctrine of Christ the Sender?[16] Put another way: Had Christ been in Paul's shoes, would he have preached that men and women are "*righteoused* by faith" and not by works of the law?

It is, of course, an outrageous and illegitimate question because the mission of the historical Jesus was mainly to Jews whereas the mission of Paul was to Jews but increasingly to Gentiles. Jesus and Paul were located in distinctly different cultures. Nonetheless, several reasons for Paul's pas-

14. Whereas the Greek word group *dikaio-* has the consistent idea of "right-," English is not able to reproduce the same verbal consistency when the verb appears in the passive voice. That consistency is lost when *dikaiōthentes* (Rom 5:1) is translated, as it must be, "[we] being justified." Hence, to make the point I have followed Stuhlmacher's "[we] being *righteoused*."

15. See chapter 3.

16. For an important discussion see D. Wenham, *Paul: Follower of Jesus or Founder of Christianity?* (Grand Rapids: Eerdmans, 1995), 73-80.

sionate advocacy that the "righteousness of God" was accessed by faith and not by works of the law was consistent with and a valid extension of Jesus' actions and teaching.

Here the principal point of continuity between Jesus and Paul is their common use of the term "kingdom of God," which occurs many times on Jesus' lips in the Gospels and eight times in Paul's undisputed letters.[17]

The one "kingdom of God" reference in Romans is relevant to this question. "For the kingdom of God is not food and drink but righteousness and peace and joy in the Holy Spirit; he who thus serves Christ is acceptable to God and approved by men" (14:17-18). Paul had just obliquely referred to a saying of the Lord Jesus that "nothing is unclean (koinon) of itself" (14:14; cf. Mark 7:15 — "there is nothing outside a man which by going into him can defile [koinōsai][18] him"). This "good" truth, however, was capable of being used unhelpfully by the "strong" in the Roman house churches, to the injury of those "weak in faith" (Rom 14:1). It was a "good" that was being "spoken of as evil" because it strained relationships between them; the "strong" wanted freedom to eat and drink what they chose although this was breaking fellowship with the "weak" who did not feel the same freedom (14:16). To overcome this pastoral obstacle to unity Paul calls on the "strong" to refrain from such eating and drinking that would offend the weak (presumably when they met together). Accordingly he enjoins, "Do not, for the sake of food, destroy the work of God. Everything is indeed clean (kathara; cf. Mark 7:19 — 'thus he declared all foods clean [katharizōn]'), but it is wrong for any one to make others fall by what he eats; it is right not to eat meat or drink wine or do anything that makes your brother stumble" (Rom 14:20-21).

It appears that the "strong" were relying on a teaching of Jesus to justify their freedom in eating and drinking whatever they chose (in the company of the "weak"), regardless of the social impact of that freedom.

Paul, however, defines the "kingdom of God" (Jesus' key referent for his gospel — e.g., Mark 1:14) as "not food and drink but *righteousness* and peace and joy in the Holy Spirit" (Paul's key referent for his gospel — Rom 1:16-17). It is not difficult to demonstrate that "peace and joy in the Holy

17. Rom 14:17; 1 Cor 4:20; 6:9, 10; 15:24, 50; Gal 5:21. On one occasion Paul refers to "his [God's] kingdom" (1 Thess 2:12). And a further five times also in the disputed letters (Eph 5:5; Col 1:13; 4:11; 2 Tim 4:1, 18).

18. The koinos, koinoō language dominates the pericope about the dispute over "defiled" hands (Mark 7:2, 5, 15, 18, 20, 23).

Spirit" are adjunct blessings to the "righteousness of God" as declared in Paul's gospel.[19]

Furthermore, it can hardly be a coincidence that Jesus used both terms together, as in "seek first [God's] *kingdom* and [God's] *righteousness*" (Matt 6:33); both his kingdom and his righteousness are his "gifts."[20]

In short, Paul displays awareness of the centrality of Jesus' preaching of "the kingdom of God" (a term rarely used in Second Temple Judaism), which he expounded in his own terms as the "righteousness of God."

This, however, prompts two further questions. For Paul the "righteousness of God" was entirely dependent on the mercy of God; it was decidedly independent of "works of the law," in particular circumcision. So, can it be demonstrated, first, that Jesus' "kingdom of God" message was based on mercy (alone), and secondly, that Paul knew it was? The answer to the first question is straightforward. The Gospels demonstrate the mercy-based nature of the "kingdom of God" in Jesus' table fellowship with "sinners" independent of the ritual demands of the Pharisees (Sabbath keeping, fasting, washings). We must regard as indisputable the texts that articulate the Pharisees' attitude to Jesus when they said, "This man welcomes sinners and eats with them" (Luke 15:2), and that he was reputed to be "a friend of tax collectors and sinners" (Matt 11:19).

B. F. Meyer's observation is apposite: "Jesus' central proclamation [of] the reign of God was God's supreme and climactic gift to Israel and the world, not just goodness but boundless goodness."[21] Commenting on Jesus' table fellowship with sinners, Meyer observed that "the Pauline account of God as the one who 'justifies (*dikaiounta* = acquits, makes righteous) the ungodly' (Rom 4:5) . . . has its concrete presupposition in Jesus' revolutionary contact and communion with sinners."[22]

The connected question as to whether Paul displays knowledge of Jesus' dispute with the Pharisees over the grace-based nature of the "kingdom of God" is less straightforward. The answer is likely found in the Corinthians' slogan "All things are lawful" (*exestin* — 1 Cor 6:12; 12:23). This appears to reflect the Corinthians' knowledge of the Pharisees' repeated objection "it is *not* lawful" (*ouk exestin*) to Jesus' refusal to observe various

19. See, e.g., "May the God of hope fill you with all *joy* and *peace* in believing, so that by the power of *the Holy Spirit* you may abound in hope" (Rom 15:13).

20. See R. A. Guelich, *The Sermon on the Mount* (Waco: Word, 1982), 86.

21. B. F. Meyer, *The Aims of Jesus* (London: SCM, 1979), 144.

22. Meyer, *The Aims of Jesus*, 160.

ritual and ethical requirements (Mark 2:24, 26; 3:4; 10:2; cf. 12:14). If, as it appears, the Corinthians knew of Jesus' free attitude to ritual matters, we must assume that Paul himself was their source, even though the Corinthians twisted freedom into license. Paul's employment of the "lawful" language suggests that he knew about the currency of that word in the disputes between Jesus and the Pharisees.

We conclude from the above discussion (i) that Jesus' proclamation of the "kingdom of God" was mercy-based toward sinners, and (ii) that Paul's use of the word "lawful" likely means that he was aware of the strife between Jesus and the Pharisees over the mercy of God for sinners, *independent of ritual requirements.*

It must not pass unnoticed that the opponents of Paul in the Jerusalem-based Jewish Christian countermission were "believers who belonged to the party of the *Pharisees*" (Acts 15:5) and that when Paul visited Jerusalem in the late 50s the elders of the church informed him of "how many thousands there are among the Jews of those who have believed . . . all zealous for the law" (Acts 21:20). Believing Jews who are "zealous for the law" can mean only one thing: believers who are Pharisees or who are sympathetic with Pharisaism. In other words, the ritual requirements of the Pharisees toward sinners (that Jesus opposed) were replicated in the ritual demands of Pharisaic believers toward Gentiles (that Paul opposed).

We conclude, therefore, that Paul's employment of his key concept "righteousness of God" was consistent with and in genuine extension of Jesus' key concept "kingdom of God" and that both were grace-based and ritual-free.

Conclusion

Despite its global character, Paul's letter to the Romans is not so much a compendium of doctrine (in the abstract) as it is a comprehensive response to the alternative theology of the Jewish-Christian countermission.

Was Paul's insistence that the "righteousness of God" is grace-based in line with Jesus' insistence that his proclamation of the "kingdom of God" was likewise mercy-based?

It is likely significant that the Jewish Christian mission opposing Paul was composed of Pharisees (or Pharisee sympathizers). It appears that the Pharisees' insistence on ritual observance for sinners (Sabbath keeping, fasting, washings) continued in principle in the countermission's insistence on ritual observance of Gentiles (in circumcision). In opposing the Pharisee mind-set in his mission, Paul followed his Master in opposing the Pharisee mind-set in his.

TWELVE

Paul's Achievement

Put the whole world on one side of the scale and you will see that the soul of Paul outweighs it.

John Chrysostom

Paul's apostolate effectively ended around A.D. 57 when he wrote his letter to the Romans. He would spend most of his seven remaining years in various prisons with all but four of his letters already written and in circulation and the greater part of his church planting also already done.

In Romans he looked back on twenty-five years as a man "in Christ" and as a missionary of the Messiah, Jesus (Rom 15:14-21). Through Paul's words and deeds Christ had "fulfilled the gospel" from Jerusalem in an arc around to Illyricum (the Balkans).

Yet we must divide those twenty-five years unequally. For the first decade and a half (ca. 34-47) Paul was confined to the Levant (Damascus, "Arabia," Judea, Syria-Cilicia), where Paul appears to have limited his ministry to Jews and Jewish sympathizers (Godfearers) within the circle of the synagogues (which explains why his synagogue beatings seem to be restricted to these years — 2 Cor 11:24).

Had Paul stayed within the Jewish orbit of the eastern Mediterranean, he would likely have remained at best a footnote of history; he wrote no letters (that have survived from this period) and would not have attracted the heroic admiration of the author of Acts. Indeed, it is unlikely that there would have been that second volume of Luke's work apart from Paul, and equally unlikely there would have even been a first volume!

It was during that second phase, however, that glorious decadelong burst of energy (ca. 47-57), that Paul made his great mark. Within those few years Paul established his churches in four Roman provinces and wrote his various letters to them as well as to that group of mission supporters in Rome.

Among Paul's many achievements let us consider six.

Gospel Herald to the Greco-Roman World

Paul was the first missionary to take the "light of the gospel" westward into the Greco-Roman world, into the provinces of Anatolia and Greece. His time in those regions, however, was quite brief, which makes his a pioneering role for the sake of those who came after him.

That role would fall to John the "holy theologian," who appears to have come to Roman Asia soon after Paul but who remained there for the next forty years. John was a profound influence on the Byzantine churches, which prospered under the protection of the Constantinople-based Byzantine Empire, which encompassed the region from the Balkans to North Africa and was to continue for the next millennium and a half. Paul's great contribution was to be the founding apostle at the heart of what would become that great theocratic empire. John built on the foundations that Paul had laid.

Exemplary Missionary

Nonetheless, Paul the missionary became the great example for centuries of those who would leave the security and comfort of home for the perils and uncertainty of the itinerant missionary. Regardless whether we consider the early missions to Egypt, China, and Russia, or the early medieval Irish missions to Europe or the missions that accompanied European colonization in the Americas, Africa, and Asia, the main inspiration and example for them all was Paul, as narrated by the book of Acts and by Paul's own letters. Paul was and remains the exemplary missionary.

Iconic Convert

Paul's radical turnabout whereby the persecutor and would-be destroyer of the church and its faith became its greatest promoter and protector (cf. Gal 1:13-23) has marked him out for all time as the iconic convert. "Damascus Road" has become part of world cultural language to portray the phenomenon of radical conversion, whether political or religious.

Paul is thus a symbol of the hope and possibility of divine redemption from a destructive to a creative life.

The question of guilt is sometimes raised in respect to Paul. The powerful example of Luther's deliverance from guilt to liberty of conscience was easy to read back into Paul's conversion. Guilt for misdemeanors was likely a major factor within Paul's psyche, though surprisingly it was a guilt that more likely affected him *after* rather than before Damascus Road. Careful reading of Paul suggests that he was only minimally affected by his moral failure regarding the law of God before his conversion. Retrospectively, however, as a man "in Christ" with a now sensitized conscience (through the indwelling work of the Spirit of God), he appears to have become aware of his own lifelong moral debility and, not least, of his shameful participation in the death of Stephen and in the violent attack on the disciples in Jerusalem.

After Damascus, however, he became (as he said) "a new creation" (2 Cor 5:17).

Missionary Theologian

Paul's greatest and abiding influence, however, is to be found in his letters, which soon became incorporated in the Christian Bible and have exercised a powerful influence throughout two millennia. As discussed in chapter 1, it is by no means easy to rank the items in Paul's teachings so as to create a "theology" of Paul.

Nonetheless, we can readily discern the following important elements for which we owe a significant debt to Paul the practical theologian and pastor.

   a. Paul redefined the God of Israel who is "One" (1 Cor 8:6) as the Father who "sent forth his Son" into the world and "the Spirit of his

Son" into human hearts, "crying, 'Abba, Father!'" so as to redeem former slaves to sin to become God's own children (Gal 4:4, 6). God has revealed himself in a "vertical" downward hierarchy ("the head of Christ is God" — 1 Cor 11:3).

b. In relation to God Jesus is "his Son" (1 Thess 1:10), the long-awaited Christ/Messiah of prophetic promise (2 Cor 1:19-20) who became sin so that sinners might become "righteousness of God" in him (2 Cor 5:21) and find "peace with God" (Rom 5:1). This resurrected Jesus is the Lord whose return believers await (1 Thess 1:10).

c. Due to human moral debility as children of Adam, the work of salvation is God's from first to last (Rom 8:28-30). Apart from the grace of God in Christ, as mediated through the gospel, man lies at the mercy of sin and death, unable to rescue himself. Deliverance is found only in Christ, so that no ritual requirement (such as circumcision) is made of believers. The descendants of Adam are "righteous" in Christ, by faith alone.

d. Believers congregate with one another in the name of Christ for love-motivated ministry and encouragement so as to be "built up" in faith and character and to support and strengthen one another and to be reminded of Jesus' death and coming again in the Lord's Supper (1 Cor 11–14). Paul placed great emphasis on unity, joy, and familial fellowship within the churches.

   Those who exercise particular leadership functions do not do so on a hereditary basis (as in the Aaronic priesthood) nor as a separate, ontologically priestly class, but on the basis of perceived "gifts" and proven Christian character (1 Thess 5:12-13).

e. Paul placed great emphasis on purity in sexual behavior, lifelong marital fidelity (1 Thess 4:3-8; 1 Cor 7:1-16) in husband-wife relationships patterned on the reciprocal relationship between Christ and his church (Eph 5:21-33).

f. Paul taught believers to work to support themselves and not to be dependent on others, and he set the example in insisting on working and not receiving payment for his ministry (1 Thess 4:11-12). The work ethic that is the basis of a functioning society is owed in no small measure to Paul.

g. Paul enjoined good relationships with those who are without (Col 4:5-6), with special emphasis on submitting to the powers that be (Rom 13:1). He encouraged believers to seek the salvation of others, based on thoughtful consistency and inoffensive behavior (1 Cor 10:23–11:1).

h. Paul was a great exemplar of prayerfulness for his churches, and he encouraged a reciprocal prayerfulness for himself (Rom 1:9; 15:30-32).

This sample of Paul's emphases reminds us of the comprehensive nature of the instruction we find in his letters. While incomplete, it does nonetheless remind us that it was Paul in particular who brought the religion of Jesus to the world at large, and who interpreted his Master's salvation and teaching for Gentiles. It is worth reflecting how one-sided our grasp of Christianity would be without the inspired wisdom and insight of the apostle Paul that we find in his letters.

Savior from Proto-Ebionism

No contribution to the future was greater than Paul's steadfast defense of the circumcision-free gospel for Gentiles throughout the years of his ministry. The Jewish-Christian countermission was so strong on occasion that it silenced otherwise faithful leaders like James, Peter, and Barnabas. The turbulent religious nationalism in Judea that emerged from the mid-40s created an environment where anti-Paul feelings would have flourished.

It is reasonable to suppose that without Paul's resistance the circumcision cause would have prevailed, making Christianity a subset of Judaism and effectively closing the door to a majority of Gentile males, who would have balked at the demand for circumcision. Paul's opposition to the countermission kept the door open for the Gentiles and made it possible for Christianity to become the religion of the Roman Empire and, beyond that, a world religion.

By the next century a form of Jewish Christianity emerged known to its critics as Ebionism,[1] which likely developed out of the conservative Jewish Christianity that Paul had opposed. According to Irenaeus, writing around 180, the Ebionites (i) used only the Gospel of Matthew, (ii) repudi-

---

1. Ebionism is derived from the Hebrew word *ebion*, meaning "poor"; it was likely attached to these Jewish Christians by their critics in the Gentile churches to signify their "poverty" in understanding.

ated Paul as an apostate from the law, (iii) practiced circumcision and other rituals from the law, (iv) regarded Jerusalem as the "house of God," and (v) rejected the virginal birth of Christ.[2] Tertullian, circa 197, stated that Ebionites rejected the deity of Christ.[3] Hippolytus, circa 225, observed that "the Ebionites . . . conform to the custom of the Jews, alleging that they are justified according to the Law."[4] Ebionism as a form of Jewish Christianity was neither Judaism nor Christianity, and after some centuries died out.

The early church fathers Irenaeus, Tertullian, Hippolytus, and Origen refer to Ebionism as a heresy. While other NT writings[5] played their part in anticipating the dangers of Ebionism, the letters of Paul written against the Jewish-Christian countermission were likely important in informing the Christian leaders of the second and third centuries.

Fulfiller of Jesus' Vision

Paul's greatest achievement, however, was that he fulfilled the vision of Jesus in taking the gospel of the kingdom of God to the Gentile nations. In Jesus' mind the "bread" of the kingdom must be available "first" for the "children" and then for the "dogs" (= Gentiles; Mark 7:27). Throughout his apostolate Paul faithfully followed Jesus' "Jews first, but also for the Greeks" priority.[6]

Jesus' approach to "sinners" was mercy-based and ritual-free (as touching washings, fastings, Sabbath keeping), in defiance of the demands of the Pharisees. Paul's gospel to the Gentiles was grace-based and circumcision-free, in defiance of the Pharisaic demands of the "circumcision party" within the Jerusalem church. The leading apostles occasionally crumbled before the pressure of the countermission wing of the Jerusalem church, notably at the "incident at Antioch." Paul, however, resisted the circumcision demand on Gentiles from beginning to end, true to the vision of Jesus for the lost.

Furthermore, Paul pursued his mission conscious that he was "in

2. Irenaeus, *Against All Heresies* 1.26; 3.25, 21; 5.1.
3. Tertullian, *On Prescriptions against the Heretics* 1.33.
4. Hippolytus, *Refutation of All Heresies* 7.22.
5. The overt anti-Judaism of the Gospel of John would have had the same effect.
6. See chapter 7.

Christ" and that Christ was achieving *his* missionary purposes "through" him (Rom 15:18-19). For Paul apostleship was no empty "office." He sought to replicate Christ as he represented Christ, for example, in "meekness and gentleness." Christ's own sufferings spilled over from Golgotha and afflicted Paul the preacher wherever he went. Paul preached Christ crucified and risen, and he saw his missionary experience in similar terms, as "Christoform." Paul embodied the Christ-centered message he preached.

In short, Paul, who was both "converted" and "called" at Damascus, became a true missionary of Jesus.

"Saul, Who Is Also Paul" (Acts 13:9)

As a Roman citizen, Paul would have had three names (the *tria nomina*).[1] A majority of authorities argue that his cognomen is Paullus (or, in Greek, *Paulos*) but that his nomen and praenomen are unknown to us.[2] The cognomen was an extra name given for a variety of reasons, including by the emancipating slave owner or by the wealthy benefactor. By the time Paul became an apostle, Roman citizens were frequently known only by their cognomen. The more formal nomen (or clan name) and praenomen (given name) were slipping out of routine use.

According to this view, then, from his birth he was Saul in home and synagogue and Paul in his public persona as a Roman boy in Tarsus. Neatly, Paul's letters give only his Roman name while the book of Acts calls him by his Jewish name until the Cyprus incident in about 48 when the author comments tersely, "Saul, who is also Paul. . . ." Acts knows him by only that name thereafter.

It must be asked, therefore, why the book of Acts notes the name Paul only after he had figured in the Acts narrative for a decade and a half.

---

1. The use of the *tria nomina* had become quite complex in the East by the NT era, where for a variety of reasons many Greeks were given Roman citizenship. See E. A. Judge, "Latin Names around a Counter-Cultural Paul," in *The Bible and the Business of Life*, ed. S. Holt and G. Preece (Adelaide: AFT Press, 2004), 68-84, with extensive referencing.

2. E.g., C. Hemer, "The Name of Paul," *TynBul* 36 (1985): 179-83; A. Nobbs, "Cyprus," in *The Book of Acts in Its Graeco-Roman Setting*, ed. D. Gill and C. Gempf (Grand Rapids: Eerdmans, 1994), 287-89; R. Riesner, *Paul's Early Period: Chronology, Mission Strategy, Theology* (Grand Rapids: Eerdmans, 1998), 143-46.

If his cognomen had always been Paul, why does the author not tell us beforehand? Everyone knows, of course, that Acts introduces the Roman name Paul on Cyprus in the context of the conversion of the Roman proconsul, Sergius Paulos. It is customary to explain the newly introduced name Paul either as appropriate to "new" Paul's Rome-ward missionary thrust,[3] or as a coincidence.[4] It has to be said, however, that if it is a coincidence, it is a large coincidence.

Even the casual reader would assume there was some connection between Sergius Paulos and the comment "Saul, who is also Paul." Various discoveries demonstrate that relatives of Sergius Paulos were prominent landholders in the region of Pisidian Antioch,[5] the city to which Paul immediately went after leaving Cyprus.[6] There were a number of Roman cities with Jewish colonies that Paul bypassed in going directly to Colonia Antiocheia. We readily imagine that Paul carried letters of introduction to the relatives of the proconsul of Cyprus, adding to the likelihood that Paul had taken his name as his own (or been given it) from that time.

As a Roman, Saul of Tarsus doubtless had the *tria nomina* from birth, including a cognomen. Here, however, the chronological issue may be important. If, as I hold, he came to Jerusalem as a young teenager and was thus domiciled there for the next seventeen years, his Roman identity would have been dormant though of course not forgotten. In that case, Paul as a Diaspora Jew living in the Holy City was in effect an expatriate Hellenist (as I argued in chapter 2) with the *tria nomina* a distant memory of early days in Tarsus.

If the case argued above is correct, it means we do not know those names, but only his Jewish name Saul. It would mean that whatever cognomen he had received at birth, from the time of the meeting with Sergius Paulos he was known by the name Paul. In that case, his new name Paul would have been an *agnomen,* a new practical alternative to Saul, and a way of identifying himself with this high-ranking Roman.[7] It must be acknowl-

---

3. So Riesner, *Paul's Early Period,* 144.

4. J. A. Fitzmyer, *According to Paul* (New York: Paulist, 1992), 2, calls the name change a "sheer coincidence."

5. Riesner, *Paul's Early Period,* 137-43.

6. See, e.g., S. Mitchell, *Anatolia* 2 (Oxford: Oxford University Press, 1995), 6-8; E. Schnabel, *Early Christian Mission: Paul and the Early Church* (Downers Grove, Ill.: InterVarsity, 2004), 1088.

7. The phrase "Saul, *who is also (ho kai)* Paul" was used stereotypically in the sense of

edged that few authorities subscribe to this view.[8] Nonetheless, arguably it makes better sense than the "coincidence" explanation.

It is just possible that the Paulli dynasts of Pisidia had earlier contacts with Paul's father or grandfather and bequeathed the cognomen Paul to them.[9] After all, Cilicia is not remote from Pisidia. Moreover, there must have been some reason that Barnabas and Paul went from Antioch to Cyprus (to convert a noted Paulli?), rather than going overland into Anatolia through Tarsus and the Cilician Gates (the more direct route that Paul followed in his next missionary tour).

"alias" (see Riesner, *Paul's Early Period,* 144 n. 52), or in modern terminology "a.k.a" ("X also known as Y"). This, however, does not demand that the newly introduced name was a technical cognomen.

8. See Riesner, *Paul's Early Period,* 143. Among distinguished advocates of the view are Mitchell, *Anatolia* 2, 7 (for which, however, he is criticized in passing in the review by G. H. R. Horsley, "Anatolia, from the Celts to the Christians," *Ancient History: Resources for Teachers* 36, no. 1 [1997]: 62 n. 17).

9. E. A. Judge and G. S. R. Thomas, "The Origin of the Church at Rome: A New Situation?" *RTR* 25, no. 3 (1966), reflect on the possibility that Paul may have been "a Sergius Paulos of freedman descent, and therefore under his patronage" (84). This (conjecture) would explain (i) why Paul and Barnabas went to Cyprus when their ultimate destination was likely Anatolia (which would have been more quickly reached by an overland route); and (ii) why Paul went specifically to Pisidian Antioch where the family of Sergius Paulos were known to have been wealthy landowners who could afford protection for Paul and Barnabas (cf. Mitchell, *Anatolia* 2, 6-8).

The Acts of the Apostles
and the Letters of Paul

How should we think about the relationship between Paul (and his letters) and the author of the book of Acts, who is the only narrative source for Paul's life? There are few comparable relationships between a biographer and letter-writer from those times.[1] Plutarch's life of Cicero the orator and letter-writer provides an example that casts some light on the relationship between Luke and Paul.

Cicero and Paul were both public speakers and letter-writers. Plutarch and Luke both admired their subjects and portrayed them with edifying intent. Plutarch's Cicero was honorable and good; he faced his murderers with stoical courage. Luke's Paul was likewise admirable for his courage and as the instrument of his exalted Lord to bring the light of the gospel to the Gentile nations.

Apart from these superficial common elements, Luke and Plutarch have little else in common in their respective portrayals of Paul and Cicero. First, Plutarch writes with moralistic intent, setting Roman and Greek subjects in twenty-three sets of parallels, in this instance between Cicero and

---

1. See T. Hillard, A. Nobbs, and B. Winter, "Acts and the Pauline Corpus 1: Ancient Literary Parallels," in *The Book of Acts in Its First Century Setting 1: Ancient Literary Setting,* ed. B. W. Winter and A. D. Clarke (Grand Rapids: Eerdmans, 1993), 183-213, who discuss the relationships between Cicero and Sallust (for the Catilinarian rebellion), Favorinus and Gellius/Philostratus (regarding Favorinus's reputation), and Julian and Ammianus Marcellinus (regarding Julian's career). These comparative examples raise important issues for the historian about the "dovetailing" use of, as against possible preference for, these respective sources.

Demosthenes. Luke, however, regards his two-volume opus (which focuses on Jesus in the first part and Paul in the second) as a continuation and conclusion of the divine salvation history going back to the beginning of history.

Second, Luke is not writing Paul's *bios*/"life"; he does not fulfill the expected conventions of a biographer. For example, Luke supplies no information about Paul's parentage, and details of his early years appear only incidentally, later in the narrative (Acts 21:39; 22:3; cf. 9:11). Again, whereas biographers typically narrate their subjects' deaths, Luke is silent about the death of Paul.

Nonetheless, Paul dominates the book of Acts. His preaching to the Gentiles in Luke's second volume fulfills the hope of his first volume, that is, the promise of "a light for revelation to the Gentiles" (Luke 2:32; cf. Acts 13:46-47; 26:16-18). Luke devotes the greater part of his second volume to Paul's missions (chapters 13–20), followed by his years of imprisonment in Caesarea and Rome (chapters 21–28). Clearly, when considered in relationship to Luke-Acts overall, Paul's missions are highly significant to the author.

Third, the author of Acts sends a clear signal that he knew Paul and was his fellow missionary and travel companion for extended periods. Luke does this by changing from the third-person narrative ("they," "them") to the first person ("we," "us") in various passages. The so-called "we" passages indicate that Luke traveled with Paul from Troas to Philippi in about 49 (Acts 16:10-16); from Philippi to Jerusalem circa 57 (20:9–21:37); and from Caesarea to Rome circa 59-62 (27:1–28:14).[2] We reasonably assume that Luke remained in contact with Paul during his imprisonments in Caesarea and Rome, a period of about five years total. Plutarch (A.D. 46-120), however, was born about a century after Cicero's death (in 43 B.C.).

In other words, Luke knew Paul at *first hand;* he did not merely know *about* him, and write about him from a distance, as Plutarch did about Cicero.

The implications of this Luke-Paul nexus for historical analysis are considerable. It means, first, that Luke's narrative about Paul must be regarded as reliable; Paul was Luke's direct (oral) source. Paul's letters and the book of Acts form the basis for establishing a chronological sequence

---

2. For the historical significance of the "we" passages, see Barnett, *BC*, 192-93.

for Paul's mission. In consequence, secondly, we are able to plot the time and place Paul wrote (many of) his letters to the churches. To be sure, there are gaps. Yet a practical chronological sequence is possible.[3]

3. For an outstanding reconstruction of Pauline chronology based on a positive attitude to the integrity of Acts, see R. Riesner, *Paul's Early Period: Chronology, Mission Strategy, Theology* (Grand Rapids: Eerdmans, 1998).

Mind and Spirit:
How Paul Made Decisions

Paul's letters reveal the man, at least to a degree. Whether they agree with his teaching or not, most people today would concur with the Corinthians' opinion that "his letters are weighty and strong" (2 Cor 10:10). The density, yet brevity, of his argument points to a man of significant intellect, and dozens of citations of or allusions to the OT disclose the mind of a biblical scholar steeped in the sacred texts.[1] No reader, ancient or modern, will doubt Paul's intellectual capacity based on a reading (for example) of 1 Corinthians or Romans.

It comes as a surprise, therefore, to discover the degree to which Paul engaged in or was a recipient of what we would consider paranormal (or nonrational) activities.

Year	Event	Reference
34	Damascus Christophany	Gal 1:16[2]
	Damascus: Paul's vision of Ananias	Acts 9:12
36	Jerusalem: vision of the Lord, who said, "Depart . . ."	Acts 22:17-21
43	Tarsus (?): caught up to third heaven/ paradise	2 Cor 12:1-4

1. See, e.g., R. N. Longenecker, *Biblical Exegesis in the Apostolic Period* (Grand Rapids: Eerdmans, 1999), 88-116.

2. See earlier, 58.

47	Antioch: a revelation to go to Jerusalem	Gal 2:2/Acts 11:28-30
49	Deflected from Asia and Mysia to Troas	Acts 16:6-8
	Troas: vision of man of Macedonia, "Come over . . ."	Acts 16:9-10
50	Corinth: vision of the Lord, who said, "Do not be afraid . . ."	Acts 18:9-10
57	Caesarea: Agabus prophesied danger for Paul in Jerusalem	Acts 21:11
57	Jerusalem: vision of the Lord, who said, "Take courage . . ."	Acts 23:11
60	At sea: vision of angel of the Lord, who said, "Do not be afraid . . ."	Acts 27:23-24

It scarcely needs saying that this list states only the visions, etc., that Luke or Paul chooses to mention; there may have been other such occasions. The point is that Paul experienced multiple "visions and revelations" (2 Cor 12:1).

The paranormal also accompanied Paul's proclamation of the gospel throughout the quarter of a century, as in his brief review to the Romans:

> For I will not venture to speak of anything except what Christ has wrought through me to win obedience from the Gentiles,
>> by word and by deed,
>> by the power of signs and wonders,
>> by the power of the Holy Spirit,
> so that from Jerusalem and as far round as Illyricum
> I have fully preached [better, fulfilled] the gospel of Christ.
>
> (Rom 15:18-19)

Paul's reference to "by deed" *(ergō)* is further explained as "by the power of signs and wonders" *(en dynamei sēmeiōn kai teratōn),* which in turn are attributed to "the power of the Holy Spirit" *(en dynamei pneumatos* [*theou*]). This remarkable (and falsifiable) claim is supported by another claim by Paul (2 Cor 12:12 — "The signs of a [true] apostle were performed among you in all patience, with signs and wonders and mighty works"; cf. Gal 3:5) and by references in Acts (see below). These indicate that, by the power of God, Paul worked miracles in various places.

Year

47/48	Iconium	Acts 14:3
	Among the Galatians (?)	Gal 3:5
	Cyprus, Pisidia, Lycaonia	Acts 15:12
50-51	Corinth	2 Cor 12:12

Once again, the references are likely incomplete, especially in light of the comprehensive assertion that "signs and wonders" accompanied his preaching throughout the previous quarter century, from Jerusalem around *(en kuklō)* to Illyricum (Rom 15:18-19).

To these paranormal occurrences we must add the "supernatural" elements within Paul's religious experience. He assured the Corinthians that he spoke "in tongues *(glōssais lalō)* more than" they (1 Cor 14:18), indicating an ongoing practice.

Furthermore, he recalled the incident circa 43 when he was "caught up to the third heaven/into Paradise" and heard things that "cannot be told" *(ouk exon anthropō lalēsai* — 2 Cor 12:4). Accordingly, (it would appear) upon returning to earth he spoke only in ecstatic speech about the mysteries he had heard ("if we are beside ourselves" — *eite . . . exestēmen* — 2 Cor 5:13). It appears that while the "out of the body" experience (as it likely was — 2 Cor 12:2-3) occurred only once, the ecstatic speech continued and was current when Paul wrote 2 Corinthians. Was this the same phenomenon as "speaking in tongues"? It is not possible to be certain.

What is clear, however, is that there was a paranormal (nonrational) aspect to Paul's life that stands in contrast with his otherwise impressive intellect as reflected in the close argument we encounter in his letters and the shrewd strategies he followed in choosing places to establish churches (at major crossroads or strategically located seaports).

This double-sided aspect of Paul (the paranormal and the rational) prompts the question: How did Paul make decisions about his missionary work? We have already raised this in relation to the general question of his determination to embark on sustained missionary work westward, toward Rome.[3] By observing the nonresponse of Jews to the Messiah and reflecting on OT texts related to the "hardening" of Israel and the "coming in" of Gentiles, Paul had reached his important decision.

What, then, about his decision (with Barnabas) to go to Cyprus, and

---

3. See chapter 9.

from there (directly) to Pisidian Antioch? On one hand, their journey arose from the fasting and prayer of the Antioch church and the instruction of the Holy Spirit (through a prophet, presumably — Acts 13:2). On the other hand, however, Cyprus was Barnabas's home and a logical place to begin their westward mission. So: Was the decision to go to Cyprus made by rational choice or supernatural intervention?

The question becomes potentially more complex when we learn that Sergius Paulos, proconsul of Cyprus, had powerful relatives at Paul's next destination, Pisidian Antioch, to which he went immediately upon arriving in Pamphylia.[4] Was Cyprus deliberately chosen as a stepping-stone to the major crossroads city Colonia Antiocheia, which had been in Paul's mind all along as a strategic nodal point for the spread of the gospel in central Anatolia?

Most likely we do not have to choose between Paul's modes of decision making. That he was a shrewd strategist is clear from the rapid spread of Christianity through the network of churches he quickly established. Yet it is no less true that he was subject to paranormal experiences and prophetic guidance, and that "signs and wonders" accompanied his preaching. In short, Paul had a broad intention of progressively planting churches in strategic locations as he progressed westward, but that within that overall plan he responded "opportunistically," including to promptings that cannot be accounted for in purely rational terms.

4. R. Riesner, *Paul's Early Period: Chronology, Mission Strategy, Theology* (Grand Rapids: Eerdmans, 1998), 137-43. Did Paul's family have earlier contacts with the famous Paulli family in Pisidia? Is this the source of Paul's name, which is mentioned in Acts in the setting of Paul's ministry to Sergius Paulos in Cyprus? We note that Tarsus is quite close to Pisidian Antioch. See further, appendix A.

Paul's Asian Epistles
(Philemon, Colossians, Ephesians)

Pauline Authorship of the Asian Epistles

Philemon: Pauline authorship not generally doubted
Colossians: Pauline authorship doubted by a majority of scholars
Ephesians: Pauline authorship overwhelmingly doubted
  i. Different vocabulary and literary style
  ii. Special cosmology ("principalities and powers")
  For many, Ephesians is deutero-Pauline (yet also
  "canonical"?)[1]

Common to Philemon, Colossians, Ephesians

1. Written from prison
   Philemon   9, 10, 13
   Colossians   4:3, 18
   Ephesians   3:1; 4:1; 6:20
2. Names common in Philemon and Colossians
   a. Greeting-senders
      Epaphras, Mark, Aristarchus, Demas, Luke   Philem 23
      Aristarchus, Mark, Epaphras, Luke, Demas   Col 4:10-14

---

1. For discussion on authorship of Philemon, Colossians, and Ephesians, see, e.g.,
L. M. McDonald and S. E. Porter, *Early Christianity and Its Sacred Literature* (Peabody,
Mass.: Hendrickson, 2000), 482-85.

b. Greeted one
   Archippus   Philem 2;
                                                     Col 4:15-17

c. Common mentioned one
   Onesimus   Philem 10;
                                                     Col 4:9

Comment: Items a-c indicate that Philemon and Colossians were written at the same time, from the same place, and to the same place, Colossae.

3. Common envoy (amanuensis?) in Colossians and Ephesians
   Tychicus   Col 4:7-8;
                                                     Eph 6:21

Comment: The common envoy Tychicus indicates that Colossians and Ephesians were dispatched at the same time or at similar times.

Conclusion on Authorship

These three letters were written at the same time and from the same place. Since Philemon is authentically Pauline, it follows that Colossians is likewise authentically Pauline. Because Colossians and Ephesians were delivered by the same envoy (Tychicus) and because the letters share verbal and theological elements between them, it follows that they have a common author. It is reasonable to conclude that each letter was written by Paul.

Place of Paul's Imprisonment

There are problems with the places of known imprisonment:

Caesarea — there is no reason a fugitive slave (Onesimus) would go there.

Rome — it is too great a coincidence that Onesimus and Paul were in the same prison at the same time in so large a city as Rome.

The case for Ephesus as the place of imprisonment (even though not mentioned in Acts) is:

   a. People in the letters who were in Ephesus/Asia
      Aristarchus (Philem 23; Col 4:10) was in Ephesus (Acts 19:29).
      Tychicus (Col 4:7; Eph 6:21) was an Asian (Acts 20:4).
   b. Paul's ministry in Ephesus was long enough (three years) and turbu-
      lent enough (1 Cor 15:32; 16:9) to accommodate a brief imprisonment
      (under house arrest?).
   c. It is more readily imaginable for Paul to envisage release for a hospi-
      tality visit to Philemon in Colossae from Ephesus than from either
      Caesarea or Rome (because of distance).

Problems of Non-Pauline Style

   1. Since Paul was known to be opposed to letters "as if" written by him
      (2 Thess 2:2), the suggestion that Ephesians was pseudonymous
      (written by a friend) must be received with caution.
   2. The presence of Paul's signature on Colossians (Col 4:18; cf. 2 Thess
      3:17) and its absence from Ephesians as well as that letter's more gen-
      eral character are consistent with the latter as a circular letter.
   3. Imprisonment (in Ephesus) would imply an external amanuensis
      (Tychicus?) who went to see Paul in prison seeking his general ideas
      for Colossians and Ephesians, which the scribe expressed in his own
      idiom (different from Paul's).
   4. The unusual "principalities and powers" language of Ephesians and
      Colossians might be explained by the influence of (Jewish)
      Gnosticism (evident in Col 2:8-23), whose language Paul adopted in
      that letter and which may have colored the language in Ephesians.

Ephesus as Base for Paul's Mission

   1. Paul spent his longest time in Ephesus. Was this because of its geo-
      graphical centrality to the churches of Galatia, Macedonia, Achaia,
      and Asia?
   2. From Ephesus Paul wrote three letters to the Corinthians (including
      the lost "previous letter" and "tearful letter") and the "Asian Epistles"
      (Ephesians, Colossians, Philemon).

Paul's Names for Jesus

Names	References[1]
[The] Christ	Too frequent to list
Lord	Too frequent to list
One Lord	1 Cor 8:6
Son of God or his [own] Son	Rom 1:3, 4, 9; 5:10; 8:3, 32; 1 Cor 1:9; 15:28; 2 Cor 1:19; Gal 1:16; 2:20; 4:4, 6; 1 Thess 1:10
God	Rom 9:5
Righteous judge	2 Tim 4:8
Cornerstone	Eph 2:20
Stone of stumbling	Rom 9:33
Rock (that followed Israelites)	1 Cor 10:4
Head of the body	Eph 1:22; 4:15; Col 2:19
Savior	Phil 3:20; Eph 5:23; 2 Tim 1:10; Titus 1:4; 2:13; 3:6
Mediator	1 Tim 2:5
Passover	1 Cor 5:7
Propitiation	Rom 3:25

1. See V. Taylor, *The Names of Jesus* (London: Macmillan, 1953), whose list and sequence are followed.

Image of God	(Rom 8:29); 2 Cor 4:4 (cf. 3:18); Col 1:15
Firstborn among many brothers	Rom 8:29
Firstborn from the dead	Col 1:18
Power and wisdom of God	1 Cor 1:24
Last Adam	1 Cor 15:22, 45; cf. Rom 5:14
The Beloved	Eph 1:6

BIBLIOGRAPHY

Akenson, D. H. *Saint Saul: A Skeleton Key to the Historical Jesus.* Oxford: Oxford University Press, 2000.

Aus, R. "Paul's Travel Plans to Spain and the 'Full Number of the Gentiles' of Rom 11:25." *NovT* 21 (1979): 232-62.

Barnett, P. *Jesus and the Logic of History.* Grand Rapids: Eerdmans, 1997.

————. *The Second Epistle to the Corinthians.* Grand Rapids: Eerdmans, 1997.

————. "Paul, Apologist to the Corinthians." In *Paul and the Corinthians,* edited by T. J. Burke and J. K. Elliott, 313-26. Festschrift for Margaret Thrall. Leiden: Brill, 2003.

————. "Indications of Earliness in the Gospel of John." *RTR* 64 (2005): 61-75.

————. "Romans and the Origin of Paul's Christology." In *History and Exegesis,* edited by San-Won (Aaron) Son, 90-103. Festschrift for E. E. Ellis. Edinburgh: T. & T. Clark, 2006.

Beale, G. K. "The OT Background of Reconciliation in 2 Corinthians 5–7 and Its Bearing on the Literary Problems of 2 Corinthians 6:14–7:1." *NTS* 35, no. 4 (1989): 550-81.

Bockmuehl, M. "Antioch and James the Just." In *James the Just and Christian Origins,* edited by B. Chilton and C. A. Evans, 155-98. Leiden: Brill, 1999.

Boring, M., et al. *Hellenistic Commentary to the New Testament.* Nashville: Abingdon, 1995.

Bruce, F. F. *New Testament History.* London: Oliphants, 1969.

————. *Paul, Apostle of the Free Spirit.* Exeter: Paternoster, 1977.

Brunt, P. A. "Procuratorial Jurisdiction." *Latomus* 25 (1966): 461-87.

Carson, D. A., P. T. O'Brien, and M. Seifrid. *Justification and Variegated Nomism: A*

Fresh Appraisal of Paul and Second Temple Judaism. WUNT 140. Tübingen: Mohr Siebeck, 2001.

Cerfaux, L. *Christ in the Theology of St. Paul.* New York: Herder and Herder, 1959.

Chester, S. *Conversion at Corinth.* Edinburgh: T. & T. Clark, 2003.

Chilton, Bruce, and Craig A. Evans, eds. *Studying the Historical Jesus,* 155-78. Leiden: Brill, 1994.

Chilton, B. D., and J. Neusner. "Paul and Gamaliel." *BBR* 14, no. 1 (2004): 1-43.

Chow, J. K. *Patronage and Power.* JSNTSS 75. Sheffield: Sheffield Academic, 1992.

Corley, B. "Interpreting Paul's Conversion — Then and Now." In *The Road from Damascus,* edited by R. N. Longenecker, 1-13. Grand Rapids: Eerdmans, 1997.

Dickson, J. P. *Mission-Commitment in Ancient Judaism and the Pauline Communities.* WUNT 159. Tübingen: Mohr Siebeck, 2003.

Donaldson, T. L. *Paul and the Gentiles: Remapping the Apostle's Convictional World.* Minneapolis: Fortress, 1997.

Drane, J. "Why Did Paul Write Romans?" In *Pauline Studies,* edited by D. Hagner and M. Harris, 209-27. Festschrift for F. F. Bruce. Exeter, Devon: Paternoster, 1980.

Dungan, D. L. *The Sayings of Jesus in the Churches of Paul.* Oxford: Basil Blackwell, 1971.

Dunn, J. D. G. "The Relationship between Paul and Jerusalem according to Galatians 1 and 2." *NTS* 28, no. 4 (1982): 461-78.

———. "The New Perspective on Paul." In *Jesus, Paul, and the Law: Studies in Mark and Galatians,* 183-206. London: SPCK; Louisville: Westminster John Knox, 1990.

———. *The Theology of Paul.* Grand Rapids: Eerdmans, 1998.

Dupont, J. "The Conversion of Paul, and Its Influence on His Understanding of Salvation by Faith." In *Apostolic History and the Gospel,* edited by W. W. Gasque and R. P. Martin, 176-94. Exeter: Paternoster, 1970.

Ellis, E. E. "Paul and His Opponents." In *Christianity, Judaism, and Other Greco-Roman Cults,* edited by J. Neusner. Festschrift for Morton Smith. Leiden: Brill, 1975.

———. *Prophecy and Hermeneutic in Early Christianity.* WUNT 1/18. Tübingen: Mohr, 1978.

Evans, C. A. "Paul and the Prophets." In *Romans and the People of God,* edited by S. V. Soderlund and N. T. Wright, 115-28. Grand Rapids: Eerdmans, 1999.

Fitzgerald, J. T. *Cracks in an Earthen Vessel: An Examination of the Catalogues of Hardships in the Corinthian Correspondence.* SBLDS 99. Atlanta: Scholars, 1988.

Fitzmyer, J. A. *According to Paul.* New York: Paulist, 1992.

Fraser, J. W. *Jesus and Paul.* Abingdon, Berks, England: Marcham Books, 1974.

Furnish, V. P. "The Jesus-Paul Debate: From Baur to Bultmann." In *Jesus and Paul,* edited by A. J. M. Wedderburn, 11-50. JSNTSS 37. Sheffield: JSOT Press, 1989.

Gardner, P. *The Religious Experience of St. Paul.* London: Williams and Norgate, 1911.

Gardner, P. D. *The Gifts of God and the Authentication as a Christian.* Lanham, Md.: University Press of America, 1994.

Goodman, M. *The Ruling Class of Judea.* Cambridge: Cambridge University Press, 1987.

Gorman, M. J. *Cruciformity.* Grand Rapids: Eerdmans, 2001.

———. *Apostle of the Crucified Lord.* Grand Rapids: Eerdmans, 2004.

Guelich, R. A. *The Sermon on the Mount.* Waco: Word, 1982.

Gundry, R. H. *Mark.* Grand Rapids: Eerdmans, 1993.

Hall, D. R. "A Disguise for the Wise." *NTS* 40 (1994): 143-49.

Hanson, A. T. *Jesus Christ in the Old Testament.* London: SPCK, 1965.

Hemer, C. "The Name of Paul." *TynBul* 36 (1985): 179-83.

Hengel, M. *Between Jesus and Paul.* London: SCM, 1983.

———. *The Johannine Question.* London: SCM, 1989.

———. *The Pre-Christian Paul.* London: SCM, 1991.

———. *The Four Gospels and the One Gospel of Jesus Christ.* London: SCM, 2000.

———. "The Stance of the Apostle Paul toward the Law in the Unknown Years between Damascus and Antioch." In *Justification and Variegated Nomism,* vol. 2, *The Paradoxes of Paul,* edited by D. A. Carson, P. T. O'Brien, and M. A. Seifrid, 81-83. Tübingen: Mohr Siebeck, 2004.

Hengel, M., and A. M. Schwemer. *Paul between Damascus and Antioch.* London: SCM, 1997.

Hillard, T., A. Nobbs, and B. Winter. "Acts and the Pauline Corpus 1: Ancient Literary Parallels." In *The Book of Acts in Its First Century Setting 1: Ancient Literary Setting,* edited by B. W. Winter and A. D. Clarke. Grand Rapids: Eerdmans, 1993.

Jeremias, J. *Jesus' Promise to the Nations.* SBT 24. London: SCM, 1958.

Judge, E. A. "Latin Names around a Counter-cultural Paul." In *The Bible and the Business of Life,* edited by S. Holt and G. Preece, 68-84. Adelaide: AFT Press, 2004.

Ker, D. P. "Paul and Apollos — Colleagues or Rivals?" *JSNT* 77 (2000): 75-97.

Kim, S. Y. *Origin of Paul's Gospel.* Grand Rapids: Eerdmans, 1982.

———. "God Reconciled His Enemy to Himself: The Origin of Paul's Concept of Reconciliation." In *The Road from Damascus,* edited by R. N. Longenecker, 102-24. Grand Rapids: Eerdmans, 1997.

———. *Paul and the New Perspective*. Grand Rapids: Eerdmans, 2002.

Köstenberger, A. J., and P. T. O'Brien. *Salvation to the Ends of the Earth*. NSBT 11. Downers Grove, Ill.: InterVarsity, 2001.

Kraftchick, S. "Death in Us, Life in You: The Apostolic Medium." In *Society of Biblical Literature 1991 Seminar Papers*, edited by E. H. Lovering. Atlanta: Scholars, 1991.

Litfin, D. *St. Paul's Theology of Proclamation: 1 Corinthians 1–4 and Greco-Roman Rhetoric*. SNTMS 79. Cambridge: Cambridge University Press, 1994.

Longenecker, R. N. *Biblical Exegesis in the Apostolic Period*. Grand Rapids: Eerdmans, 1999.

Maccoby, H. *The Mythmaker: Paul and the Invention of Christianity*. London: Weidenfeld and Nicholson, 1986.

Martyn, J. L. "A Gentile Mission That Replaced an Earlier Jewish Mission." In *Exploring the Gospel of John*, edited by R. A. Culpepper and C. C. Black, 124-44. Louisville: Westminster John Knox, 1989.

Meyer, B. F. *The Aims of Jesus*. London: SCM, 1979.

Millar, F. *The Roman Near East, 31 BC–AD 337*. Cambridge: Harvard University Press, 1993.

Miller, R. "The Romans Debate, 1991-2001." *CurBS* 9 (2001): 306-49.

Mitchell, M. M. "New Testament Envoys in the Context of Greco-Roman Diplomatic and Epistolary Conventions: The Example of Timothy and Titus." *JBL* 111 (1992): 641-62.

Murphy-O'Connor, J. *Paul: A Critical Life*. Oxford: Oxford University Press, 1996.

Nobbs, A. "Cyprus." In *The Book of Acts in Its Graeco-Roman Setting*, edited by D. Gill and C. Gempf, 287-89. Grand Rapids: Eerdmans, 1994.

O'Brien, P. T. *Colossians, Philemon*. WBC 44. Waco: Word, 1987.

———. *Commentary on Philippians*. NIGTC. Grand Rapids: Eerdmans, 1991.

———. "Was Paul Converted?" In *Justification and Variegated Nomism*, vol. 2, *The Paradoxes of Paul*, edited by D. A. Carson, P. T. O'Brien, and M. A. Seifrid, 360-91. Tübingen: Mohr Siebeck, 2004.

Polhill, J. B. *Paul and His Letters*. Nashville: Broadman and Holman, 1999.

Ramsay, W. M. *The Cities of St. Paul*. London: Hodder and Stoughton, 1907.

Richard, E. "Polemics, Old Testament and Theology." *RB* 3 (1981): 340-67.

Richardson, P., and J. C. Hurd, eds. *From Jesus to Paul*, 1-21. Festschrift for F. W. Beare. Waterloo, Ont.: Wilfred Laurier University Press, 1984.

Riesner, R. *Paul's Early Period: Chronology, Mission Strategy, Theology*. Grand Rapids: Eerdmans, 1998.

Rosner, B. S. "Temple Prostitution in 1 Corinthians 6:12-20." *NovT* 60 (1998): 336-51.

Rosner, B. S., and R. Ciampa. "The Structure and Argument of 1 Corinthians: A Biblical/Jewish Approach." *NTS* 52, no. 2 (2006): 205-18.

Sanders, E. P. *Paul and Palestinian Judaism.* Philadelphia: Fortress, 1987.

Savage, T. *Power through Weakness: Paul's Understanding of the Ministry in 2 Corinthians.* SNTSMS 86. Cambridge: Cambridge University Press, 1996.

Schnabel, E. *Early Christian Mission.* Downers Grove, Ill.: InterVarsity, 2004.

Schnelle, U. *Apostle Paul: His Life and Theology.* Translated by M. Eugene Boring. Grand Rapids: Baker Academic, 2005.

Segal, A. *Paul the Convert.* New Haven: Yale University Press, 1990.

Stendahl, K. "The Apostle Paul and the Introspective Conscience of the West." *HTR* 50 (1963): 199-215.

————. *Paul among the Jews and Gentiles.* Philadelphia: Fortress, 1976.

Stuhlmacher, P. *Paul's Letter to the Romans.* Louisville: Westminster John Knox, 1994.

Taylor, V. *The Names of Jesus.* London: Macmillan, 1953.

Thiselton, A. T. *The First Epistle to the Corinthians.* NIGTC. Grand Rapids: Eerdmans, 2000.

Thompson, M. *Clothed with Christ.* JSNTSS 59. Sheffield: JSOT Press, 1989.

Thrall, M. E. *II Corinthians.* ICC. Edinburgh: T. & T. Clark, 1994.

Turcan, R. *The Cults of the Roman Empire.* Oxford: Blackwell, 1996.

Van Unnik, W. C. "Tarsus or Jerusalem, the City of Paul's Youth?" In *Sparsa Collecta* 1: *Evangelia — Paulina — Acts,* 259-320. NTSupp 29. Leiden: Brill, 1973.

Vermes, G. *Jesus the Jew.* Glasgow: Collins, 1973.

————. *The Religion of Jesus the Jew.* London: SCM, 1993.

Wenham, D. *Paul: Follower of Jesus or Founder of Christianity?* Grand Rapids: Eerdmans, 1995.

Wilson, S. G. "From Jesus to Paul: The Contours and Consequences of a Debate." In *From Jesus to Paul,* edited by P. Richardson and J. C. Hurd, 1-21. Festschrift for F. W. Beare. Waterloo, Ont.: Wilfred Laurier University Press, 1984.

Wolf, C. "True Apostolic Knowledge of Christ: Exegetical Reflections on 2 Corinthians 4:14ff." In *Paul and Jesus,* edited by A. J. M. Wedderburn, 84. JSNTSS 37. Sheffield: JSOT, 1989.

Wrede, W. *Paul.* Boston: American Unitarian Association, 1908.

Wright, N. T. *The Resurrection of the Son of God.* London: SPCK, 2003.

Yeung, M. W. *Faith in Jesus and in Paul.* Tübingen: Mohr Siebeck, 2001.

INDEX OF SUBJECTS

INDEX OF MODERN AUTHORS

INDEX OF SCRIPTURE
AND OTHER ANCIENT WRITINGS

Ezekiel	
36:24-27	63

Hosea	
11:1	104n.16

Amos	
9:11-12	100n.4

Micah	
4:1-2	155n.40

Habakkuk	
2:4	66

Zechariah	
8:20	140
8:20-23	52n.18
8:22	140

NEW TESTAMENT

Matthew	
1:16	19
4:12-17	107
5:5	164n.10
5:20	140
6:32	106n.25
6:33	195
7:6	104n.17
7:13-14	140
7:21	140
8:5-13	103, 108n.26
8:10-12	106, 107
8:11-12	111
10:5	106n.25
10:5-6	37n.39, 105, 110, 111
10:18	106n.25
11:19	195
11:29	19, 164n.10
12:18	106n.25
12:21	106n.25

15:21-28	103
15:24	105, 110, 111
17:2	19
18:3	140
19:17	140
20:18-19	106n.25
21:5	164n.10
21:43	106n.25
23:15	37n.39
24:7	106n.25
24:9	106n.25
24:14	106n.25
25:32	106n.25
28:18-20	104, 106
28:19	105, 106, 111

Mark	
1:14	194
2:24	196
2:26	196
3:4	196
3:6	90n.29
3:9	104n.18
3:14	19
4:1	104n.18
6:52	140n.16
7:2	194n.18
7:5	194n.18
7:15	194
7:18	194n.18
7:19	194
7:20	194n.18
7:23	194n.18
7:24-30	103
7:24–9:29	103
7:27	103, 105, 111, 112, 113, 203
8:17	140n.16
8:27-30	19
9:2	19
9:43	140
9:45	140
9:47	140
10:2	196

10:15	140
10:20	27
10:23-25	140
12:13	90n.29
12:13-17	31
12:14	196
13:10	104, 105
14:9	104, 105
15:7	32n.22

Luke	
1:2	108, 113
1:32	18n.24
1:68-70	18n.24
2:1-5	30n.17
2:32	108, 209
2:42	18n.24
3:6	108
3:23	18n.24
3:38	108
4:16-30	108
7:1-10	108n.26
13:1	32n.22
15:2	195
17:17	103
24:44-49	104, 108

John	
1:11	109n.29
3:5	140
4:1-42	103
4:38	109
7:5	85
7:35	37n.39, 109
9:22	51n.16
10:16	109
11:48	109n.27
11:50	109n.27
11:51	109n.27
11:52	109
12:20	109
12:40	140n.16
12:42	51n.16
14:12-13	109